Ancient Roots, New Shoots

Endogenous Development in Practice

Ancient Roots, New Shoots

Endogenous development in practice

Bertus Haverkort, Katrien van 't Hooft and Wim Hiemstra (eds)

Published in 2002 by ETC/Compas in association with Zed Books Ltd.
ETC/Compas, P.O. Box 64, 3830 AB Leusden, The Netherlands
Zed Books, 7 Cynthia Street, London N1 9JF, United Kingdom
and Room 400, 175 Fifth Avenue, New York 10010, USA.
Distributed in the USA exclusively by Palgrave, a division of St Martin's
Press, LLC, 175, Fifth Avenue, New York, NY 10010, USA in 2003.

Ancient Roots, New Shoots
Endogenous development in practice
Bertus Haverkort, Katrien van 't Hooft and Wim Hiemstra (eds)
Leusden: ETC/Compas
London: Zed Books
2003

ISBN 1 84277 334 8 cased
ISBN 1 84277 335 6 limp

A catalogue record for this book is available from the British Library.
Library of Congress Cataloging-in-Publication Data is available.
Keywords: biodiversity, endogenous development, sustainable agriculture,
indigenous knowledge, culture, health, natural resource management,
traditional practices

Seeking knowledge

The cautious guest
who comes to the table
speaks sparingly.
Listens with ears
learns with eyes.
Such is the seeker of knowledge.

Eddaic poem AD 800

CONTENTS

1. INTRODUCTION

Over the last 5 decades the development activities of rural and urban people, local leaders, NGOs, government agencies, as well as international research and support agencies, have led to a situation in which more people have food, better health, longer lifes, more access to education and faster communication. And yet, more people than ever before live under circumstances of extreme poverty. Education, healthcare, markets, and employment systems often function poorly. At global level, the environmental problems are alarming, the differences in wealth between countries are enormous, social and cultural systems are disintegrating, while political and ethnic tensions are increasing [Beemans in Harper, 2000].

In addressing these problems, a great number of initiatives and approaches aim at an economically feasible, socially just, ecologically sound, and culturally acceptable development path. Often these initiatives are carried out by networks working on a particular theme such as poverty reduction, participatory development, natural resources, low external input and sustainable agriculture, energy, biodiversity, indigenous rights, cultural diversity, or language. These initiatives give considerable attention to traditional knowledge, although the focus is often limited to the technical part of it, while the socio-cultural and spiritual aspects of these knowledge systems often receive little attention.

Compas. The Compas programme has its roots in innovative initiatives with low external input agriculture, based on local knowledge and practices. Since 1997 Compas functions as an international network that supports initiatives for endogenous development, or 'development from within'. The partners in this network are NGOs and universities based in Latin America, Africa, Asia and Europe. They link theoretical reflections about development with practical interventions in the rural areas, thus contributing to the emergence of insights and effective methodologies. The approach of the Compas programme can be described as 'action-research on endogenous development'. It aims at supporting the growing movement towards sustainable and endogenous development. Through the Compas Magazine and regular workshops, Compas also contributes to the international intercultural dialogue on development.

Endogenous development is based on the local initiatives to use resourses. Key aspects of supporting endogenous development are: building on local needs, improving local knowledge and practices, local control of development options, identification of new development niches, selective use of external resources, retention of benefits in the local area, exchange and learning between cultures, training and capacity building, networking and strategic partnerschip, understanding systems of knowing and learning. This book presents the experiences and insights gained with endogenous development during the Compas programme: between 1997 and 2002.

Ancient Roots and New Shoots. In the course of mankind's history, several cultures, each with their own religion, worldview, scientific concepts and technologies, have emerged. The introduction of agriculture eventually resulted in the building of towns, the emergence of trade, as well as writing and accounting, the development of specialised professions, scientific discoveries, and schools. Several early civilisations reached high degrees of sophistication and influence, especially in the Middle East, Mediterranean, South Asia and China. Later, the Greek-Roman, Mayan, Inca, Arab and western cultures gained influence. The rise and fall of civilisations, with their domination, control and exchanges of cultures and technologies, seems to be a phenomenon of all times throughout the world.

The last couple of centuries have witnessed the incomparable dominance of the western culture. Western economic mechanisms, values, science and technology increasingly replace traditional cultures and knowledge systems throughout the world. These traditional systems are rejected, or regarded poorly, while little is done to strengthen their dynamics for local development. The capacity of local knowledge systems is further weakened when the younger generation is attracted by the dominant culture, and decides to move away from their cultural background.

At the same time, the traditional cultures display remarkable resilience. Though not always openly expressed, traditional values, knowledge, concepts and practices still play an important role in the decision making process of rural people in many parts of the world. Traditional leaders are influential, and their cultural values - often quite different from those which dominate in the West - prevail in many rural societies. This of course, includes both the positive and more negative aspects of traditional practices. Meanwhile, the limitations of the western culture and technologies are also becoming clearer. The persistent problems of industrialised agriculture, such as environmental degradation, loss of biodiversity, lack of animal welfare, and the disintegration of rural communities, strengthen the call for innovative rural development approaches.

Diversity and co-evolution as important keys. There is growing awareness that technologies developed under one set of conditions may not be effective under other economic, ecological and socio-cultural situations. Instead of applying fixed technology packages under all conditions, more importance is now attached to the concept of 'diversity': diversity in values, scientific concepts, technologies, development approaches, farming styles, biological systems, cultural expressions and lifestyles. Diversity is increasingly considered to hold important keys towards solving major global problems.

The ultimate result of basing development actions on this concept can be a diversity of sciences, practices and cultures, which co-exist and co-evolve. This diversity allows for a variation of options and solutions according to the specifics of local situations. Combining the efforts of innovative rural people, development organisations and policy-making bodies is required to bring this concept one step further, and to relate it to our increasingly globalising world.

This book

The book provides insights into some of the cultures and knowledge systems on the different continents. The authors from Asia, Africa, Latin America and Europe have learned that traditional cultures and knowledges - we deliberately use this word in plural - of the local people can be the starting point for local development activities. In doing so, two risks need to be avoided: the risk of romanticising local traditions and the risk of rejecting them. This, of course, is also true for modern technologies, which can be romanticised or rejected. Taking knowledge systems seriously implies a constructive and critical position, one that searches for possibilities to improve upon them. Strengthening the capacity for learning, experimenting and changing is an important task for all those involved in the process of enhancing endogenous development. Experiences presented here provide important insights in endogenous development

Acknowledging the importance of equitable and just international relations, this book does not emphasise confrontation between the knowledge systems of the West and the rest. Instead, it presents a critical analysis of the mechanisms required for endogenous development, which includes both traditional and modern knowledge and practices.

Content. The first three chapters of this book provide a historical perspective of cultures and knowledges in the world, a description of the endogenous development approach, and the background of the Compas programme. The chapters on the geographical regions (4, 5, 6 and 7) describe the most important aspects of the cultures, knowledge and technologies prevailing in Asia, Africa, Latin America and Europe, with specific reference to those areas where Compas partners are building up experiences. This includes the worldview of the peoples, their knowledge and concepts, as well as the demographic and political context. Special attention is given to the history of each region.

These Ancient Roots continue to influence the present situation, and give rise to New Shoots in endogenous development. The case studies in the same chapters present practical experiences of rural people and development staff in enhancing endogenous development. The insights gained into traditional practices and values are described together with the local constraints related to human welfare, ecology or economy, and the results of the wide variety of interventions to improve upon them. Though the major focus is on agriculture, health and natural resources, the activities also include a variety of other aspects, such as tourism, crafts and marketing.

An analysis of these efforts, as well as the mechanisms for creating an enabling environment for endogenous development is presented in the concluding chapters (8 and 9). The annexes provide information on the Compas partner organisations, and present an explanation of some of the most important concepts used in this book.

Limitations. This book presents a snapshot of the learning process in the 14 countries in Asia, Sub-Saharan Africa, Latin America and Europe, where Compas partner organisations are implementing their activities. At present, Compas is working only in countries where English or Spanish is spoken. Information about other cultures, such as the Arab world, the Chinese, the Aboriginals, the North American natives, to name but a few, are absent in this volume.

In the process of writing this book, we have not been able to overcome all our cultural biases, as the editors and most of the authors have been trained in the western way of thinking. The very process of describing the historic context in the various regions confronted us with striking cultural differences, for example, in the concepts of time. Such cultural differences also exist in the scientific approaches. A scientist in the West is supposed to accumulate knowledge by using the five senses - smell, taste, hearing, touch and sight - while in other scientific traditions, the senses may be complemented with consciousness, religious experiences and intuition.

Readability has been the argument for reducing the number of local terms, or for translating them into English, and in the process the original significance may have been somewhat distorted. Moreover, although the editors have tried to prevent generalisation, writing about cultures may have in places done just that. Despite these limitations we feel that the experiences and insights presented here provide valuable insights on endogenous development. The authors are aware that much still needs to be learned in this field, and are open for comments and reactions. The Compas programme produces the six-monthly Compas Magazine as a medium for the dialogue on endogenous development.

Acknowledgements

The book has been written by a great number of authors who are directly involved in practical field work of the Compas partner organisations. The work towards endogenous development is a challenging, difficult and energy absorbing activity. The fact that we have been able to present the experiences here is proof of the dedication and determination of all involved in the Compas network, as well as other actors in the movement.

Valuable basic ideas and comments for the book were provided by the regional co-ordinators of Compas - David Millar (CECIK), Cosmas Gonese (AZTREC), A.V. Balasubramanian(CIKS) and Freddy Delgado (AGRUCO). A reference group in the Netherlands, consisting of Karin Boven (Nuffic), Coen Reijntjes (ILEIA) and Edith van Walsum (ETC), guided the writing process, while scientific support was provided by Niels Röling and Jan Douwe van der Ploeg from the Wageningen University, and Ton Dietz from the University of Amsterdam. Language editing was done meticulously by Chesha Wettasinha, while editorial support was provided by Désirée Dirkzwager. The lay-out and page making was done by Marijke Kreikamp. We are grateful for their dedication.

The Compas programme has been funded and sponsored by DGIS-DDE, DGIS-DCO, Novib, SDC, CTA and UNESCO. Without their generous financial and moral support the programme would not have been possible.

2. CULTURES, KNOWLEDGES AND DEVELOPMENT A HISTORICAL PERSPECTIVE

An impressive variety of civilisations exists across the globe, each with its own knowledge and value system. Some of these can be traced back more than 10,000 years when agriculture emerged, followed by towns, crafts, trade, scripts and other technologies. Religion played an important role in determining the values, systems of governance and scientific methods on which these cultures were based. This chapter presents an overview of some important ancient civilisations, as well as more recent developments, such as the colonial period, the enlightenment and the present process of globalisation. These historical roots determine the cultural identity, and play a crucial role in the choices of development options of rural communities today.

Some 2.5 million years ago tool-making hominids emerged on the earth, and the first known tools are chipped pebbles from East Africa. Evolutionists believe that around 100,000 years ago, modern man (Homo sapiens sapiens) emerged in Africa, and by 30,000 years ago man was present throughout large parts of the world, including the Americas and Australia [Scarre, 1991]. When the last ice age came to an end, some 10,000 years ago, the earth's temperature rose, and allowed people to inhabit its northern parts as well. Ever since appearing on the earth, man has been learning to master the environment. This process started with the use of hand tools, building of shelters and the knowledge of fire, passed through to the development of agriculture, pottery, metallurgy and building of towns and steam engines, and has finally evolved to the use of nuclear power and electronics.

Emerging cultures

Around 10,000 years ago agriculture developed on the different continents: in the Fertile Crescent (the territory stretching from the Persian Gulf to Mesopotamia and Palestine), the Indus and Gangetic Valleys, as well as the plains of northern China. Later, it spread to Central America and the Andes, north western Europe and sub-Saharan Africa. Only the deserts did not allow for farming; here, hunting and gathering, in combination with nomadic systems, exist even today.

The development of the first urban, literate civilisation in southern Mesopotamia, around 5,500 years ago, was to have profound consequences in history. Within a few centuries, similar processes led to the emergence of advanced civilisations in Egypt, the Indus Valley and northern China, which shared certain features. They were centred on fertile alluvial plains with high potential to support an increasing population. The people lived in cities, which were ruled as independent states, or as part of a larger empire, while differentiation of occupations and crafts, as well as international trade emerged. Similar processes took place around 3,000 years ago in the Andean highlands and Central Mexico. The agricultural practices in these different ancient civilisations varied greatly: in Egypt and the Indus Valley the annual flooding was used to provide water and fertility - crops could be planted on receding waters - while in Mesopotamia, China and the Americas, water scarcity led to the development of irrigation systems.

Trade went hand in hand with the development of towns and craftsmanship. Trade brought Mesopotamia in direct contact with Egypt and then with the Indus. In the Near East and in China, writing appeared for the purpose of keeping business accounts. During the first millennium BC large empires emerged in the Middle East, the Mediterranean, the Indian subcontinent, China, Central America and the Andes. During several thousand years these empires controlled large geographical areas through military occupation and trade relations. Due to a variety of reasons these empires collapsed over time. Polynesia, Australasia, northern Asia, the northern part of the Americas, and sub-Saharan Africa remained largely unaffected by these ancient imperial structures.

Religions and knowledges

The world has known and still knows a large variety of religions: basic religions as well as formal religions, such as Hinduism, Buddhism, Taoism, Confucianism, Shintoism, Judaism, Christianity and Islam. These religions have largely determined the worldview, values and knowledge concepts of their adherents, including the concept of time, the ideas about destiny, soul and life after death, as well as the relationship between humans, the spiritual world and nature These concepts largely determine their technologies, ways of doing research, and the way people look at the present, past and future.

Without pretending to be complete, we will briefly outline some basic aspects of the most important religions, as well as the concepts on which their knowledges are based. We use the word 'knowledges' in plural, to indicate that knowledge does not have only one way of expressing itself, but manifests itself in a variety of ways. In the overview chapters on each continent (chapter 4, 5, 6 and 7) we will go deeper into this subject.

Basic religions. The religions of prehistoric peoples embraced a variety of beliefs and practices, including animism, totemism and the belief in many Gods [Hopfe and Woodward, 1998]. Animism is the belief that nature is alive with spirits and Gods that can be communicated with. It is one of the most common religious experiences, both in the early human civilisations and in the various ethnic groups throughout the world today. People believe that animals, trees, stones, rivers, mountains, heavenly bodies, as well as the earth itself, possess a spirit. These spirits communicate, can be flattered or offended, and therefore can either hurt or help humans. People consider themselves dependent on these forces to which they can pray, worship, or make sacrifices for support. Totemism is part of most basic religions, in which a tribe or clan identifies itself with an animal species, plant or natural phenomenon. The totem can be considered as the ancestor of the clan, and the relationship between the clan and the totem often implies certain taboos in eating or hunting the species involved.

In many early civilisations, such as the Egyptian, Mayan, Inca or Celt, enormous energies and resources were spent on building temples, astronomic observatories, graves and places of sacrifice to appease the Gods and spirits. Spiritual leaders were influential, not only in religious matters, but also in governance, justice, education, health, and agriculture. These health and agricultural practices directly referred to the relationship between

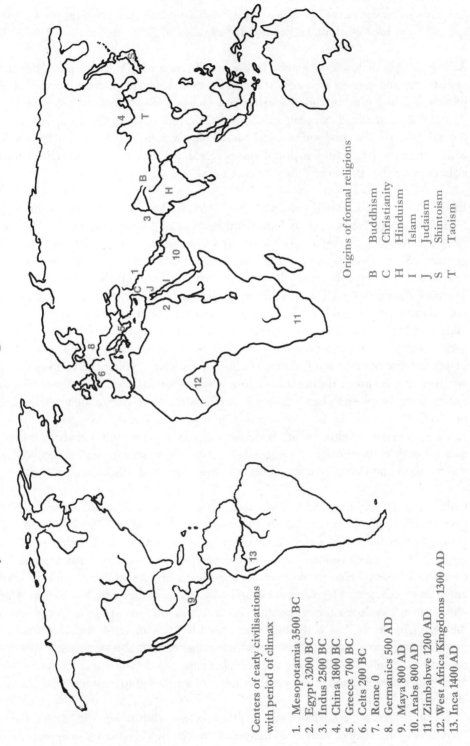

Early civilisations and formal religions mentioned in this book

Centers of early civilisations
with period of climax

1. Mesopotamia 3500 BC
2. Egypt 3200 BC
3. Indus 2500 BC
4. China 1800 BC
5. Greece 700 BC
6. Celts 200 BC
7. Rome 0
8. Germanics 500 AD
9. Maya 800 AD
10. Arabs 800 AD
11. Zimbabwe 1200 AD
12. West Africa Kingdoms 1300 AD
13. Inca 1400 AD

Origins of formal religions

B   Buddhism
C   Christianity
H   Hinduism
I   Islam
J   Judaism
S   Shintoism
T   Taoism

mankind, nature and the spiritual forces. In the present-day belief systems of many indigenous peoples throughout Asia, Africa and Latin America, animism plays an important role, and is often combined with a formal religion.

Africa. In addition to the widespread influence of Islam and Christianity, traditional belief systems are still present in most African societies. Animistic and totemic practices are often combined with ancestral worship and sacrifices to the natural Gods and spirits. Traditional political and spiritual leaders, as well as spirit mediums, play important roles in the daily life of the communities and households. Ethnic affiliation and links with the land, where the family and ancestral spirits reside, are considered important. Chapter 5 elaborates on the African religions in more detail.

India. Besides the animistic beliefs of the different tribal societies, India is the origin of several formal religions, such as Hinduism, Jainism, Buddhism and Sikhism. These religions are based on a belief in many Gods and in a system of reincarnation. The ultimate goal of these religions is to be released from 'the cycle of life, death and re-birth', which can be achieved through appropriate actions of the believer and assistance of the Gods. The divine manifests itself in evolution. The human race, though currently at the top of the evolutionary pyramid, is not seen as separate from the earth and its biodiversity. Hinduism is permeated by a reverence for life and awareness that the great forces of nature - earth, sky, air, water and fire - as well as plant, animal and human life, are all bound together within the rhythm of nature. Hindus believe that all plants and animals have souls and that people should do penance before killing plants or animals for food. Buddhism differs from the other Indian religions as it rejects the caste system, denies the relevance of the Gods and the necessity of worship and sacrifice. The ultimate goal of each individual is to reach 'enlightenment'. Buddhism implies a relationship between humans and nature based on reverence and compassion. Chapter 4 presents more information on the major Indian knowledge systems: Hinduism, Buddhism and tribal animism.

China. Formal religions and philosophical systems from China and Japan are Taoism, Confucianism and Shintoism. Like in other societies, the earliest religions of the Chinese people were based on the animistic recognition of many Gods and spirits, especially the Gods of the Heavens and the Earth, which controlled the universe. In spring and fall the emperors of early China would perform elaborate sacrifices to these Gods, which were intended to ensure the fertility of the soil and bountiful harvests. The ancient Chinese philosophers developed the concept of *Yin* and *Yang*, the two opposite forces that make the universe operate. Yin is the negative natural force: dark, cool, female, related to the moon and the earth. Yang is the positive force in nature: light, bright, warm, male, dry and related to the sun. Yin and Yang are complementary, and the balance between Yin and Yang brings harmony and 'life energy', or *Chi*. Chi is believed to exist in all living and non-living things.

Similarly, Taoism, founded some 2,500 years ago, emphasises the natural harmony, unity and spontaneity of nature. Man and nature can be in harmony since both humans and nature obey the same laws. When perfect balance and harmony exists between the Yin and Yang qualities, growth of all living things flourishes, and Chi enhances the environment. These concepts have developed into a complex science known as *Feng Shui*, which can be considered as an early form of ecology based on the sustainability of natural resources. Taoism also stood at the basis of the eloborate Chinese medical theories and health care practices. The Chinese philosopher Confucius, who was primarily concerned with society and interpersonal relations, called for people to act in a proper manner and to take care of nature. According to him, people could assist the harmonious balance between heaven and earth by leading a moral life.

The most developed sciences in ancient China were astronomy, mathematics, medicine and agronomy. In fact, the science and technology developed in China were dominant in the world before the 15th century. Chinese discoveries during that period comprised more than half of the total number of new inventions, and included the compass, gunpowder, paper and printing. These innovations, when introduced to the west, had great impact on its economic and political developments. The Chinese had special values related to learning: the most important criterion for learning was its usefulness for humanity. This differed strikingly from the ancient Greek, who studied for the sake of knowledge in itself, not necessarily for its direct practical application. [Berger and Yang di Sheng, 1997]. This volume does not provide any further information on the Chinese knowledge systems, because Compas does not work with partner organisations in China.

Middle East. The Middle East is the origin of the Zoroastrianism, Judaism, Christianity, Islam and the Bahai faith. These formal religions believe in one supreme creator God, and in one life on earth. They have a linear view of time and believe in the divine judgement of the world.

Christianity is the largest religion of the world, with almost 2 billion followers, followed by Islam, with about one billion. Both Christians and Muslims believe that creation is the act of God, who continues to take care of all aspects of existence. People have only one life in which to determine their destiny after death: either eternal bliss in heaven or torment in hell. Humans may explore and exploit nature, but may not destroy it: people should act as stewards of natural resources. Values like thrift, planning for the future, and working hard to reach specific goals in this life, were developed and presently dominate in Christian societies. Christian and Islamic religions are dominated by men; women do not fulfil important roles in the rituals and priesthood [Hopfe and Woodward, 1998]. Meanwhile, Christianity has also gone through a number of reformations and changes. At present Christianity presents itself in a wide range of denominations, and its influence on European society is no longer as prominent as in the past. In western cultures the church and the state are separate identities. Christian values, such as the linear time concept, attitude towards nature, and the emphasis on the material world still have a major impact on western cultures today.

Islam was founded as a religion in Mecca in the 7th century AD. Arab armies and merchants carried Islam to the entire Middle East, India, Pakistan, Bangladesh, China, Spain, North Africa, as well as central and south-east Asia. The Arab world has known a period of high scientific achievements from the 7th to the 9th century. Around the year 800 AD, Arab mathematics, geography, astronomy and medicine flourished, and became an important source for European scientists. Christian and Muslim armies have been fighting each other in search of political and religious control for several centuries. During the 15th century the Muslims conquered Constantinople and the Christian crusaders were defeated. Northern Africa was engulfed in Muslim missionary activities during the 19th century, as abuses of the Africans by the colonial powers opened the doors to Islam.

In order to be a good Muslim one has to obey what is referred to as 'the five pillars of Islam': repetition of the creed, daily prayers, giving alms, fasting during Ramadan, and pilgrimage to Mecca. For the Muslim, humans are the creation of Allah, or God, and must be obedient to Him. Righteous persons must submit to His will, and humanity's role on earth is that of a *khalifa*, or trustee of God. The earth belongs to God, and He has entrusted mankind with its safekeeping, the integrity of the earth, its flora and fauna, its wildlife and natural environment. The khalifa is answerable for his/her actions, and for the way in which this 'trust of God' is used or abused. Allah is unity; and this unity is also reflected in the unity of humanity, and the unity between humanity and nature. As in all other religions, there are many different ways of experiencing and practising Islam. This book does not provide further information on the Islamic knowledge systems because Compas does not work with partner organisations in areas where this religion is dominant.

Central and South America. In the traditional worldview of the native Americans all nature is alive with spirits. At the heart of nature is Mother Earth, or *Pacha Mama*, who gives life and should also be revered, in order to reciprocate her gifts. This 'mutuality' is seen as an important principle, while good human behaviour and making sacrifices to the Gods are seen as another precondition for harmony between humans, nature, and the spiritual world. Harmony in the cosmos is optimal if harmony exists within the human sphere, the natural-material sphere and the spiritual sphere, as well as between each of these spheres. Mountains, water bodies and other places considered sacred are used as places of worship. The farmland, or *milpa* (central America) and *chacra* (Andes), is considered a sacred place, where animals, plants and human beings live in mutual dependence. Here, traditional farmers have a most intimate relationship with Mother Earth, which is expressed in numerous beliefs and rituals throughout the year.

Early civilisations of the Maya and the Aztecs in Central America, and the Incas in the Andes, built impressive temples that were used for rituals, sacrifices and as astronomic observatories. The *Popol Vuj* is the ancient Mayan text that describes the story of the creation of mankind, in which maize plays an important role as the sacred crop. Similarly, potatoes are considered sacred in the Andes. The Latin American indigenous knowledge concepts include the spiral notion of time, the importance of community festivals and rituals, the sacred aspect of nature, the polarity between opposite forces such as hot-cold and male-female, the importance of bio-diversity, and the mutuality between human beings and other living organisms. The morality of the people is considered an important factor in explaining the processes related to farming, health and community welfare.

These worldviews and concepts are still alive among the native peoples in northern, central, and south America. After the conquest by the Spanish and Portuguese, traditional lifestyles, beliefs and practices have been replaced by, or complemented with Christianity and western values. Also ethnically, most indigenous peoples of Latin America have been replaced by, or mingled with European settlers. The *ladinos*, or *mestizos*, now form the largest population group in most Latin countries. But, syncretism prevails, and within most indigenous groups, such as Mayas in Mexico and Guatemala, as well as Quechuas, Aymaras and Mapuches in the Andes and Chile, traditional beliefs and religious practices go hand in hand with Christianity. Chapter 6 provides more details on the background of American religions and knowledges.

Western Europe. Some 7,000 years ago, agriculture was well established in western Europe, where its original peoples, such as the Celts and Germanics, built places of worship based on animistic religions. The first European urban-based civilisation emerged in Crete, around 4,000 years ago. The Greek developed an elaborate religion with a pantheon of Gods, semi-Gods, and giants, and laid the basis for modern scientific thinking by the development of 'logic': a system of propositions and deductive arguments. From the 3rd century onwards the Roman empire became the stronghold of Christianity. Western Europe was christianised from the 7th century AD onwards. In contrast to the pre-christian religions, this new faith was dominated by men, and women could no longer fulfil roles in the rituals and priesthood. This combination of pre-Christian and Greek-Christian worldviews in Europe allowed the emergence of a culture where thrift, planning the future, hard work, and technological enquiry were held in high esteem. Between the 10th and 14th century many universities were founded with theology as their main intellectual pursuit. These values, combined with missionary zeal, led to colonisation of large parts of the world in the 16th and 17th centuries.

The Enlightenment

During the middle ages, the European local rulers were generally appointed, sanctioned or ordained by the Church. The Church also controlled the educational systems and science according to its own dogmas and concepts of life. Scientific insights that were in contradiction to the beliefs held by the church were rejected and scientists presenting such insights were prosecuted. For example Galileo, who provided evidence that the planet earth turned around the sun, instead of the sun around the earth, was condemned by the Inquisition, a church-based court of justice. In the 18th century, a number of scientists decided to work without the limitations imposed on them by religious dogma. Francis Bacon, Isaac Newton and Descartes, considered the founders of modern science, formulated a new scientific paradigm: they shifted from the concept of a world controlled by God to the concept of a material world, which functions like a machine.

Francis Bacon formulated his theory of the 'inductive procedure': general conclusions drawn from experiments can be tested in further experiments. Thus, well designed experiments can force nature to reveal its secrets. Isaac Newton formulated the 'law of gravity', and on that basis formulated the astronomic concept of the sun, planets and their satellites, which are kept in place through the laws of gravity. He developed the prism, discovered the spectrum of light, and formulated the mechanistic worldview. Descartes believed in the certainty or 'absolute truth of scientific knowledge'. His method, also called the Cartesian worldview, is reductionist: all aspects of a complex phenomenon can be understood by reducing it into parts, and understanding each constituent part. He made a clear distinction between mind and matter, and replaced the notion of the 'divine plan of the creator' by the 'mathematical order of nature'. For Descartes the material universe was comparable to a machine. There is no purpose, life or spirituality in matter. Nature works according to mechanical laws and everything in the material world can be explained in terms of the arrangement and movement of its parts.

Bacon and Descartes agreed that the aim of science is to dominate and control nature, and assumed that scientific knowledge could be used by humans to render themselves the masters and possessors of nature. To describe nature mathematically, they had to restrict themselves to studying those aspects that can be quantified by shape, weight, number or movement. Other properties like colour, taste, smell, and especially emotional or spiritual values were considered subjective projections, to be excluded from the scientific domain. This mechanical picture of nature became the dominant paradigm of western science, and from then on guided the scientific observations and theories in the western world. This new paradigm is called Enlightenment, as it implies an optimistic view on the potential of the human being, based on its rationality. In this perspective, humans can use science to dominate and control nature. Through western dominance, this paradigm was to become a central element for science and development across the world in the centuries to come.

Process of colonisation

Throughout history, Christianity and Islam have been particularly active in their missionary activities. The Christian missionaries within Europe were led by the Church of Rome. As on other continents in their subsequent invasions, in Europe too they were faced with a widespread animistic belief system of its original inhabitants, in which worshipping different Gods and spirits, the sun and other elements in nature, were common elements. The strategy for gaining control over these indigenous western European peoples, such as the Celts and the Germanics, shared similarities with that of the conquest of the Americas, Africa and parts of Asia by European Christian nations, and the Muslim invasions in other parts of the world.

Strategies of colonisation. The colonising empire would build up an economic and military power with a strong link to its religion. The indigenous cultures and religions of the colonised peoples would be declared inferior, and their belief systems 'superstitious'. The new religion would then be presented as a means of liberalisation for the colonised peoples and as a benefit to them, which in turn justified the dominationover them. The indigenous populations of Europe were called 'barbaric' by the Roman colonisers; similarly the black people of Africa and the indigenous populations of the Americas were considered inferior by the Europeans colonisers.

Many dominated cultures that were confronted with powerful intruders, perceived the actions of the latter in terms of their own constructs of the supernatural, and thus subdued to them. In the conquest of the Aztec Empire, for example, the Spanish invasion leader Hernan Cortes, as well as the horses his soldiers were using, were considered to be supernatural powers. Their arrival had been predicted by traditional seers and was therefore welcomed by part of the people. In other parts of the Americas, as well as in Africa, the native peoples considered the missionary priests as shamans, and their books as tools to manipulate nature and supernatural forces.

The colonising power would make alliances with the local political leaders, while legal systems were forced to take on board the new morality and values. At the same time indigenous traditional leaders were declared demonic, clairvoyant women were called witches to be prosecuted and killed, while non-believers in the new religion were convicted. During the Christian colonisation of Europe, and later on in the Americas, a church-based court of justice could condemn and punish - even to death - those who practised traditional 'heathen' rituals, or those who did not comply with the laws of the church. Colonial rule in the 18th and 19th centuries often included laws to forbid witchcraft in African colonies. Sacred places and places of worship of the original religion were destroyed and replaced by churches on the same location. For example, the Christianisation of northern Europe was impacted strongly when Irish missionary Bonifatius destroyed a sacred oak of the Germanics in Kassel. Similarly, sacred places of the Incas and Aztecs were destroyed and turned into Christian churches, using the same building materials. Sacred shrines and groves in Africa were rejected and where possible demolished by the colonial occupants.

Meanwhile, the strategy of the colonisers also implied that traditional practices, which were not wholly in contradiction with the new religion, were given a new label, and gradually integrated into it. This syncretism can be observed in medieval Europe and Latin America, and to a lesser extent in Africa, where the church tolerates certain indigenous festivals and practices. In Latin America this syncretism is still very much part of the reality. For example, the Mayas in Guatemala and the Quechuas and Aymaras in the Andes have a wide range of traditional festivals and agricultural rituals, that are incorporated into expressions of Christianity. Hence, it could also be argued, that these peoples have absorbed Christianity into their traditional belief systems as a survival mechanism. In contrast, the traditional religious practices in Africa have been suppressed strongly by the formal churches, and syncretism is not as common and open as in Latin America.

Through education, welfare and technological innovations, the religion of the coloniser would gain popularity and over time create a new local elite educated in the new system. These new leaders had the tendency of rejecting the old religion even more vigorously than the missionaries before them, as their new position and status depended on it. The new elite was often trained by church-based institutions, as was the case in Africa, where the church-based education systems and development programmes often perform better than the state-based institutions. Even today, acknowledging the presence and relevance of indigenous knowledge and practices is often more difficult for the local elite than for outsiders.

Meanwhile, many traditional practices, leaders and institutions continued to function in parallel or secretively; the new religion and value system could not wipe out all traditions of the colonised population. Though often under threat, traditional leaders continued to perform their roles as spiritual leaders of the people in the local communities. This can still, and quite clearly, be observed in Latin America, Africa and Asia. Europe was no exception to this rule. But 700 years of domination by Christianity and the subsequent social, economical and political developments, has reduced the original indigenous belief systems in to a vague memory for most Europeans.

Colonialism, western science and knowledge. The industrial revolution and the resulting economic development of Europe, as well as the spread of European trade and colonisation from the 16th century onwards, was the start of the inter-linked world economy. Innovations in maritime technology, as well as the feeling of superiority of the European people, enabled European ships to transport slaves from Africa to the Americas, to bring silver from the Americas, porcelain from China, and spices from the East Indies to the flourishing cities of western Europe. These processes culminated in European colonialism and imperialism of the 18th, 19th, and 20th centuries, which together with industrialisation, mark the birth of the modern world we know today [Scarre, 1991].

In the Encyclopedia of the History of Science, Technology and Medicine in Non-Western cultures [Selin, 1997], Micheal Adas presents an overview of the way in which western science played a role in European expansion, explaining how this has affected the diversity of knowledge systems in the dominated cultures. Adas asserts that, besides economic and religious expansion, scientific curiosity was one of the major motives for the European expeditions and conquests. Astronomers and cartographers often sailed with the merchants to test new instruments, take astronomical and nautical readings, and chart unknown regions. As European armies and administrators advanced inland in the Americas, Africa and Asia, geologists and botanists followed, and brought home specimens of exotic plants and minerals etc. The information gained was used to accumulate wealth in Europe and to build a new vision on the earth and the cosmos. Ethnological studies became the basis for allegedly scientific, and invariably hierarchic, classifications of human types, usually termed races. As western Europe's need for markets and raw materials grew, fields like meteorology, geology, chemistry and applied mathematics became important in the colonial enterprise.

With only a few exceptions, the European colonial scientists and policy makers were generally unreceptive to non-western ways of thinking and interacting with the natural world. They perceived western science as value neutral, objective in its procedures, privileging abstractions and reason, empirically grounded, transcending time and space, and therefore universally valid. These attributes gave the practitioners and scientists the confidence that the spread of this epistemology - and the institutions and procedures associated with it - to the rest of the peoples of the earth was both beneficial and inevitable. It was seen as a strategy to rationalise the world, and to banish superstitious, subjective, and intuitive epistemologies. Western science was as aggressively intolerant to non-western epreligions and sciences, as it had been to the culture of the original European peoples.

The process by which western science was diffused, and its impact on other societies, differed greatly. The Muslim leaders in the Middle East, for example, integrated western concepts in their knowledge, while the Chinese and Japanese resisted their introduction. This difusion process depended on various aspects, such as the timing of European interaction with the non-western culture, the colonisers' assumptions about the level of sophistication of indigenous technologies, as well as the actual attainments of the colonised peoples in science and technologies. In India, China and the Middle East, the European colonisers recognised some aspects of the ancient civilisation - writing, the specialised intellectual elite, cities - which fed mutual curiosity and exchange. In China, the European Jesuits studied Chinese astronomy, chemistry and medical techniques, while the Portuguese and Dutch merchants in India consulted the local physicians, and accepted their superiority in treating tropical diseases.

Nonetheless, in all of the settlement colonies, indigenous systems for understanding, learning, teaching and experimenting were pushed to the periphery. Ethnologists studied indigenous belief systems for their antiquarian value, not because they had something to learn from it. The research agendas in the colonies were set by the scientific societies and institutions in Europe and served the needs of uncovering and extracting the great natural wealth. Meanwhile, racist assumptions about the mental capacity of the indigenous peoples ensured that little or no training in science was made available. Though in India surveyors, engineers and medical practitioners received training and worked for colonial administrations or firms, in much of the rest of Asia, sub-Saharan Africa, Latin America and the Pacific islands, the opportunities for advanced training were minimal. In these areas, scientific work was the monopoly of the European coloniser. This left most colonised peoples ill-prepared for the post-colonial world, where the western concepts of science, law, nation building and administration were dominant. This has limited their capacity in economic competition, development planning and intellectual discourse [Adas, 1997].

Several other authors have also studied the impact of colonialism on indigenous peoples. Ubiratan d'Ambrosio [1997], for example, refers to the exploitation of lands, resources and peoples of the American colonies. *"The conquerors had no concepts to explain and understand what they observed in the newly found lands. They marvelled at the construction, urban organisation, clothing, and ornamentation of these peoples. The colonisers brought with them traditional European agricultural and mining techniques. The means of production were changed, native religions destroyed and food habits modified. Latin America was the recipient and not the producer of scientific advances. Also after independence, the peripheral position of the countries was maintained. The colonial style and submission of the native population was continued and education was modelled on the former imperial system"*. Gloria Emeagwali[1997] states: *"Colonialism has weakened the African capacity in experimentation, problem solving and the creation of utilitarian objects and processes. It has left an educational system more geared to the reproduction of Christian values and alienation, than the further development of the African scientific and technological capacity"*.

The impact of colonisation, did not end when the independent nation states were contributed. For example, scientific thinking in present day India has absorbed the western concept of man's control over nature [Guha, 1994]. The roots of this phenomenon do not only lie in the Judeo-Christian ethics of the colonisers, but also in the process of gaining independence from the British in 1947. The post-independence process of development considered it a national challenge to reduce the gap between independent India and the industrialised countries. Rapid industrialisation was conceived as the basis of this development, as well as the technical and social sciences related to it. These western based sciences and concepts replaced the Indian scientific traditions to a considerable extent.

Postmodernity

The scientific paradigm that emerged during the Enlightenment is still equalled by many to 'modern'. The impact of the technologies developed by this approach has been tremendous, and has ensured food security and accumulation of wealth in various parts of the world. At the same time the limitations of this materialistic-mechanistic worldview are now clearly visible, such as the increasing poor-rich divide, environmental pollution, loss of biodiversity, and the break down of social structures in rural areas throughout the world. There is a growing need for more sustainable food production systems and economies, which calls for a new approach.

In the early 20th century Einstein formulated his laws of thermodynamics and the theory of relativity, thereby laying the foundation of new physics and of post-modernity. Development in quantum mechanics, pioneered by Niels Bohr and Werner Heisenberg, further modified the hitherto conventional concepts of time and space, matter, gravity and cause-effect relationship. They concluded that subatomic particles have a dual nature: depending on how we look at them they can appear as particles (matter), or as waves (energy). Bohr, therefore, considered the particle and the wave as complementary descriptions of the same reality. Heisenberg postulated the 'uncertainty principle', which is based on the finding that at subatomic level matter does not exist with certainty at definite places, but rather shows tendencies to exist, and atomic events show tendencies to occur. In contrast to the former mechanistic Cartesian worldview, this post-modern worldview can be characterised as holistic: the universe is no longer seen as a machine, made up of a multitude of objects that can be controlled, but as one indivisible, dynamic whole whose parts are interrelated.

In the 1980s the General Systems Theory emerged, in which an organic, living system is not considered a machine that can be managed and controlled once its dynamics are known, but rather a combination of living, interacting and self-organising elements. Competition, symbiosis, self-renewal and innovative creativity are important processes in a living system [Röling, 1992]. Chaos can be a necessary step in the evolution of a system towards a new order of higher complexity and quality [Prigogini, 1984]. The notion of Gaia [Lovelock, 1979] assumes that earth behaves like a living organism, and her properties and processes cannot be understood and predicted from the mere sum of its parts. In this notion, the reductionist description of organisms can be useful and necessary, but is considered dangerous when taken as the complete explanation of reality. Reductionism and holism, analysis and synthesis, are seen as complementary approaches, which, if used in a proper balance, help us to gain a deeper understanding of life [Capra, 1983]. Ruppert Sheldrake [1994] has elaborated the theory of morphogenetic fields and resonance. Other authors, like Ken Wilber [1998], are elaborating holistic theories to link science and spirituality.

This is combined with an increased interest and influence of the scientific concepts of eastern knowledges. For example, Capra [1983] points at the relationship between the Systems Theory and Taoism, and concludes that the dualism observed at sub-atomic level, coincides with the Taoist concept of Yin Yang duality. Others look at eastern sciences based on completely different concepts, to find ways of complementing western science.

For example, they look at Ayurvedic medicine, in which completely different categories are used and the analytical methods are not limited to the five senses (smell, taste, hearing, touch and sight). Instead, complete awareness is sought at a level of perception, by which the observer both reaches out and looks within, establishing a subjective flow between the observer and the observed.

The boundaries and potential of post-modern science are difficult to indicate. New paradigms are sometimes difficult to defend, prove or explain in the conventional paradigm; some may be speculative and many meet with resistance. Yet, post-modern science presents an interesting panorama of diverse approaches, perspectives and theories. Moreover, western science is increasingly interested in understanding the human condition with an emphasis on the local. In fields as varied as physics, ecology, history, feminist theory, literature, anthropology, economy and politics, more attention is paid to understanding the specific characteristics of each locality. Yet, in the vast majority of centres of formal education, both in the North and the South, positivist thinking and materialistic values are still dominant.

Globalisation

Global co-operation, exchange and conflicts between groups and nations have existed since the emergence of the first urban centres in Mespotamia some 5,500 years ago. The industrial revolution and colonial system in the 16th and 17th century led to the first worldwide trade and communication system. Though the colonial system formally came to an end by the second part of the 20th century, the economic relationships between the new nation states and their former colonisers did not become equitable. Transnational enterprises did little to invest in the South, while export subsidies and import levies prevented access of tropical countries to the northern markets. Later on, development co-operation became the responsibility of the governments of the rich countries, but without a radical change in trade relations, was insufficient to alleviate poverty, or to help stimulate local economies.

Meanwhile, ongoing technological and commercial developments increased the incorporation of regional and local economics, as well as communication, into the global systems. Especially the innovations in transport and telecommunication have allowed a multiple exchange of ideas and goods: the global market has penetrated all parts of the globe. This contemporary process of increased global communication, application of internationally accepted technologies, and the uniformity of commercial products and values, is now commonly understood as 'globalisation'.

Globalisation offers opportunities to link people across the globe, to exchange information and goods. It provides the opportunity to link production systems in a complementary way and allows production to take place in those areas with a comparative advantage. In the present global information system, people can inform and learn from each other, assist each other in decision-making, or join forces in negotiation and lobbying. Globalisation contributes to fast and intensive communication and greater knowledge about different societies, cultures and ecosystems in the world. It also contributes to an increased awareness of the fragility of the earth's ecosystem, and the recognition that indigenous knowledge and traditional cultures may contain key characteristics for meeting the global challenge of re-establishing biological and cultural sustainability. The present-day trends aimed at diversification of biological and socio-economic systems, and at revitalisation of local cultures, can be understood as an effect of globalisation.

Globalisation and poverty. Though globalisation has contributed to overall economic growth, this growth is clearly not found everywhere on the globe, and certainly not all social categories have benefited from it. Many are forced to migrate whilst numerous traditional life forms are driven into the background. Almost half of the world's 6 billion people live on less than US$ 1 per day. Poverty can be expressed in the increased lack of purchasing power, political power, ill health, high child death ratio, low education, economic dislocation, personal violence, political extremism and poor resilience to natural disasters in large parts of the world.

Economic growth demands space, energy and resources, and puts stress on the global climate, waters, biodiversity and vegetation. The resulting and ongoing erosion of natural and biological resources is accompanied by diminishing cultural diversity. Many traditional societies break up and numerous customs, cultural expressions and languages are vanishing. More than half of the 6,000 languages currently spoken is unlikely to survive the 21st century. Global awareness of these problems, and recognition of these by governments, have led to a considerable number of international conventions and initiatives on biodiversity, desertification, water and climate change.

But, despite efforts to liberalise world trade, international trade relations are still far from equal. Export subsidies and import levies are still imposed on the poorer countries by the major economic blocs in the North. One cannot speak of equal chances for most tropical countries in accessing the global economy. Integration of the poorer countries into the global market often implies the supply of low income jobs to foreign companies and the specialisation in bulk production of raw materials. This produce is then exported to the rich countries, where the processing and commercialisation take place, and where most of the benefits in terms of added value remain. Besides social and economic injustice, this process also implies massive international transport, high energy costs and health risks.

Another effect of globalisation is that rural communities experience a change in their local markets. Under the influence of mass media and education, a general westernisation of taste and consumption patterns is taking place. Urban consumers in developing countries increasingly consume western (fast) food and drinks more than their traditional products. At the same time, local producers find it difficult to access national consumer (super)-markets due to different quality standards and supply systems. Similar processes are taking place in relation to traditional dress, crafts and architecture, as well as traditional human and animal health practices. The economic opportunities for these local products are increasingly being taken over by the international markets, resulting in further poverty as well as loss of traditional skills and experience. In the process traditional leadership is loosing its impact on local management of natural resources, leading to further deterioration of the local eco-systems and the income that can be derived from them.

The spread of global science. Present day scientific concepts and approaches are no longer specific to a certain region. Today, global knowledge and science is the result of global processes of knowledge generation, application and technology development. It is the product of regional specialisation, and global integration of communication, production and trade. Scientists from all over the world communicate, co-operate and exchange concepts, theories and research results. Whether based in Europe, USA, Japan, India or any other country in the South, East or West, the concepts, approaches and contributions can be chosen depending on the particular expertise and price of the researcher.

At the same time, access and contribution to this global knowledge is not spread equally over the globe; it is dominated by western-based organisations whose research and development activities are financed by trans-national commercial enterprises. Although virtually all countries in the South have established institutions of academic education and research, they differ greatly in sophistication and effectiveness. In many cases, university education and research are based on western scientific standards, rather than on their own scientific traditions, local resources and knowledge systems. Curricula and research protocols are often poorly adjusted to the needs and possibilities of the local people and their knowledge systems. As a result research and development activities have the tendency to enhance technologies for international systems, rather than to support the technological, economic or cultural needs of the specific region. In general, low literacy rates, colonial history, economic status, national budgeting and planning, and political instability contribute to the problem. The processes of privatisation and liberalisation have put health services and agricultural inputs beyond the reach of many rural people.

The outcome of these processes is that those sections of the population that want to develop their local economy and cultural identity find it increasingly difficult to achieve their goals. This lack of development options in the rural areas has led to an increase in rural poverty, and migration in search of greener pastures. Internationally, the large numbers of political and economic refugees put pressure on the western states for accommodation, education, employment and safety. Policies to control the number of asylum seekers and multi-culturalism are hot political issues in most of the western countries today.

Reactions to dominance. When faced with pressures from a dominant foreign society and its culture, people respond in a variety of ways, varying from total acceptance to total rejection, with partial acceptance and a combination with their own traditions in between. Each of these positions can be expressed in a different way: silently or vocally, collectively or individually. Often the rejection of the dominant culture takes place in a hidden or secret way. Therefore, in most traditional societies that are dominated by a foreign culture one can observe underground systems of traditional value systems and leadership, which guide the decisions of rural people. Representatives of the dominant system, however, are often inclined to believe that these traditional values and practices largely belong to the past.

Meanwhile, traditional societies are not uniform. Often there is a communication gap, or marked difference of opinion, about the best way forward. This is often the case between generations, and between family members with formal or informal education: the younger and the (formally) educated people are often inclined towards the western-based knowledge system. This contradiction can also be observed between local and formal governance and jurisdiction systems. Sometimes the acceptance of the dominant system is based on the conviction that it will bring a genuine improvement, a liberation from the negative aspects or 'ties' of tradition.

The problems associated with the introduction of modern, or Green Revolution agriculture, such as declining soil fertility, health hazards, declining producer prices, increasing input prices, and reduced income, may explain the increasing tendency to revive traditional knowledge and practices. Revivalism may be expressed as a genuine belief that parts of the past may be important to develop the cultural identity and local economy, possibly in combination with certain elements and practices from other origins. But, revivalist tendencies can also take other shapes: it can become a fundamentalist reaction, which reduces the capacity to look for improvements of local practices, and to adjust to changing circumstances.

The position of Compas presented in this book is the acceptance of the existing diversity of cultures as a fact that offers a wide range of opportunities. Intercultural contacts can lead to dominance, control and disappearance of cultures, but, if these contacts are managed in a different way, they can also lead to productive and respectful learning. In the process of enhancing endogenous development, respect for differences in cultural values and concepts is a precondition. But, respect does not imply the unconditional acceptance of all differences. Instead, it implies the willingness to listen, openness to learn and be responsive, and the capacity to criticise, respectfully, when necessary [Fay, 1996].

Relating the local and the global. Western science has succeeded in transforming the world and livelihood systems in a way that no other system has so far. The success of western science is embedded in its ability to move and apply the knowledge it produces beyond the site of its production. However, at the end of the 20th century the high cost of such a scientific hegemony was observed - especially in terms of increasing environmental degradation and ethnocide. Turnbull [1997] states, for example: *"Without the awareness about local differences, we will lose the diversity and particularity of the things themselves. We need a new understanding about the dialectical tension between the local and the global. We need to develop forms of understanding, in which the local, the particular, the specific and the individual are not homogenised, but are listened to and enabled to talk back."*

Speaking about indigenous knowledge, practices and leadership does not assume that all is positive. As with other knowledge systems, indigenous knowledge of different cultural backgrounds does not have all the answers to the present day problems, and certainly has its limitations. Its adaptability to present needs may be limited, while it is often not uniformly distributed in the communities. The access to specialised knowledge may be limited to certain persons, who may not always use it to the benefit of the community. Differences in power structures, access to land, knowledge and medicine may be very difficult for certain classes, or castes. Many traditional systems are dominated by male leaders and the position of women is marginal, while some traditional practices justify the exploitation and abuse of women.

Over the past decade a renewed interest in the technical aspects of traditional knowledge and practices in agriculture and health has emerged. Many indigenous techniques on a variety of subjects, such as soil and water conservation, natural pesticides, inter-cropping, agro-forestry, food processing, as well as ethno-veterinary and human health practices, have been documented and can be improved successfully [Reijntjes et al., 1994]. A number of such documented indigenous practices, especially related to the use of medicinal herbs, are now available in computerised databases, readily accessible to governments and scientific communities. Though this so-called *ex situ* conservation approach has an important function in demonstrating the relevance of indigenous knowledge, it also carries the risk of extracting the knowledge from local communities. The data can easily be used for the benefit of outsiders, who may even patent it. Moreover, the focus is often limited to the biophysical side of indigenous knowledge, while the way local people interpret the world, their traditional leaders and spiritual practices, as well as their ways of learning, teaching and experimenting are often not considered. The endogenous development approach, on the contrary, implies the so-called *in situ* conservation and development of indigenous knowledge (see chapter 3).

Meanwhile, an increasing number of universities and development agencies, such as the World Bank, UNESCO, IFAD and FAO, now have programmes that focus on indigenous knowledge. Also United Nations conventions, such as UNCBD and UNCCD, acknowledge the importance of indigenous knowledge and practices in their declarations. A recent publication of UNDP specifically addresses the need for integrating local and global knowledge as one of the challenges for technical co-operation [Fukuka-Parr et al., 2002].

Towards a co-evolution of cultures

Therefore, there is an urgent need for new initiatives and paradigms of development with a balanced view on traditional sciences, technologies and knowledge systems. While modern science and technology are spreading, the vast majority of the people in the world still survive on the material and intellectual sustenance from their own indigenous traditions. These practices have their potentials as well as their limitations, but few efforts are undertaken to test and improve them on basis of the worldview of the poeple involved. We need to thoroughly re-evaluate the indigenous traditions of science and technology, free from the prejudices and preconceptions of the western scientific outlook.

This chapter has shown a great diversity of knowledge systems that co-exist and co-evolve, that influence, absorb or neglect each other. While the interest in non-western knowledge, and the call for synthesis between global and local knowledge is increasing, a number of agencies are emphasising the importance of endogenous development. This is a development based mainly, but not exclusively on locally available resources, such as land, water, vegetation, local knowledge, as well as the values and preferences of the local people. Supporting endogenous development does not imply a narrowly defined development approach, nor does it romanticise or reject traditions. Endogenous development is an approach that takes place complementary to the ongoing global processes, and can thus be seen as an effort to bring together global and local knowledges.

The next chapters present the Compas programme, and elaborate on the characteristics and methodologies for endogenous development, as developed by the Compas partners. Chapters 4, 5, 6 and 7 present an overview of the worldviews in Asia (with a focus on the Indian sub-continent), Sub-Saharan Africa, Latin America and Europe, as well as case studies of the Compas partner organisations in these areas. An analysis of the results of these efforts and ways for creating an enabling environment for endogenous development are presented in the concluding chapters.

Participants Compas International Workshop (2001). **Kneeling, left to right:** Selvaraj *India*, David Nkanda *Uganda,* Marthen Duan *Indonesia,* Nestor Chambi *Peru,* Krishna Prasad *India.* **First row, left to right:** K. Vijayalakshmi *India,* H. Saraswathy *India,* T.S. Suma *India,* Manasi *India,* Katrien van 't Hooft *the Netherlands,* Vanaja Ramprasad *India,* A.V. Balasubramanian *India,* G. Bhupathy *India,* Felipe Gomez *Guatemala,* Damodaran *India,* S. Arumuga Swamy *India.* **Second row, left to right:** Nirmala Arunkumar *India,* Sophia Solomon *India,* Dora Ponce *Bolivia,* Yovita Meta *Indonesia,* Maragarita Correa *India,* Nanditha Ram *India,* C.B. Shrivatsa *India,* Jaime Soto *Chile,* Freddy Delgado *Bolivia,* Batuuka Samuel *Uganda,* O.T. Kibwana *Tanzania,* Upendra Shenoy *India,* Maheswar Ghimire *Nepal,* Arjuna de Zoysa *Sri Lanka,* David Millar *Ghana,* G.K. Upawansa *Sri Lanka,* Tirupati Rao *India.* **Third row, left to right:** Thambi Durai *India,* James Handawela *Sri Lanka,* Bomber Mamba *Swaziland,* Aruna Kumara *India,* Wim Hiemstra *the Netherlands,* Prashanth Varma *India,* Darshan Shankar *India,* A.S. Ananda *India,* K.A.J. Kahandawa *Sri Lanka,* Cosmas Gonese *Zimbabwe,* Bertus Haverkort *the Netherlands,* Coen Reijntjes *the Netherlands,* P.M. Unnikrishnan *India,* Abdul Hafeel *India.*

3 THE COMPAS APPROACH TO SUPPORT ENDOGENOUS DEVELOPMENT

The Compas programme is an international network of field-based organisations that support endogenous development. It has learned that enhancing endogenous development implies a number of requirements, such as building on local resources and complementing them with appropriate external resources, maximising local control, enhancing the dynamics of local knowledge systems, and retention of benefits in the local areas. This process also implies networking and lobbying for policy reforms, training of staff and theoretical reflections on the lessons learned. The Compas partners have agreed on a code of conduct, which aims at minimising the risks related to working on the basis of indigenous knowledge.

The ongoing process of globalisation involves the entrenchment of western modern knowledge systems and technologies throughout the world. The dominant education and research systems are based on western knowledge and value systems. As a result, development activities have tended to enhance technologies with international standards, rather than support the needs of specific regions or populations. In agriculture, the use of external inputs has increased due to extension and subsidy policies. In health, western bio-medicine has reached out to all corners of the globe. Although these efforts have led to definite improvements, awareness related to the problems of this approach is increasing. Environmental pollution is a major problem, while privatisation and liberalisation have put health services and agricultural external inputs beyond the reach of large groups of rural people. Many young people are leaving rural areas in search of greener pastures. These processes strain local economies as well as the social and cultural inheritance of the local communities.

Globalisation at local level

At local level, many rural communities are experiencing a change in market opportunities. In their quest to access a share of the market, they are not only confronted with cheap subsidised products from elsewhere, but also with changing patterns of local consumption. Under the influence of mass media and education, a general 'westernisation' of taste and consumption is taking place. Urban consumers increasingly prefer western (fast) food and drinks to traditional food items. As western practices continue to be adopted, the confidence in traditional human and animal health practices is declining. Moreover, as the strength of local cultures and traditional authority structures is undermined, social cohesion and local conflict resolution mechanisms are being endangered. But evidence in Europe shows that the real impact of globalisation depends on the responses developed at the grassroots. Though the modernisation model was well internalised by many regions and groups of farmers, it was also deconstructed and reshaped by others. Some groups of farmers in Europe have taken distance from what appears to be a dominant blueprint, thus contributing to the heterogeneity of European agriculture [van der Ploeg et al., 2002].

The same phenomenon can be observed in tropical areas too. Despite the apparent acceptance of dominant technologies, a number of indigenous institutions have survived and a wealth of indigenous knowledge still exists. It is consistently observed by the Compas partner organisations, that, although under threat, there is still substantial indigenous knowledge, cosmovision and traditional leadership. These still form the basis for the decisions made by the majority of rural people. Therefore, for development organisations to be effective in supporting endogenous development, they need to understand the basic characteristics of the indigenous knowledge systems, and the worldviews that they are founded on. This, in fact, should be the starting point of development.

As indicated in chapter 2, indigenous knowledge and practices cannot provide all the answers to the present day challenges faced by rural people. The limitations and setbacks need to be analysed and taken into account. Indigenous knowledge and leadership need to be taken seriously, while ensuring that these are not romanticised.

Compas and endogenous development

The Compas partner organisations have ongoing programmes in the domains of poverty reduction based on participatory development, local management of natural resources, low-external-input and sustainable agriculture, biodiversity, local health systems, indigenous knowledge, and cultural diversity. Based on their experiences the partners have concluded that the conventional approach to support development, consisting of the transfer of technologies from the 'modern' to the 'underdeveloped' world, needs to be revised. They are of the opinion that traditional knowledge with its technical, social and spiritual dimensions needs to be accepted as the starting point for development.

Endogenous development refers to development that is mainly, though not exclusively, based on locally available resources and the way people have organised themselves. External knowledge and resources are often used to complement these local resources. Endogenous development, therefore, does not imply isolation; nor does it limit its attention to local processes. It actively uses the opportunities provided by globalisation. The approach of the Compas programme can be described as 'action-research on endogenous development'. It attempts to be complementary to the many organisations that have a similar focus but often restrict themselves to research or to the technical aspects of indigenous knowledge. It thus hopes to support the growing movement towards endogenous development.

Indigenous worldviews. The Compas partners realized that most indigenous knowledge systems are based on the understanding that the living world is made up of three worlds: the human world, the natural world and the spiritual world (see box 3a). The human (social) world implies the social life of the people in all its dimensions, such as community life, family ties, ethnic groups, and traditional leadership and organisation. The natural (material) world includes nature in all its forms, including agriculture, as well as the natural phenomena. The spiritual world can be composed of different spirits, ancestral spirits, or Gods, often with different functions and tasks. In reality these worlds are interrelated: certain natural places are considered sacred, as sites where spiritual forces can communicate with humans through animals and habitats.

Together these notions form the worldview or cosmovision that describes the role of the supernatural powers, the perceived relationship between the humans and nature, and the way natural processes take explained. On the basis of these perceptions people organise themselves and determine their interventions in nature as well as their religious activities.

Box 3a   Indigenous worldviews

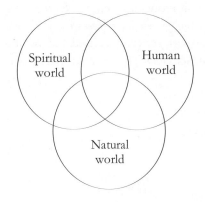

Local use of resources. To a large extent the local capacities to use the local resources is thus determined by this worldview. Recent insights have drawn the attention to the capacities and opportunities of rural people to improve their livelihoods in a systematic way based on their local resources. It was learned that the more successful rural livelihoods are characterised by relatively successful efforts to get access to resources such as credit, land, skills, labour, and the opportunities to turn these resources into livelihood enhancement. Examples are accessing labour- or product markets, and better terms in transactions, by renegotiating power relations. Access to kin and ethnic network, social organisations, intermediate state and NGOs and markets are important means for rural people to strengthen their negotiation power [Bebbington, 1999].

This analysis distinguishes six different types of resources: Natural resources (land, ecosystem, climate, plants animals); Human resources (knowledge and skills, local concepts, ways of learning, teaching and experimenting); Produced or human-made resources (buildings, infrastructure and equipment); Economic-financial resources (markets, incomes, ownerships, price relations, credit); Social resources (family, ethnic organisations, social institutions and leadership); and Cultural resources (beliefs, norms, values, festivals and rituals, art, language, lifestyle). This division is an elaboration of the concept of the three worlds, as used in the Compas approach.

Endogenous development, development defined by the choices and opportunities of the local people, implies a process of identifying, getting access to, and making good use of these resources. Rural people have developed their own mechanisms to get access to each of these resources, to claim, defend, and transform them. Individuals, households and organisations, that have gained access and control over these assets, can interact with the state organisations, civil society or market, and use them for the improvement of their livelihoods. A balanced development process includes all these types of local resources.

Field work for enhancing endogenous development

The Compas partners started their work by systematically learning with and from rural people about their knowledge, practices and worldviews. Hereby they gained insights into the local ways of reasoning, the methods of experimentation, and the systems of learning and communication on which they are based. This meant that field staff participated in local activities with an open mind, in order to understand the concepts used and the values behind them.

Subsequently, a participatory diagnosis on the actual situation, the changes taking place and the risks involved was made. On the basis of the findings, development options to improve the situation of the different population groups were chosen. These options were then tested in a systematic way. Initiatives were taken to test and improve traditional practices and to find innovative development niches for income generation. Networking and training was done and a number of workshops and publications have led to a further systematising of the experiences. The efforts of local people to use their resources can thus be supported by development organisations. The support activities carried out by the Compas partners could be divided into 10 different activities as indicated in the diagramme below.

Box 3b   Activities in supporting endogenous development

1. Building on local needs. Generally, increased economic growth or income generation is the primary objective of conventional development approaches. For rural people in many cultures of the world, however, the level of income is not the only parameter for defining their well-being. Other aspects, such as social cohesion, health, children, natural resources, and harmonious relations with the spiritual world, may be of equal importance in their development decisions. Therefore, the general goals for endogenous development may vary and include a combination of aspects, such as poverty reduction, diminished ecological exploitation, increased equity and justice, as well as cultural and spiritual goals. These aspects often vary according to sex, social position and age groups. The process of gaining insight into the diversity of needs of the different population groups, overcoming contradictions, and finding common acceptance of the development goals requires time, but is a crucial step for sustained development.

2. Improving local knowledge and practices. Endogenous development aims at enhancing in situ development of indigenous knowledge and practices, to support people in adapting their practices to meet today's challenges. Local resources are not static, but are dynamically transformed on a day to day basis by the people who depend on them. This implies that people carry out experiments with local resources, and with combinations of local and external resources, in adapting to the ever-changing circumstances and opportunities. The outcome of these experiments vary to a great extent, according to the perceptions and circumstances of each person, family, community, and culture, but are invariably based on the peoples' own experiences and ways of explaining reality. This methodology respects, but also challenges both tradition and modernity. The Compas partner organisations have developed several innovative methodologies for the in situ development of local knowledge and practices.

The capacities of rural people to make observations, to explain certain situations, to design and test possible innovations, to exchange experiences, as well as to teach them to younger generations, are crucial elements for success. Therefore, enhancing the support of local knowledge systems is important. Rural people and development workers can do this by combining the outcome of experiments with possibilities to improve the processes of learning, teaching and experimentation.

3. Local control of development options. Conventional development models have the tendency of introducing externally developed innovations to local communities. Endogenous development, in contrast, aims at local control and decision-making, and implies that members of the communities use their own mechanisms to make decisions regarding control. Traditional authorities play an important role in this process, while the community itself manages internal power conflicts, and comes to grips with gender balances and leadership systems. Acceptance or rejection of external support and practices will be a decision of the community.

This process of local control and decision making, of course, cannot avoid the problems raised by differences in interests and values amongst the various groups within a community. In some cases rural people themselves consider the use of local knowledge and resources as a step backwards. They fear that this will deny them the opportunities represented by external resources. Decades of development rhetoric and commercial influence have created a strong association between 'development' and the use of western style development alternatives. Nevertheless, subcultures abound and differences in gender, class, caste, ethnic subgroups, age, geographic origin, religious affiliation, language, education, wealth and power inevitably lead to different needs and objectives. Addressing these subcultures is a delicate process.

The role of the Compas field workers is to facilitate the community's role in decision making, monitoring and evaluation of the activities. Empowering local communities and local leadership can, however, lead to leadership tensions or go against the implicit politics of national governments. Governments and formal religious establishments have

often considered traditional leadership a hindrance to the development of local communities. Re-valuing the role and experience of the traditional leaders is therefore an activity
that requires careful negotiation and strategic choices.

4. Identification of new development niches. Many conventional development
approaches consider rural families as potential producers of a variety of products. Local
farmers are stimulated to produce agricultural products that can be processed and com-
mercialised in a uniform way for the (inter)national market. Endogenous development
looks at ways of generating additional income based on specific ecological and cultural
local resources. Stimulating the production, processing and marketing of region-specific
products opens a reservoir of untapped local opportunities. New development niches may
include local food items, traditional crafts, crops, and domestic animal breeds, as well as
locally managed tourism. Identifying and opening market possibilities for these local
resources are important activities.

5. Selective use of external resources. It is obvious that in many cases local knowledge
and resources have their limitations, and can benefit from the combination of specific
external inputs. A local system can benefit, for example, by the use of cement, a bicycle,
a pump, transport systems, electricity, fertilisers, seeds, chemical pesticides, or drugs. Loan
facilities may provide the financial means for obtaining the external inputs, while external
advisors can be useful when the local community does not have the required expertise, for
example in marketing. Most rural families experiment with combining local and external
inputs to utilise their land and other local resources more efficiently. But selecting the
appropriate external resources is crucial. A good example is the great number of farmers
who have lost their land due to their inability to repay the loans provided for fertilisers, or
other external inputs. A tractor may appear to be a very beneficial, but without the necessary spare parts it may bring more disillusion than benefits.

Therefore, the first questions to be asked in the endogenous development process are:
is it feasible to solve the identified problem by using local resources, and what are the
advantages and risks of using solutions from outside? What possibilities exist for building
up the local capacity to reproduce the external technology? And what experiences can be
found in other communities, regions, or cultures, for solving the identified problem?

6. Retention of benefits in the local area. Development initiatives are often taken by
outsiders who, consciously or unconsciously, aim at their own benefit and may extract
knowledge and resources from the community. Patenting the property rights related to
certain species of medical plants is, of course, one of the most flagrant examples of such
extraction. But more subtle extraction of benefits also take place, for example through
conventional tourism activities, which do not take the local community into account.
Activities to protect intellectual property rights, eco-tourism in which the community plays
a definite role, and enhancing the production, processing and marketing of local foods,
are examples of keeping benefits in the local area.

Prices for local produce may vary greatly throughout the year. In many subsistence
economies food prices fluctuate and producers have to sell part of their produce at low

prices just after the harvest. In times of food deficit they often have to buy back the same food at much higher prices. Therefore, enhancing storage facilities as well as credit to buy food items during the cheap post-harvest period often result in increased local benefits and food security. In the process of searching and building up new development niches, the opportunities for retaining the benefits of the activities within the local area need to be continually assessed.

7. Exchange and learning between cultures. The exchange of experiences and world-views between different cultures is part of the current Compas programme. Comparing the concepts behind the local health traditions in various cultures, for example, has resulted in finding striking similarities, which has enhanced the self-esteem and dynamics of the often marginalised local health practitioners. In this process representatives of marginalised traditional health systems have been able to learn from the experiences and insights of the more privileged traditional health systems. In general, the sharing between rural people, farmers, field staff, managers and researchers leads to cross cultural exchange, learning and co-operation.

8. Training and capacity building. The way pupils and students are schooled or taught differs according to each country and culture. Despite the many years that have passed since decolonisation, western concepts of education still play a dominant role in the teaching curricula in many 'developing' countries, while local knowledge and practices are not given attention as study objects. This is stronger in the universities than in the primary and secondary schools, but even in the latter, mathematics, physics, economy and religion are often taught according to the western value system. This is further eroding the local knowledge systems.

As a result, most development workers are trained in methods of transferring knowledge, rather than in ways of learning from and with the rural people. They are usually better equipped in technical subjects than in social processes, or in methods to enhance the dynamics of local knowledge and culture. Therefore, a systematic training and possibly de-schooling process needs to be considered for all field staff involved in endogenous development.

9. Networking and strategic partnership. Endogenous development acknowledges the importance of linking regional, national and international processes, while looking for synergy between the different knowledge systems and practices. Local market opportunities are often influenced by international trade relations, while national policies and research priorities may be largely determined by international conventions and agreements. Endogenous development at local level can, therefore, only thrive with a positive political environment. Networking, co-operation and advocacy can enhance the establishment of such a political environment. Examples of activities in this domain include: linking with likeminded NGOs, establishing strategic alliances with government agencies, presenting experiences at (international) fora, approaching funders, suggesting changes for policy or research programmes, and building up partnerships with commercial, political or religious organisations.

10. Understanding systems of knowing and learning. All traditional knowledge systems use different paradigms, which manifest themselves in the knowledge of everyday life, in the way this knowledge is used and changed and in the philosophy of science [Mouton, 2001]. The Ayurvedic, Andean, Mayan, Chinese and African medical practices, for example, have their unique ways of perceiving health and disease. The same applies to agriculture, nature and to socio-spiritual practices. These ways of knowing have been achieved within a specific worldview and by using a specific research methodology. As a result of different theories, concepts and definitions, striking differences in the notion of time, the relationships between cause and effect, or the importance of quantification, intuition and conscience in the experimental process, can be observed. This can easily lead to controversies in the collection and interpretation of data.

Understanding the basic concepts of the various indigenous knowledge systems, therefore, is important for international co-operation and research. The western knowledge system has gone a long way to develop powerful technologies. But its limitations are also obvious, and other knowledge systems may provide important elements for solving the major problems the world is facing today.

Box 3c   A code of conduct for enhancing endogenous development

Experience has learned that the work with indigenous practices and knowledge as an outsider implies certain risks, such as disturbing the status-quo at community level, extracting local knowledge for purposes not in the interest of the rural people, domination of local processes by outsiders, prying too much into people's private matters, or the introduction of lifestyles that are not consistent with local values. Therefore, in their work with the rural people the Compas partners have agreed to:
- Accept the idea that local communities have indigenous knowledge systems with its own rationale and logic, and will be prepared to learn from them.
- Commit to work in the interest of the local communities. Programmes will only be implemented after approval of the local community and its leaders.
- Accept the rules and regulations set by the local community for attending and receiving visitors, and respect the limitations set by local leaders.
- Accept and seek complementarity between external knowledge and the local knowledge systems. Avoid the domination of external over the local knowledge and value systems.
- Accept the fact that in many cases new methods will have to be developed, as the conventional approaches for research and development may not be the most appropriate.
- Pay attention to the attitudinal changes that may be required for staff and accept that all involved are students with the local people, leaders and experts as their tutors.
- Learn empathetically from the local knowledge systems, analyse it and enter into a respectful and constructive dialogue about the positive and negative aspects, the possibilities for improvement, as well as the epistemologies and paradigms.
- Accept the guidance of local leaders to ensure that the information collected will be used in the interest of the community, thus respecting traditional Intellectual Property Rights.
- Accept the importance of exchange of experiences within and between rural communities. Publish experiences for other audiences only after approval of the communities involved.

4. KNOWLEDGE AND BELIEF SYSTEMS IN THE INDIAN SUBCONTINENT

A.V. Balasubramanian, CIKS, India

A large number of cultures exist in Asia. Here only the civilisationss from the Indian subcontinent will be elaborated. The Indian traditional knowledge systems have been documented in ancient texts known as the Vedas. A large number of traditional practices still exist in India and cover a variety of disciplines such as medicine, agriculture, architecture, metallurgy, music and arts. The traditional Indian sciences place special importance on linguistics and logic. The research methods and concepts within Indian science, such as Ayurveda, are different from those used in modern western science. This calls for an analysis of, and if possible, synergy between the different scientific traditions.

Asia is the continent with the largest population on the globe. It has a great diversity of landscapes, ecosystems and cultures. The brief historical overview presented below gives a glimpse of how this diversity came to be. But, before the historic facts as understood by conventional archaeology and history are presented, an important note has to be made in relation to the Indian concept of history and time. In the traditional Indian concept, time is considered cyclic. Classical epics reveal the story of creation of the Universe: once created, the universe passes through a number of cycles of growth and decay, and at the end is drawn back into *Brahman*, or Supreme God. This cycle of creation and disappearance of the universe is repeated according to the pre-defined flow of time. Within this large cycle, there are a number of shorter cycles. The total cycle constitutes 4,320,000 years and thousands of such cycles make merely one day of Brahma.

This cyclic concept of time is in contrast to that of the western civilisation. In the latter, dates of important events, ranging from the birth of Christ to the fall of an empire, are marked with respect to commonly accepted eras. While there may be differences between scholars on the exact dates of events, the importance of recording such dates is not disputed. When time is perceived as cyclic, however, the exact moment at which an event has occurred does not have the same unique status. This may explain why remarkably little importance is given to marking the exact dates of events in Indian history. Moreover, the spans of time conceived are so stupendously large, that the magnitude of the life of a human being or even the rise and fall of a civilisation, is considered insignificant. In a sense, one may say that a major lesson of the Indian time concept is the concept of the smallness of man in relation to the Universe. Similar notions of the cyclic nature of time are found amongst other indigenous peoples throughout Asia, Africa and South America.

Historical overview

Conventional archaeology indicates the earliest evidence of hominid occupation in two regions of East Asia: Youanmou in western China and Sangiran in Java, Indonesia. Also in Thailand, Korea and Vietnam, traces of early hominid occupation have been found. As the sea level in that period was much lower than at present, human expansion to the south-eastern part of Asia, as well as to Australia and the Americas was possible.

The first agricultural systems on the globe are reported in the territory stretching from the Persian Gulf to Mesopotamia and Palestine, with the domestication of wheat, barley and sheep. This system allowed the growth of human population and the emergence of towns, as well as craftsmanship and trade. In northern China agriculture started with the domestication of foxtail and broomcorn millets, rice, cabbage, plums and hazelnuts, as well as pigs and dogs. Evidence of early farming in the Indian subcontinent was found between the hills of Baluchistan and the Indo-Gangetic plains, with grazing resources for sheep, goats and cattle, and crop production in the fertile plains. Rice cultivation started in the Ganges valley. The rise in sea levels after the last ice age created new coastlines and islands in South East Asia. This benefited the hunter-gatherer communities along the coast and estuaries.

For millennia, Asia has seen the rise and fall of large civilisations. Empires of great size and power emerged in the near East, followed by the Persian and the Greek empire of Alexander the Great. The Indian subcontinent was united for the first time under the Mauryan empire, while the Mediterranean and other parts of western Europe fell under the sway of the powerful Roman empire. China witnessed a period of empires over the last few centuries B.C. under the Han dynasty. The different Asian cultures were in contact through trade relations, exchanging political and cultural influences. As agriculture developed further, irrigation and terracing systems emerged, animals were used for traction, and the plough facilitated open field cultivation and increased agricultural yields. Salination and soil erosion were serious side-effects of these agricultural activities, to the extent that large parts of Anatolia, the Middle East and other parts of Asia turned into deserts. The decreasing population, together with warfare between different powers, most likely caused the decline of the early Asian civilisations [Scarre, 1991].

All major religions, such as Hinduism, Buddhism, Judaism, Christianity and Islam, as well as Taoism and Confucianism, were founded in Asia. They have all put their marks on the continent. It goes beyond the scope of this book to present detailed information about each knowledge and belief system throughout the continent. Here, we put emphasis on the most widespread traditional knowledge systems in the Indian subcontinent: Hinduism, Buddhism and the animism of tribal peoples. Other important knowledge systems and cultures in the area, such as the Chinese knowledge system and Islam, are briefly described in chapter 2.

Image of Hindu Goddess Dhanwantri holding a leech. In Ayurveda leeches are used for blood letting treatment.

Hinduism

Archaeological excavations in northwest India revealed an ancient and advanced civilisation with several cities along the Indus river. The total complex of cities and villages covered nearly half a million square miles and may represent the largest political entity before the Roman empire [Hopfe and Woodward, 1998]. The cities were made of fired brick and were supported by advanced agricultural communities that made use of irrigation. This population had a written language, which has not been deciphered.

We can sum up some characteristic features of today's dominant Hindu civilisation as follows: the society is organised into four *varnas*, loosely translated as castes, which include *brahmins* or priests, *kshatriya* or rulers, *vaishyas* or trading class, and *shudras* or the labour class. Over a period of time, the category of outcastes, or *Dalit,* became a striking phenomenon in India. Other key features of Hinduism are the doctrine of transmigration of the soul, and the doctrine of *karma*, which includes the concept that the current status of every human being has been decided by his or her past actions and deeds, not only in this life but also in previous lives. Similarly, future births are decided by actions in the present life. In the Hindu concept, the soul is essentially divine and migrates from one living form to another through rebirth. This has profound implications for the Hindu understanding of life in which human, animal and plant life are considered aspects of the divine. The Buddhist worldview, in contrast, includes the concept of transmigration, but the 'soul' is replaced by the concept of 'the ever-changing stream of consciousness'.

In many parts of Asia, Hinduism and Buddhism, as well as Islam and Christianity, co-exist with what may be considered animistic or shamanistic practices. Hinduism does not view these practices as a challenge to its legitimacy. In fact, it appears that such animistic practices and what may be considered as 'mainstream Hinduism' have often influenced each other. This process has resulted in a variety of religions, beliefs and modes of worship, which seem to fit within the broad framework of Hindu thought.

The Vedas. Traditional Hindu knowledge in India has been traced to the vedas, ancient texts that include a collection of hymns, mantras and prayers written in Sanskrit. They are considered the results of divine revelation to visionary sages, who have collected them over a period of 7,000 years. India has the largest collection of ancient manuscripts in the world; some estimates indicate that there may be as many as 300 million manuscripts, which today can be found in monasteries, universities and other institutes. They pay a great deal of attention to agriculture, livestock, rains and harvests. There are a total of fourteen *sastras*, or branches of knowledge: the four vedas, the four *upavedas*, or auxiliary vedas, and the six *vedangas*, or limbs of the vedas. The four upavedas are: ayurveda, literally 'the science of life', which constitutes the ayurvedic medical system; *arthasastra*, which includes political theory; *dhanurveda*, which includes the art of warfare, and *gandharvaveda*, including music, drama and the fine arts.

Similarly, the six branches of the vedangas, or the limbs of the vedas, explain the knowledge required for understanding, interpreting, and applying the vedas. They are *vyakarana* or grammar; *chandas* or metrics; *siksa* or phonetics; *nirukta* or etymology; *kalpa* or ritual and *jyotisa* or astronomy and mathematics. These vedangas are essential, as the vedas had to be understood correctly (needing etymology and grammar), pronounced and chanted accurately (needing metrics and phonetics), used properly in various contexts (needing ritual), and with the correct timing of these performances, related to time and planetary movements (needing astronomy and mathematics). In the following sections, we will discuss a few aspects of the vedic knowledge system that illustrate its basic nature.

Traditional medicine

We can use the case of traditional medicine to understand various aspects of Indian traditional knowledge systems. The most remarkable characteristic of the Indian medical tradition is that it prevails at two different levels: the classical and the folk system. By the classical system, we refer to the codified systems such as Ayurveda, Siddha and Unani. They are characterised by institutionally trained practitioners, a body of texts originating since ancient times, and highly developed theories to support the practices. These traditional medical systems encompass knowledge of life, health and disease of all living forms, not only human but also of animals and plants. The branch dealing with traditional medicine for animals is known as *mrgayurveda*.

Ayurveda is also present outside India, especially in other parts of Asia, such as China, Thailand, Cambodia and Indonesia, and is increasing in the western world. The Unani system, which came up during the Arab period, also enjoys great popularity and over time has interacted successfully with the Ayurvedic system. Both systems of medical tradition are supported by a rich textual base. It is estimated that there are 10-30 million manuscripts in Sanskrit alone, many of them relating to medicine. The Tamil University at Thanjavur has made a catalogue of 24,000 Tamil manuscripts in libraries and public collections, including 8,000 related to science and technology, of which 4,000 pertain to medical sciences. Most of these have not been printed. In addition, innumerable manuscripts exist with individuals and families of *vaidyas*, or traditional healers.

Parallel to these systems, folk traditions exist, which have been transmitted orally in tens of thousands of our villages throughout the ages. These folk traditions are rich and diverse and include specialised practitioners as well as home remedies for common ailments. These traditions include knowledge and beliefs regarding the relation between food and health, as well as yoga and other physical practices of a preventive nature. Specialist practitioners work with specific diseases, bone setting, poisoning treatment and birth attendance. A conservative estimate stipulates that there are around 70,000 traditional bonesetters throughout the country, who attend to over two-thirds of the fractures, as modern orthopaedic facilities are few in number and concentrated in cities and urban areas. Some 600,000 traditional birth attendants perform home deliveries.

In the tribal areas the folk medical practices include herbal treatments, often in combination with reciting certain verses called *mantras* and the use of symbols, such as ritual chalk drawings or *gondas*. Often the sacred stick and rings are used to invoke the blessings of the Gods for healing. Moreover, there is a tremendous depth of tribal knowledge regarding the use of natural resources. The tribal communities alone use over 9,000 plant species, including some 7,500 species of plants for medical properties. Besides this, a considerable number of materials of animal and mineral origin are used in traditional medicine.

It is important to note that Ayurveda, Siddha and Unani do not devalue or suppress these folk traditions, but have a symbiotic relationship with them. These codified medical systems and folk traditions draw from and get enriched by each other's practices and insights.

Categories of understanding in Ayurveda

Various traditions of sciences and technology have adopted different categories for studying the same phenomena. If one were to describe the nutritional properties of food substances in modern biochemistry, it would be done in terms of proteins, carbohydrates, fats, vitamins, minerals, and calorific values. Medicinal plants would be described in terms of active ingredients. Moreover, in the western tradition, the scientific temper is limited to the use of the five senses: smell, taste, hearing, touch and sight.

In Ayurveda completely different categories are used, while the analytical methods are not limited to these five senses. Complete awareness is sought at a level of perception, by which the observer both reaches out and looks within, establishing a subjective flow between the observer and the observed. Thus, in Ayurveda, the senses are complemented with the mind, preferably free of the six prejudices: lust, anger, greed, intoxication, delusion and jealousy. The senses make it possible to decipher the world around us, while the mind moves inwards and outwards [Shankar, 1999].

Ayurveda is also based on the recognition of a range of fundamental principles, known as *dravya, guna, rasa, veerya* and *prabhava*.

- Dravya refers to the 'nature of the substances', based on the tunderstanding that all is composed of the five elements: earth, water, wind, fire and ether or space, in varying combinations. In the Indian case, each of these categories is defined in the texts of Indian logic, and each one is correlated with one of the five sense organs.
- Guna refers to 'properties of matter' that can be evaluated using the sense organs; describing it in terms of cold, heavy, stable, rough, hard, dry, or oily.
- Rasa refers to 'taste': sweet, bitter, sour, salty, hot and astringent. Each of these is attributed certain nutritional or therapeutic properties. For example, sweet substances help in tissue building, bitter substances help to purify blood, and hot substances kindle the digestive capacity.
- Veerya refers to 'hot' or 'cold'. This does not imply the direct temperature of the material, but the metabolic impact on ingestion. Thus, raw papaya is considered hot, while cow's milk is considered to cool the body. These significant properties have direct application in food, medicine and even agriculture.
- Prabhava refers to 'special properties' of substances. For example, a substance may be described as deepana, meaning increasing digestive capacity, *muthrala*, meaning increasing the output of urine, or *Chaksusya*, beneficial to eyesight.

Moreover, according to the Ayurvedic classification, all beings - humans, plants and animals - can be classified according to three different types of constitution, or *doshas*: *vaatha*, *pitta* and *kapha*. These characteristics also exist within every living organism and, if in good health, are well balanced. The vaatha constitution is slender and tall, light and dry. The pitta constitution is medium in size, weight, colour and height, and is warm and dry. The kapha constitution refers to organisms that are short, bulky, humid and cold. The Ayurvedic treatments in case of disease are based on re-establishing the balance between these three doshas within the organism.

Traditional Plant science, or Vrkshayurveda. Vedic literature also pays attention to plant sciences. The texts are vast, detailed and varied, and include subjects such as seed collection and selection, germination, cultivation, sowing, planting, nursery techniques, soil, manuring, pest and disease management, as well as the traditional names and description of plants. It is a real challenge to interpret and use these texts in today's context, as the prescriptions are often not described with enough detail to understand them directly.

Recently there has been a revival in the interest for traditional practices relating to agriculture and natural resources management. The Compas partners CIKS and KPP have started to collect material on vrkshayurveda, and are testing selected practices. In this process it is important to perceive these traditional agricultural practices as more than a mere collection of technologies, and understand their theoretical foundations (see chapters 4.1 and 4.4).

Tribal knowledge systems

In tribal cosmovisions food crops are seen as gifts from ancestors and divine beings. The Peepal leaf (Ficus religiosa) symbolises Mother Goddess Devi.

According to the 1991 census, around 6% of the Indian population, some 53 million people in 550 ethnic communities, have a tribal background. Many of them have maintained traditional lifestyles, knowledge and values. They believe in the existence of a wide range of divine beings and ancestral spiritual forces with benevolent and malevolent characters that inhabit houses, villages, agricultural fields, burial grounds and surrounding forests. The tribals believe that these divine beings are beyond human control and able to help or harm nature and human beings. The tribal people also believe that the good and bad ancestral spirits always watch over them and may help them in times of danger and distress. Therefore, the tribal people perform certain rites and rituals to appease the divine beings and ancestral spirits, thereby protecting themselves and getting rid of evil influences. They do not start constructing a house, distributing land, felling trees, performing a marriage, or going hunting until they have performed the appropriate rites.

The tribal people believe they are the children of Mother Nature and that she protects and guides them. Some trees, such as tamarind and mango, wild animals, such as the Indian bison, tiger and common langur (monkey), peacock and dove, are considered to be holy and to contain sacred elements. Besides this, they also believe in sacred hills, forests, streams, mountains and caves which are inhabited by divine beings. Hence, they are worshipped through rituals, ceremonies and fairs.

The majority of the tribal cosmovisions contain beliefs related to their agro-ecological and health practices. Certain crops, such as the major and minor millets, hill paddy and red gram, are not only perceived important as food crops, but also as sacred gifts from their ancestors and the Goddess of nature and earth. Hence any ritual would not be complete without offering these grains to the divine beings and ancestral spirits, both good and bad.

The indigenous knowledge, values and cosmovision of the tribal population also found expression in the form of a rich tradition in arts, such as music and visual presentations. The subjects included in traditional knowledge and practices include management of natural resources, herbal medicine, agriculture, animal husbandry and aspects of the relationship between people and every other facet of the universe. The Compas partner IDEA in Andrapradesh and Orissa, and in a more limited form also Green Foundation in Bangalore, work with tribal peoples. In their chapters (4.9 and 4.7) a more detailed description of the knowledge and belief systems of these tribal populations is presented, as well as the practical experiences of enhancing endogenous development.

Buddhism

De Zoysa [2002] describes the main characteristics of Buddism in the following way. The teachings of Buddha began in India some 2,500 years ago, from where it spread to China, Japan, Korea and South-East Asia. Buddhism persists in many parts of Asia, though in India the number of followers has reduced considerably. Buddhism differs from the other Indian religions because it rejects the caste system, denies the relevance of the Gods and the necessity of worship and sacrifice. The ultimate goal of each individual is to reach enlightenment. Buddhism teaches the relationship between organism and environment,

Image of Buddha in Anuradnapura, Sri Lanka.

human and nature, which is based on reverence and compassion. Therefore an ethic for a sustainable society is implicit in Buddhism, recognising the limits of resources, compassion for life in all of its diversity, and action out of the responsibility of the individual for nature.

The knowledge systems, which emerged during the 'enlightenment' period in Europe, place utter-most importance on knowledge based on verified theories and propositions. This is also called 'propositional knowing'. In contrast, in the ancient systems from the East, knowledge is derived from direct experience, which is also called 'experiential knowing'. According to the Buddhist viewpoint, experiential as well as propositional knowledge has to be ultimately experienced by the knower, and meditation is used as a methodology to accomplish this. The question of subjectivity is dealt with in Buddhism by developing *sila,* or the correct ethical attitudes and behaviour in the experiencing individual. Without such parallel ethical development, experiential knowledge will merely lead to individualism and result in a bias fashioned by individual desire. An ethically informed process can lead to validity beyond the limits of individuality [De Zoysa, 2002].

Box 4a   Experiential knowing in Buddhism

Buddhist philosophical discussions emphasise the importance of experiential knowing. This is expressed, for example, in the text of the Kalama Sutta: *"Come, Kalamas. Do not go upon what has been acquired by repeated hearing, nor upon tradition, nor upon rumour, nor upon what is in scriptures, nor upon surmise, nor upon specious reasoning, nor upon a bias toward a notion that has been pondered over, nor upon another's ability, nor upon the consideration 'The monk is our teacher'. Kalamas, when you yourselves know; 'these things are good; these things are blameless, these things are praised by the wise, undertaken and observed, these things lead to benefit and happiness, then enter on and abide in them".*
(Kalama Sutta, Soma Thera)

The second important point of departure from modern systems of knowledge lies in the theory of substances. Modern science is strongly materialistic, and does not take into account phenomena which can be recognised as part of 'consciousness'. Buddhism recognises the world as a collection of phenomena, devoid of substance, and the human mind as a sixth sense. Consciousness is the organising force of all six senses. De Zoysa, therefore, concludes that modern science with its insistence on propositional knowledge, may be a poor candidate for understanding, interpreting and developing the use of traditional knowledge systems, when compared to other scientific systems in the world.

Tradition, modernity and change

Indian Hindus have a long-standing belief that the divine repeatedly incarnates in various forms to lessen the burdens of the earth. Sometimes the complexity of the world becomes too much to bear, the sense of right and wrong gets clouded, and the natural balance of life, or *Dharma*, is lost. At such times, according to the Indian beliefs, the divine incarnates on earth, to help restore the balance and to make life flow smoothly once again. It is therefore not surprising that, when Mahatma Gandhi arrived in India in 1915, many

Indians saw him as another *Avatara of Vishnu*. The state of India at that time seemed to many as beyond redress through mere human efforts, and ripe for divine intervention.

Mahatma Gandhi coupled an acceptance of traditional Indian social structure with the recognition that it needed to be changed and reformed. Thus, he accepted the Dharma of the traditional Hindu society, while starting his battle against the discrimination of the lower castes. At the same time other approaches were present, such as from Dr Ambedkar, who claimed that the 'untouchables' could not obtain justice within the Hindu society, and initiated a movement for their conversion to the Buddhist faith. In a sense, even in modern India, one can find movements in science, technology and development, with roots that can be traced to these two modes of thinking.

Bruun and Kalland [1995] conclude that India and most other Asian societies are in a process of rapid change. The aspirations of the Asian governments usually include large-scale industrialisation, as well as rapid modernisation of agriculture and other economic sectors. The economies of the 'Asian tigers' Japan, South Korea, and Taiwan, have had formidable growth rates. Huge world financial centres and large cities with highly sophisticated life styles are surrounded by simple peasant economies.

"It is good to swim in the waters of tradition, but to sink in them is suicide." (Mahatma Gandhi)

Sections of the population seem to feel so overwhelmed by the external forces of modernisation which have brought about powerful changes, that there is a tendency to withdraw into their inner space rather than to interact with the outside world. Though rarely explicitly stated, some sections of traditional society tend to wait and 'bide their time', in the hope that modernity will 'exhaust itself'.

Simultaneously, the ecological challenges are enormous. Industries are producing toxic wastes, while forest cover and biological resources are declining. Even scarcely populated countries like Nepal and Tibet are facing deforestation and pollution at an alarming rate. The environmental degradation is also the result of a change in power relations, as rural people increasingly loose influence over the natural resources on which their life depends. Local communities not only face competition from the state and its agencies, but also from the urban elite, who want to use the countryside for hunting and other forms of recreation. The environmentalists sometimes care more for the survival of endangered animal and plant species than for human welfare, while business sees great profits by turning nature into a commodity for tourism, housing and industry.

In this process, rural people are becoming increasingly alienated from efforts to conserve their bio-resources and biodiversity. But, the study of Bruun and Kalland also reveals that respect for nature and natural processes is still explicit in many rural communities, in which environmental concern is often expressed in religious terms. Yet, these values do not always result in sound environmental behaviour. The appeal of material gain, promoted by governmental policies, mass media and the educational system, can be stronger than traditional values. Still, today's increasing attention for traditional cultures and values also expresses a general sense of renewed interest in 're-finding one's cultural identity' as well as the local natural resources, as a reaction to the cultural domination of the West. This process implies a strong cultural creativity, which is absent in the case of 'pure' ecological environmentalism.

Indian and western scientific knowledge systems

In any scientific discourse it is essential to achieve precision and rigour. In the western tradition, the geometry of Euclid is considered a supreme example of an ideal theory. In contrast, in Indian tradition, an attempt was made to use natural language and to sharpen its potential by technical operations. As a result, particularly in Sanskrit, even the most abstract and metaphysical discussions regarding grammar, mathematics, or logic, are written in natural language. Therefore, in traditional Indian knowledge systems, the science of linguistics occupies the central place, which, in the west, is occupied by mathematics.

Identifying the different Indian traditional scientific concepts, as well as the cultural values implicitly included in them, may be a good starting point for endogenous development. This can be compared to the western scientific and cultural concepts. Complementing different knowledge systems is not a matter of simply comparing them. Complementary lines of action can only be achieved after the contradictions, misperceptions and anomalies in terms of domination and control of each knowledge system are corrected. In this respect, the practice of prospecting knowledge, as well as the methodology of research and the scientific concepts for understanding reality, should be analysed for each knowledge system.

Prospecting indigenous resources and knowledge. Research on traditional knowledge by scientists from 'mainstream' western science and technology institutions is not a new phenomenon. A lot of this research, however, suffers from the limitations of a mind set, which essentially looks upon physical resources, as well as the technologies and knowledge of the local communities, as raw material that needs to be scanned, prospected and refined, in order to get incorporated into the modern/western framework. Over the past centuries, a large number of herbs have been screened in this way for their potential pharmacological action, leading to some outstanding success stories, such as quinine from the Cinchona bark. At the same time, many perceive that these research activities do not lead to the revitalisation of traditional knowledge and endogenous development of the communities involved. Another example is given in box 4b.

> **Box 4b   Scientific research on herbal medicine**
>
> *Rauvolfia serpentina* is a plant known in Ayurveda for a very long time. This small shrub used to be widely distributed throughout India, reputed for its medical potential in treating hypertension, fever, wounds, insomnia, epilepsy and certain conditions of Kapha and Vatha (Ayurvedic categories) disorders. At the beginning of the 20th century modern research was carried out on this plant, and the 'crude drug' was fractionated into 'active ingredients'. One of these ingredients, the alkaloid Reserpene, was identified as a powerful drug for hypertension. Subsequently, the drug based on Reserpene had several undesirable side effects, which were not present in the original formulation of Rauvolfia serpentina used in traditional medicine. Meanwhile, the research and use of the plant did not lead to strengthening of the traditional knowledge of the subject, while the industrial demand resulted in over-exploitation of the plant in the wild. In fact, Rauvolfia serpentina, once growing abundantly throughout India, is today on the list of endangered species, and the traditional medical practitioners are unable to get sufficient supplies for local use. Similar cases of modern research to traditional herbal medicine have led to patenting of the knowledge and violating the intellectual property rights of the original carriers of the knowledge.

Methodology of research. Quite often we come across researchers, who claim not to oppose traditional knowledge and to be very open to it, as long as it can be examined and validated according to western scientific terms. This viewpoint implicitly assumes that the methodologies used in modern western sciences are universal, in the sense that they are 'above and beyond' all other scientific traditions. When this claim is examined in more detail, one can find that several methods, currently employed by modern western sciences, are the products of a specific historical and cultural context. For example, in researching the effect of drugs in clinical trials, the system of blind and double blind trials is widely prevalent (see box 4c). It is assumed that valid knowledge about the efficacy and use of any drug can be obtained by following such an approach. The fact that the patient is 'blinded' for the control of the trials, however, goes against the Ayurvedic notion of the active role of the patient in his own healing process.

As mentioned earlier in this chapter, there are many other differences in the conception and understanding of various aspects of health and diseases between Ayurveda and western science. These include the categories of the properties of plants, animals and humans Vaatha, Pitta and Kapha, as well as the categories of understanding the properties of food and drugs Dravya, Guna, Rasa, Veerya and Prabhava. However, once we get rid of the notion that modern western science is the only way to understand and analyse these phenomena, the search for synergy between the scientific traditions becomes an important challenge.

Synergy between multiple traditions

In retrospect, we can see that through the ages, every geographical location of the world has nurtured and produced sciences and technologies that bear the distinct stamp and character of its own people and civilisation. However, during the last few hundred years

> **Box 4c   Control experiments based on blind and double blind trials**
>
> In modern testing procedures, only one group of the patients receives the new drug, while the others are given a 'placebo'. But what if we are dealing with a medical system where the patient is not just a passive recipient of a treatment, but as an active participant in the therapy? If a patient is treated by an Ayurvedic physician, not only a drug may be prescribed, but the patient is also given advice about how to regulate his diet - to avoid certain foods or methods of preparations - and may be given specific behavioural guidelines, such as the timing of meals, the spacing between meals, or sleeping habits. This difference is even more striking, if a patient is being treated by the system of Yoga, which implies the active participation of the patient by performing certain *asanas* (assuming specific postures) or *pranayama* (regulated breathing). In such cases, it is impossible to 'blind' the patient. Hence, it appears that the system of performing blind or double blind trials is, in fact, the product of the cultural context in which the patient is the passive recipient of treatment. Therefore, we need to re-examine the assumptions behind the various methodologies of research, and determine the methods suited to the specific knowledge system.

and increasingly for a hundred years or so, a myth has developed to the effect that the western tradition of science and technology is unique and universal. This viewpoint has not only been propagated by the mainstream scientists in the West but has also been internalised by professionals in various other parts of the world, particularly developing countries. While, it is true that in the West, there is scholarship that points to multiple traditions of sciences and technologies, most often, this literature and discussions are confined only to theoreticians and professionals working in the frontiers of philosophy or epistemology of science. Meanwhile, this has not influenced the thinking of mainstream scientists, policy makers and others in any significant way.

Therefore, there is an urgent need for new initiatives and paradigms of development, with a balanced view on traditional sciences, technologies and knowledge systems. While modern science and technology has limited its benefits to a minority of people, the vast majority of the people in the world still survive on the material and intellectual sustenance from their own indigenous traditions.

The activities of the Compas partners in India and other parts of Asia may be considered a contribution to this re-evaluation of indigenous traditions of sciences and technologies. They all take traditional knowledge and values as the starting point for endogenous development. They include the cosmovisions and relationship to nature of the people whom they work with, the role of the senses and the mind, the way the fundamental principles are being used, the role of traditional leaders, the methods of scientific research, and the way these relate to western approaches. The experiences in supporting endogenous development of the five Compas partners in the Indian sub-continent, as well as the partners in Nepal, Sri Lanka and Nepal, are presented in the subsequent chapters.

4.1 ENDOGENOUS DEVELOPMENT THROUGH EXPERIMENTING FARMERS

Dr Upendra Shenoy, V. K Aruna Kumara and A.S. Anand, KPP, India

Krishi Prayoga Pariwara (KPP) is an organised group of around 5000 farmers practicing ecological farming in Karnataka State, southern India. The objective of KPP is to understand how indigenous knowledge can enhance endogenous development to meet today's challenges. To this end, experiments are carried out on topics like indigenous cattle breeds, fruit trees, cash crops, and traditional food dishes.

Shimoga district is blessed with rich biodiversity, and the people of this district are relatively well off in terms of food and income, though 30% of them still live below the poverty line. The main crops are paddy, arecanut, coconut and spices; the marginal farmers mainly grow the staple food crop, paddy, while the medium and big farmers have arecanut (Areca catechu) and, recently, vanilla as cash crops. There are numerous medicinal herbs, shrubs, trees, vines and fruit yielding trees, like mango, amla, garcinia, jamun and jak. The area receives an average rainfall of 1,800-2,000 mm, the soils are laterite in nature and shallow. Many indigenous practices and technologies are still practiced by a number of people in the field of agriculture, health and education. Some farmers consult astrological timing for sowing, transplanting, intercropping, and harvesting. They base their practices on organic manure, traditional seed treatment and mixed cropping, and manufacture their own bio-pesticides. Some consider these practices as a fashion of the times, as many modern products in the markets come as ayurvedic herbs or natural eco-friendly products. But KPP also looks at these indigenous or local chemical-free practices as a heritage, which has the potential to support increased self-reliance and sustenance of the local people.

The ancient Indian scripts: the Vedas. It is interesting to note that the ancient Hindu scripts called Vedas, consider agriculture as the most honourable of human activities: agriculture is the one area where humans and the divine co-operate with each other to sustain creation. A hymn in the Rig-Veda says: *"don't play the games of dice; get involved in agriculture. You will acquire plenty and prosperity. This will bring you fame and recognition. Thereby you will lead a happy life."* The Bhagavad Githa, another honoured script based on the Vedas says: *"If you respect and co-operate with the Gods, they will also respect and co-operate with you. By this mutual respect and co-operation you derive prosperity - both material and spiritual."*

There are two famous collections of hymns in the Vedas. In the *Bhoomi Sukta*, or earth hymns, the human relationship with Mother Earth is equated to that of a son with his mother. She expects us to worship her devoutly because she bestows us with food, water and air, the three essential requisites for our life. In the *Anna Sukta*, or food hymns, food is equated to God, as it gives us vigour to achieve our ends - both material and spiritual. Thus, according to traditional Hindu thought in India, not only the earth, but also mountains, rivers, lakes, oceans, forests, birds and animals are sacred and should be worshipped. Therefore, in traditional Indian agriculture human needs can be met, but human greed is condemned. In recent decades these norms in Indian agriculture have increasingly given way to more westernised norms and methods. The sustained propaganda in the media, the policies of the government, the teaching in agricultural universities, as well as national and international economic pressure, have all contributed to the present situation where traditional practices and values are seriously threatened.

Krishi Prayoga Pariwara

Shimoga district, where KPP's major activities are carried out, is well influenced by free market and globalisation programmes. Modern goods and comforts have changed the life style of rural and urban people. For example, branded products, such as tooth paste, soap, towels, toothbrush, oil, cosmetics, baby foods and beverages, are now common in the rural areas, whereas in the old days neem tooth sticks, local tooth and bathing powders made out of herbs, cotton towels of local mills, herbal local cosmetics, home prepared baby foods and local natural, herbal drinks were used. Meanwhile, the knowledge behind these local products is rapidly disappearing. This is also true in the case of agriculture. Farmers who aspire to maximise their economic benefits and yields depend on markets for seeds, equipment and chemical inputs. Yet, the effects of these modern inputs on their environment, soil, water and air, and their increased dependency on markets, are not given the same consideration.

KPP was initiated in the early 1990s by a farmer peer group, in a remote village in the Malnad area of Karnataka. This group of experimenting farmers concentrated on the increasing problems experienced with chemical agriculture, and aimed at finding solutions to them. The group grew informally under the able leadership of Mr Purushothama Rao, a progressive organic farmer from Thirthahalli in the Shimoga district. Today the association counts over 5,000 members. By 1996 KPP became a registered body and its vision and objective were broadened, aimed at developing practical development strategies, which are not simply economic, but also based on moral, spiritual and ecological values. KPP has three major objectives. Firstly, KPP promotes indigenous, self-reliant and organic eco-friendly agriculture, which is thoroughly sustainable. Secondly, KPP revitalises local traditions, in which safe, non-chemical agriculture and diversified ecosystems play a central role. Thirdly, KPP provides development education to young people, empowering them to play a role in constructive, non-political development.

KPP grew under the leadership of Sri Purushothama Rao, an innovative organic farmer.

KPP has a farm developed by Sri Purushothama Rao at Thirthahalli as a model farm. It comprises of 10 acres of land; 50% of the area is under local paddy varieties, while the remaining 50% is devoted to commercial crops, including arecanut, coconut, vanilla, pepper, elachi, coffee, banana and vegetables. The farm is fully organic since 1989. Nearly 50 farmers visit this farm on a daily basis, to learn about organic manure, bio-pesticide preparation, as well as sowing, planting, intercultivation, pest control, harvesting and post harvest technologies. KPP publications are available on the farm, which is also the registered office of KPP. The majority of the meetings of member-farmers and the Board of Trustees, as well as training and seminars are held here.

KPP has a Board of Trustees comprising of eight trustees. Seven of them are practicing organic farmers representing different parts of Karnataka state, and the other is a social worker who guides the whole body. This body, along with active local farmers, plans and executes the activities. Besides this, KPP presently works with two full-time staffers, who plan, advice, and direct the activities, based on good relationships with both the farmers and the academic community.

Methodology. Shimoga district has a diverse population. KPP is working with farmers of different ethnic communities, such as Idigas, Bovis, Havyka Brahmin, and Vokkaliga. These communities have their own customs, beliefs, norms and values, but all of them observe the Hindu festivals of *Ganesh Chathurthi, Dashera, Yugadi* and *Bhoomi Hunnime,* and use nature's diversity in different rituals. They worship different parts of nature, like water, soil, plants, animals, and air, in the name of Gods and Goddesses, as well as agricultural inputs like seeds, manure, farm implements and equipment. This concept of the sacredness of natural resources is still alive, even in this modern era, and this is the basis on which KPP works with the farmers on the relevance of traditional knowledge and practices in agriculture.

The objective of KPP within Compas is 'to understand how indigenous knowledge systems and techniques, as well as indigenous institutions, can enhance endogenous development'. To achieve this, various activities are executed.

- Documentation. The elders are consulted in documenting local knowledge and practices. Sometimes school children are involved, motivated through special prizes. The collected information is systematically compiled according to themes: crops, season, locality, farming operation, ethnic community, beliefs, faith and worship. To support this documentation, classical texts like *Vedas, Puranas*, and *Shastras*, as well as contemporary literature are collected. Persons, libraries, research institutes and institutions with similar interest are also identified.
- Working with research-minded farmers. KPP supports research-minded and knowledgeable farmers to find solutions to the problems that the KPP farmers face in their fields. All necessary information and expertise by way of resource persons are provided in facilitating the experimental process. KPP now works with more than 50 farmer-scientists of this kind. Their interests vary from seed selection to seed treatment, soil fertility improvement, plant protection, liquid manure, growth stimulation, fruit ripening, harvesting, storage, processing and value addition.
- Training and exchange workshops. For the last decade, apart from training workshops to the farmers, KPP has also organised meetings of farmer-experimenters in different

parts of Karnataka, in which they could highlight successful techniques and exchange their experiences.

- Organising village units. KPP has established ten village units, which consist of a minimum of five farmer families who practice organic farming. Key persons in each unit are identified and supported, to help in propagating the alternative philosophy in agriculture, which is eco-friendly, self-reliant and cost-effective. These units are supported through training to become the production centres of organic food products, and include a total of about 110 people, most of them women and subsistence farmers.
- Organising mass meetings. Mass meetings of farmers and community members are organised in the villages to present the outcomes of their activities related to organic agriculture. KPP has organised three mass meetings over the past three years: one to release the booklet on traditional recipes, another to release a pamphlet on the organic *kumkuma,* the red natural dye traditionally used on the forehead; and the third to release a booklet called *Kamadhenu,* which deals with indigenous cattle breeds.

Examples of KPP field activities

Revitalising traditional food dishes. Traditional Indian food is highly diversified; an ordinary lunch consists of many vegetables, grains and herbs. The Indian kitchen contains a wide variety of dishes, and any particular dish can be prepared in many different ways. KPP is interested in the relationship between the preparation of local dishes, human health and agriculture. In 1998, KPP invited schoolchildren to ask their mothers and grandmothers for recipes for *tambli,* traditional soup in which many local herbs are used. Nearly 160 different recipes were found! KPP listed the different types of tambli, described how they were prepared and recorded their ayurvedic background. It turned out that about 130 plant species are used in the preparation of the different tamblis. The parts used vary from tender leaves to flowers, fruits, seeds, bark and roots. The results of this research were presented during a mass meeting and in a booklet.

Home-made pickle and tender mango. Pickle is an indispensable side dish in traditional Indian food. There are many varieties, including tender mango pickle, lime pickle and vegetable pickle. The tender mango pickle is famous for its taste, the wood of the tender mango tree is used for construction and mango leaves in specific rituals. Leaves are tied around the house and in front of doors, to protect the house from the pollutants in the atmosphere. The tender leaves of mango and jak are also used in the *Kalasa,* a copper pot with water, where the leaves energise the holy water of the Kalasa. Two rather surprising facts about the use of tender mango led KPP to further study the use of this fruit tree. First, we found a large number of varieties of tender mango in the local vegetable markets: they differed in size, shape, flavour and sap content. This made us wonder about the mango varieties in the region and the quality parameters used by the local population. Second, it astonished us that local sellers harvest the tender mangoes by cutting down whole branches. The mangoes are then transported by lorry to big cities like Shimoga, Bangalore and Chennai, to be processed as industrial pickle. We wondered why people would indulge in such damaging harvesting practices. Moreover, due to industrial pickling, the technology and know-how of local pickle preparation are being lost, and the younger generation no longer interacts with the older generation in the process of pickle making. People have lost the habit of offering a gift of homemade pickle, and even during community gatherings factory-made pickle is now commonly used.

Tender mango competition

The KPP team identified and prepared a small group of local people to conduct a survey on local mango varieties: the local name, the age of the tree, its fruiting pattern, yield and propagation. In April 1999, with the help of the Karnataka Forest Department, a tender mango competition was organised. During this competition nearly 100 entries were exhibited in classes like raw tender mango, tender mango in brine (saturated salt water) and ready pickle. The judges were two farmers and two housewives, experienced in pickle preparation and tender mango selection. They judged according to

During the tender mango competition the mangoes were judged by local criteria such as flavour, size, shape and sap content.

eight local criteria: size, shape, flavour, texture, stalk length and girth, sap content, thickness of skin and seed. Nearly ten local varieties of high quality mangoes were selected during the competition. The ceremony was attended by local leaders as well as representatives of the media, while Sri Vinaya Kumar, an official of the Government Forest Department expressed his department's interest in maintaining and propagating local mango trees.

For two years after this programme, a few grafters from the KPP farmer group supplied over 2,000 tender mango seedlings to nearby farmers. The local branch of the State Horticulture Department also took interest and supplied a good number of grafted tender mango plants to farmers. Meanwhile, home-scale pickle production has increased, and KPP is involved in selling these pickles directly to the consumers. The awareness about the tender mango tree has reduced the unsustainable harvesting practices.

Promoting organic kumkuma. Kumkuma is the name for the sacred red vermillion powder, which is used widely by the Indian Hindu population. It is applied on the forehead (*Agnya chakra*, or third eye) everyday, after performing morning rituals and worship of mother Goddess. It helps to develop purity in thoughts and feelings, improves *Satwik*, or the mental properties of silence, patience and self-control, and connects the person's inner and outer worlds. The particular spot is also a well-known accupressure point, which is used to promote health, calmness of mind and happiness. Medically speaking, turmeric, an ingredient in kumkuma preparation, is a good antiseptic against various bacteria and fungi, while it improves the colour and smoothness of skin as well as eyesight, sense of

Over 15,000 women and children have been trained by KPP in the organic preparation of kumkuma, the dye applied on the forehead after morning rituals.

taste, smell and hearing. KPP resolved to revive the traditional preparation of kumkuma and found an almost forgotten traditional method of producing it on the basis of turmeric, lemon juice, borax, alum and cow's ghee. To date nearly 15,000 women have been given a course related to the social, cultural, historical and spiritual background of kumkuma based on Indian science. They were trained in preparing the pure kumkuma, which has provided some of them an added income. This, to our surprise, has spread autonomously throughout Karnataka State.

Advocating cow products. In India, the cow is greatly respected, worshipped and is believed to be the abode of all the Gods, particularly of *Laxmi*, the Goddess of wealth. In farmers' families, food is offered to the sacred cow every morning, before the day's activities begin. The cow is an inseparable part of the farming community. It is worshipped in particular during the festival of lights, *Deepavali*, in the month of October, when the cow is referred to as *Kamadhenu*, which means the animal with the power to provide whatever a person may ask for. All the products of the cow are used in agriculture. Gandhi once remarked: *"The cow was, in India, the best companion. She was the giver of plenty, the mother of life. Not only did she give milk, but she made agriculture possible."* KPP has experimented with some ideas from ancient texts, by using cow's urine (both of pregnant and non-pregnant animals), dung, milk, curd, buttermilk, ghee and whey in agriculture. The texts also advocated the use of amniotic fluid to promote growth and induce flowering. Most of these cow products are now used by the KPP farmers in one or the other way: cow's urine as a foliar spray, manure for composting, milk as an antiviral spray, curd and buttermilk to increase the microbial activity in the soil, while ghee is used in traditional seed treatment.

Improving local cattle breeds. In India there are 26 descriptive indigenous breeds of cattle as well as numerous non-descriptive breeds. Unfortunately, Jersey and Holstein-Friesian breeds have been introduced for cross breeding programmes. The farmers in KPP are disturbed, however, by the fact that these crossbred cattle do not perform well in their area, as they require more concentrates and roughage than the indigenous breeds, and often suffer from diseases and disorders for which qualified veterinarians have to be called in. Poor farmers are unable to cope with these increased costs of maintenance, and the dependency on external inputs such as antibiotics and other chemicals. The farmers associated with KPP concluded that except for a few incidental successes, crossbreeding at large is not an economically viable option. This made them decide to look at local cattle breeds afresh.

The cow in India is sacred and has multiple functions in agriculture.

A survey conducted by a KPP team concluded that the local breed, known as Malnad Gidda, can yield 3-5 litres of milk per day, comparable to 4-6 litres of milk yielded by cross bred animals in the KPP project area. Through selection and careful breeding, the yields of this indigenous breed can be improved. The National Dairy Research Institute in Bangalore has expressed its interest to support this programme. KPP has also collected relevant literature on ethno-veterinary medicine, documenting the role of indigenous cattle in family life, revitalising the local health traditions based on cow products, and disseminating all information to interested farmers. The findings of this KPP study is documented in a booklet titled 'Kamadhenu', which describes the characteristics of the four main local cattle breeds of Karnataka State. The booklet also presents several preparations from ayurvedic medicine based on cow products, and their effect on human health. Moreover, with the help of a local spiritual leader, Sri Raghaveshwara Bharathi Swamy, a centre for breeding and conservation of indigenous cattle has been established. The centre is playing a key role in the selection, breeding and distribution of local breeds, while also producing a variety of cow-based products for human health. It is supported by experienced ayurvedic doctors and by a research institute in Nagpur, Maharastra State.

Arecanut experiment. The on-farm experiment on the yellow leaf complex of areca was started in October 2000. Arecanut is a perrenial cash crop. Yellow leaf complex is a complex of diseases and disorders, first observed in early 1941 in Karnataka, which reduces the yield drastically. Within some 5 years the plot is unfit for the cultivation of arecanut. KPP has collected primary information regarding this problem, through local surveys and a review of literature. The KPP team discussed the matter with local farmers, agricultural scientists and ayurvedic doctors, and tried out treatment according to the principles of *Vrkshayurveda*, the ancient plant science. The treatment used was documented in a text published by Asian Agri History Foundation, Hyderabad: a decoction prepared of hog fat, horse hair, cow horn, cow ghee and hemp. This was applied to each plant every month on the tenth day of the ascending moon. The treated plants have shown some promising

KPP director (left) visits arecanut farmer in his garden to discuss experiments to reduce yellow leaf complex.

changes, like increased root growth, decreased nut shedding, and improved flowering and fruiting. KPP will continue these experiments in the coming 3-5 years.

Some results and conclusions

KPPs work is participatory in nature. As a farmers' organisation it is relatively easy to appreciate the cosmovision aspects of indigenous knowledge and practices of the rural people. Presently, KPP is an association of relatively well-to-do farmers, belonging to the upper castes. At the same time KPP is also supporting subsistence farmers, who have paddy as a staple crop, through training, meetings and direct distribution networks. In the next phase, more priority will be given to experiments with indigenous knowledge and practices related to paddy.

Over the past six years, the demand for the different training activities on the above-mentioned subjects in the different villages and communities has steadily increased. Many families in the communities have started to include positive practices based on indigenous knowledge in their agriculture and life style. Though operating only with two full time workers, KPP is now considered one of the leading NGOs in the area in the field of organic agriculture. There has also been special interest in conserving local cattle breeds and the organic kumkuma production. The major constraint KPP has encountered is the challenge to understand the indigenous systems and knowledge in a holistic way. It proves difficult to give a scientific basis for certain indigenous practices and beliefs. For example, in the case of kumkuma, widely used in India for its sacredness, modern science does not explain what happens by applying it on the forehead. But Indian science, which looks inwards, indicates that it enhances the *satwik* properties of a person: the mental properties of silence, patience and inner control, which connect a person's inner and outer worlds. Satwik is considered very important for one's personal health, as well as the health of society as a whole. We intensively struggle to combine these two sciences - one which looks inwards and the other which looks outwards.

In the first years of the Compas programme, KPP had indicated that it would only work on organic agriculture. But over time we realised that the knowledge and practices documented were relevant not only to agriculture, but also to health and lifestyle in general. Therefore our vision was broadened, and we started to document knowledge and practices related to the different fields mentioned above, and conducted relevant training in the community.

In the next few years farmers and communities working with KPP will be strengthened further, and also be established in regional structures, called *taluks*. KPP will continue with the training programmes on various aspects of organic agriculture, health and rural development. Based on a syllabus developed between 1998 and 2002, training will be given to youth from different agro-climatic zones of Karnataka. The youth, selected according to their dedication to organic agriculture, will be trained for two years. They will involve themselves in the process of documentation, experimentation and dissemination. After the training period, they will return to their villages to facilitate endogenous development. Another activity will be the ongoing documentation of indigenous knowledge and practices. After collecting over 1,000 ancient texts, the next step in this process is to catalogue and analyse these texts. A group of Sanskrit scholars, ayurvedic doctors, agricultural scientists and farmers are prepared to support KPP in this effort.

Conclusion. KPP has made a small and modest attempt in the area of endogenous development. The process of building on the local resources in the area and supporting the farmers from different ethnic communities and socio-economic backgrounds, was started off with organic farming. Over the years, the local production, consumption and local marketing of organic foods have increased. Other activities have had impact on groups, especially rural women. For example, the production and use of organic kumkuma has reached over 15,000 women, which has stimulated them to think about their own cultural roots and how to build on it. The work on tender mango pickle production has also benefited women in terms of work, income and self-esteem.

KPP started with a charismatic local leader, the late Sri Purushothama Rao. His farm has become the central meeting place for the organisation as well as a demonstration farm for organic agriculture, where farmers from all around come to visit and see for themselves. The strength of KPP is that it builds on farmers' own capacities and initiatives for experimentation, in seeking answers to their practical problems. Making endogenous development a reality in a wider area requires, however, policies aimed at encouraging local communities to become more self reliant, while making better use of their own local resources.

Fortunately, and due to the positive results so far, different organisations, including research and government, as well as several reputed institutions and personalities at national and international level, have shown interest in the different programmes of KPP. Some of these are co-operating actively in spreading the results. This is a slow and ongoing process. As Sri Raghaveshwara Bharati Swamy, the local spiritual leaders who guides the cattle conservation and breeding centre, explains: *"Here we have several cattle breeds that are threatened by extinction, along with the local knowledge attached to them. Nature and people want evolution and not revolution. For us this is real development."*

4.2 REVIVING LOCAL HEALTH TRADITIONS

Darshan Shankar, Abdul Hafeel, Unnikrishnan Payyappapallimana and Suma Tagadur
FRLHT, India

The mission of FRLHT, the Foundation for the Revitalisation of Local Health Traditions, is to revitalise the local practices, beliefs and customs related to health in four states of Southern India. People in India have an outstanding knowledge of medicinal plants acquired over centuries, and in the majority of rural communities illness is treated with home remedies and by specialised folk healers. Yet, such knowledge and practices are eroding rapidly under the influence of modernisation. One of the main objectives of the FRLHT-Compas programme is to document and rapidly assess specific remedies. An innovative methodology was developed, in which local healers were supported, and selected local practices were compared with western bio-medicine as well as other codified medical systems, such as Ayurveda, Siddha and Unani.

Local health traditions are practices, beliefs and customs related to health, specific to each locality and passed on from generation to generation by word of mouth. They make use of a surprisingly wide array of locally available flora and fauna. Thousands of specialised folk healers are versed in methods such as pulse diagnosis, examination of urine, specific poison treatment, and *varma kalai*, diagnosis and treatment using 'vital points' in the body.

Codified medical systems in India. Local health traditions can be found throughout India parallel to codified or classical systems of medicine. These codified systems consist of medical knowledge, which includes sophisticated theoretical foundations expressed in thousands of manuscripts. Apart form western bio-medicine, examples in India are Ayurveda, Siddha, Unani and the Tibetan tradition. Siddha is one of the oldest systems of medicine in India, largely therapeutic in nature and specialised in pharmacology. Its principles and doctrines are similar to Ayurveda. The Unani system, with its origin in Greece, was introduced by the Arabs and Persians around the eleventh century. Unani interacts closely with Ayurveda and other local medical systems. Tibetan medicine in India is primarily a regional manifestation of Ayurveda. It is estimated that there are 600,000 licensed medical practitioners of these codified systems of medicine.

Local health traditions in India

Traditional healers. In addition to these codified systems, there are over a million community-based traditional health workers, including 60,000 village bone setters, 60,000 herbal medicine practitioners (excluding spiritual healers) specialising in jaundice, paralytic conditions, children's diseases, eye diseases, poison healing, dentistry etc., and around 700,000 midwives in India [Shankar, 1992]. These are India's traditional barefoot doctors, or *Nattu Vaidyas*. They assist in around 80% of all rural deliveries, treat over 40% of broken bones and 50% of snake, scorpion and dog bites. Sophisticated therapeutic techniques include *marmam* (treatment of vital points), *agni and kshara karma* (cauterisation), *sodhana*

Patients queue at the shed of healer Murthy near Shimoga, southern India.

karma (purificatory techniques), *rasayana* (rejuvenative therapy), techniques used in the management of dislocated joints, as well as surgical management of a number of conditions. They also treat health problems in domestic animals.

Traditional healers do not undertake medical service as a full-time vocation; the typical healer may be a farmer, a barber, a shopkeeper, a blacksmith or even a wandering monk. The medical service they undertake, though not free of charge, is performed on ethical grounds and is non-commercial in nature. This low sustenance cost is one of the reasons why the tradition is so large,and widespread.

Natural resource base. Around 8,000 plant species and more than 200 animal and mineral sources are used in treating health problems in India's 4,639 ethnic communities [AICRPE, 1996]. This accounts for almost 50% of the known flowering plants of India. There are huge numbers of written documents on the usage of these resources in the codified systems of medicines. It is interesting to observe that Indian knowledge about plants and plant products is not based on the application of western categories and approaches, such as chemistry and pharmacology. It is based on an indigenous system called *Dravya Guna Shastra,* the science of biological properties of natural materials. Establishing a bridge between western biomedical science and Dravya Ghuna Shastra is complex, though functional links have been identified. Unfortunately, there is a lack of rigorous cross-cultural studies and, in fact, a well-accepted methodology for such studies is still missing.

The in-depth study to be done on a plant before it can be admitted into the indigenous Ayurvedic Materia Medica is quite impressive. It includes aspects like nomenclature, parts used, methods of purification, contraindications, effect on physiological systems, effect on body tissues, effect on organs, effect on the excretory system, qualities, metabolic activity, post-digestive effect, drug therapeutic class and processing strategies. This has resulted in around 25,000 plant drug formulations in the codified Ayurvedic system, while it is suggested that over 50,000 herbal drug formulations have been developed by India's ethnic communities.

Social and cultural aspects. The traditional Indian medical worldview recognises the existence of body, mind, spirit and soul, and the therapies and practices cover these four dimensions. The concept of *swasthya*, or perfect health, is therefore a combination of bio-

Box 4d   Healing hands of Shimoga

Generations of traditional knowledge and folk healing have been serving thousands of people faced with life threatening diseases all over the world. Near Shimoga, southern India, Mr Narayana Murthy is a living example of this. For the past eighteen years he is serving the people on Thursdays and Sundays of every week. These days are considered as Siddhi varas - days which gives good effect. The healer and his family are strong believers of God and do the daily rituals as per community rules. The blessing of the community deity (*Lakshmi narasimha*) is an important factor which influences the patient's well-being and efficacy of the medicine given.

Healer Murthy treats the patients without any charge. The family's source of income is agriculture. Patients are allowed to put money in the metal box with small opening, without any condition and this amount is later used to meet the expenses of their community temple. Most cases that come to him are diagnosed cancer of different kinds (70% according to him) and people often consider this place as a final place of hope. Some patients carry laboratory reports of clinical diagnosis and hospital discharge summaries. His one day medication for the urinary calculi and medicines for heart blocks are a well-known remedy in Karnataka and adjacent states. According to the patients, their belief in the good heart and genuine mind of the healer is essential in the healing. As they state: *"we only want the medicine from his hands"*. Students and scientists of the Government Ayurvedic Medical college in Bangalore are learning and recording Murthy's cases, treatment and effects.

The Murthy family has established 30 acres of land with naturally grown medicinal plants and tree species. Healer Murthy views the plant as a living and a life-giving organism and a specific ritual is needed when collecting the required plant part. This ritual is a *pradhakshina*, encircling the divine body of the tree. He prays for the effect of the medicine and asks permission of the tree to take its part with medicinal properties. He says that this ritual bestows the effect of medicine. The ritual is also a sincere prayer for the benefit of each patient who comes to him for treatment.

physiological principles, metabolic processes, body channels, excretory processes, mental faculties, senses and the self. It is also understood that the external and the internal world of a being share the same principles, and that health requires a balance of the two.

Traditional medical knowledge is also diverse and specific to each eco-system and ethnic community, because of the special characteristics of resources, health needs and belief systems. There are certain common features, however, such as a very strict code of conduct followed by most barefoot doctors. They extend health care irrespective of a patient's personal work, caste, money and time. Certain prayers and offerings usually follow the collection of the medicinal plants and administration. Patients believe that certain healers have special healing powers, which is known as 'the power of the hand' or *Kaippunyam* (see box 4d).

The spiritual dimension of local health traditions is also included in communal meetings with folk healers and households. For example, some human disease conditions, particularly chronic skin ailments, are believed to have both material and spiritual causes, and the healer usually advises the patient to make a particular offering to the Snake God before starting the herbal treatment. In case of diseases caused by 'wind disorders in the body' the healers recite a special *mantra*, a kind of prayer, before starting the treatment with roots of four different plants. Traditional Indian literature also emphasises the spiritual dimension of the use of plants. It is obvious that including the spiritual dimension is essential to understanding the complexities and the potentialities of local health traditions in rural India.

The healers pass on their knowledge to younger successors who are selected on ethical criteria, which include qualities such as patience, strong faith in God, courage and a love of mankind. Some sociologists see this ethical screening as being 'too secretive'. But how could this explain the fact that at the start of the 21st century India continues to have around a million carriers of the oral health traditions spread throughout the country?

Erosion of local health practices. Yet, there is a large-scale erosion of local health traditions. The average age of the traditional health worker is now over 50, and successors are limited in numbers. Even at household level, there are fewer households working with home remedies today. This deterioration of local health traditions has a major negative impact on the access to local health care, which is very important for a country like India. Despite erosion being quite evident, the reasons behind it are not clear. It is too simple to state that local health traditions are eroding because they are ineffective and unable to meet present needs. Plants have not lost their healing properties and the knowledge of plants in the traditions is still profound. At the same time there is a rapid resurgence of interest in natural medicine throughout the world. Pharmaceutical researchers acknowledge that screen-

A traditional bonesetter in his prayer room cum clinic. The average age of local healers now is over 50, and successors are limited in numbers.

ing plants on the basis of information derived from traditional knowledge saves billions of dollars in time and resources. The question, therefore, remains as to why health traditions are eroding despite their apparent potential.

The reasons for this erosion are political, economic and social rather than medical. Wild plants, wild animals and other natural resources used by traditional medicine are threatened due to degradation of natural habitats and, in specific cases, due to over-harvesting for commercial purposes. Urgent measures for conserving these genetic resources are necessary.

Influence of modernisation

Even though traditional medical knowledge serves a vast majority of the Indian population, government support for these traditions is very meagre. Only around 4% of the annual health budget is allocated to the codified Indian systems of medicines, while the existence of local healers and local knowledge is not recognised in the Indian national health policy. Up to now there has been hardly any effort to recognise and codify the local health traditions in India.

Bio-prospecting. On the other hand, the interests of the pharmaceutical industry in herbal drugs [Wilgenburg, 1998], as well as the market for natural products, is growing. Laboratories are increasingly involved in isolating the active compounds of plants with medicinal properties for developing new drugs. Most of this research ends in patents. A few important examples of such commercialisation from India are plants like *Phyllanthus niruri* for viral hepatitis, *Evolvulus alsinoides* and *Bacopa monnieri* for anxiety, *Gymnema sylvestre* for diabetes, *Garcinia indica* for obesity, and *Taxus wallichiana* for various types of cancer. It has been estimated that 74% of the commercially used plant-based drugs have been developed on leads taken from indigenous knowledge. Needless to say that in most cases the local healers, who are the carriers of this knowledge, have no say in this commercialisation. The source of this knowledge is seldom acknowledged and there is hardly any effort to share the benefits coming out of this commercialisation [Sinha et al., 1998].

Public health care system. The present public health care system in India is dominated by western, technology-centred medicine, which depends heavily on external resources. It is estimated that only one-third of the population is covered by this system. In rural areas the coverage is much lower, sometimes as low as 3%. In order to open up the rural markets for their products, companies with a western bias are actively trying to replace traditional beliefs and practices, presenting them as obsolete and irrational.

As a result of these and other developments, a section of the rural people in all social classes, including the poor, are giving up traditional health practices and turning to western medicine. But this medical system is increasingly unaffordable for common people. Moreover, in a few years time, and due to the new international trade and patents regime supervised by the World Trade Organisation, modern pharmaceutical products are expected to become much more expensive than at present. Socio-economic surveys indicate that the single and largest cause of rural indebtedness in India is on account of health expenditure. This expense can be brought down considerably by promoting effective local health practices.

FRLHT methodology for fieldwork

The Foundation for the Revitalisation of Local Health Traditions, or FRLHT, is a non-governmental organisation established in 1991, dedicated to revitalising India's rich and diverse health traditions. FRLHT's mission further includes the conservation and sustainable use of medicinal plants, building databases, as well as research on selected medical, sociological and epistemological aspects of the Indian medicinal heritage. In 1993, in response to the dwindling medicinal plant resources, FRLHT initiated a pioneering collaborative programme with the state forest departments, research institutes, local NGOs, and local communities. Since then a network of over 530 conservation sites of medicinal plants has been established across the states of Kerala, Tamil Nadu, Karnataka, Andhra Pradesh and Maharastra, covering 11,000 hectares in different forest areas. FRLHT has accumulated a wealth of researched data, as well as a unique medicinal plant herbarium and a museum of traded raw drugs. The main objective of the four-year programme with Compas was to design a participatory method for documentation of local health traditions, and to carry out a rapid assessment of some selected elements and aspects of local health traditions/cultures in a few rural communities in South India.

Identifying effective practices through elaborate pharmacological and clinical trials is a time consuming task. Validating a single practice may involve several years of laboratory research and huge capital investments. Thus in the first phase of the fieldwork, an alternative methodology without detailed laboratory and clinical studies was developed to validate health practices. The methodology consisted of 4 major steps.

Documentation. A meeting of 13 local NGOs was organised to start the documentation and assessment of the local health traditions in the states of Marahashtra, Karnataka, Tamil Nadu and Kerala. These organisations had already been involved in the conservation of medicinal plants and traditional health care, and had well-established relationships with the local communities. Operational details and responsibilities were agreed upon, NGO staff was trained, and community level support committees were established. Local communities were fully involved in these revitalisation activities.

Training field staff
A series of training workshops were held to orient the field staff in documenting local health traditions. Training was given on subjects such as cultural diversity and cosmovisions; the documentation of local health traditions and their worldviews; finding the effective health practices through participatory rural appraisal; and rapid assessment of local health traditions. Appropriate tools for documenting these practices as well as describing prevalent health conditions were discussed.

Pilot study
Next, a pilot study was carried out in four field locations, prior to the actual documenta-

tion process. Questionnaires to record the knowledge, resources and socio-cultural aspects of health traditions were field-tested. In order to record the different levels of knowledge and practice of folk healers, five subsets of questionnaires were designed for veterinary practitioners, healers treating poisonous bites, traditional birth attendants, traditional bonesetters and those healers who treat more general health conditions. The household questionnaires focused on home remedies, as well as on food practices and the health-related aspects of the daily routine.

Data collection
A total of 1,048 healers, around 80% of the folk healers in the area, were interviewed between 1998 and 1999. Moreover, the practices of around 2,000 knowledgeable house-holds were collected and documented: in three survey areas in Tamil Nadu a total of 106 health conditions commonly treated at household level were documented. The resources used in household health care practises ranged from 84 to 127 items, the majority being of plant origin (44%), the rest of animal and mineral origin. Based on this data, 96 health practices were selected for further analysis in the assessment workshops in the second phase of the project. This data collection resulted in more in-depth understanding of the local health traditions, their knowledge base, biological resource base as well as their socio-cultural-spiritual context, including prayers, mantras, usage of astrology, rituals, and the code of ethics of the traditional healers.

During the rapid assessment, the facilitator confirms the measures used in medicine preparation. The removal of distorted practices and the encouragement of positive ones are essential for the growth of any culture.

Databases

Two computerised databases emerged from this work. The first database systematises the local health traditions of the southern states of India, based on the documentation process mentioned above. This is a centralised, dynamic database in English in the FRLHT office in Bangalore, which can be used by other organisations. As this is the intellectual property of the local people, the data is being returned to the respective communities in the form of Community Health Registers. This is part of an extensive programme to protect the local knowledge being pirated for commercial purposes, without proper consent of the local communities or equitable benefit sharing. The second database lists the reference literature from Ayurveda, Siddha, Unani and modern pharmacology, aiming to serve as evidence for clinical studies based on the local health traditions.

Prioritising health conditions. As a next step, the prevailing health conditions were prioritised by means of participatory rural appraisals with groups of 35 community members each, both male and female, in five selected areas. This exercise included four steps: listing the health conditions prevalent in the community; establishing the criteria to prioritise the health conditions; developing a matrix with criteria and health conditions; and ranking, or scoring, the conditions based on each criterion. Twenty health conditions with the highest scores were selected for the assessment. The communities' understanding of these health conditions, like causes, symptoms and stages, was also discussed and documented during the exercise. The selected health conditions were screened to see what home remedies were available to prevent or cure them, and if the health condition or remedies were repeatedly mentioned during the interviews. The accessibility of the natural resources, their affordability and the effort required to prepare the remedies were also documented.

Assessment of the selected remedies. The third step, during the second phase of the FRLHT-Compas programme, was to develop a protocol for the rapid assessment of the local health traditions in order to assess the selected home remedies for subsequent promotion in primary health care. This exercise was called 'rapid', as it did not involve detailed laboratory or clinical studies. Five areas in Tamil Nadu were selected for assessment workshops on the basis of the quality of data and the diversity of practices identified. Participants of the assessment workshops, organised by the 5 participating NGOs, included community members, folk healers, practitioners of western biomedicine and of the other Indian systems of medicine (Ayurveda, Siddha and Unani), field botanists, pharmacologists, researchers, facilitators, NGO staff, reporters and FRLHT staff. The references for the selected plants, animal parts or minerals collected from literature of the different Indian systems of medicine and modern pharmacology helped the participants to comment on the local health practices under review.

During the workshop, the participants broke up into small groups and commented on a given health condition and its remedies. The NGO staff assisted in facilitating and reporting on the process. The natural resources used in the remedies were identified by the community, and the medicinal plants were documented in a voucher specimen collection. Missing data was added and cross-checked. The discussions and individual comments were also documented. In the plenary sessions each group presented its conclusions on the remedies, and commented on efficacy. Any differences of opinion were clarified until a common understanding was reached. About 96 home remedies for 20 health conditions from 5 areas in southern India were assessed through the five rapid assessment workshops. This has helped to develop the confidence of the local communities in their own traditions, and stimulated a critical but respectful way of looking at community-level traditions.

Several criteria were used to decide on the practices to be promoted. Distorted practices were discouraged. Remedies with strong positive empirical evidence from the communities, but negative assessment from the other medical systems, were subjected to further research among the communities. This category is called 'data-deficient'. Remedies with strong empirical evidence from the community and the folk healers were promoted, irrespective of whether they are supported by the other medical systems.

In the process it was found that rural people's understanding of health conditions does not always coincide with the symptoms, stages and causes mentioned by the other medical systems. For instance, the community from Virudhunagar understood that leprosy was caused by snakebite. The participatory assessment exercise gave the local community an opportunity to seek clarification on the causes and symptoms of leprosy and its transmission. Thus an inter-cultural dialogue was generated between different medical experts and members from the communities.

Traditional healing among the tribal population of Orissa involves herbs, mantras and offerings.

Mainstreaming the findings. Another major step in the methodology was to find ways of introducing and promoting the practices that were positively assessed within the mainstream public health system. In January 2001, the methodology and findings of the documentation and assessment process were presented to a forum of scientists, policy makers and development-oriented NGOs. During this workshop, which received considerable attention from the press, a strategy for the revitalisation of community-based local health traditions in rural and urban households was designed. In addition, databases on local health traditions were also prepared, and along with comprehensive reports of the rapid assessment exercises, were released during public meetings.

Presently the FRLHT-Compas programme is implementing an action plan to promote this methodology of selecting best practices and medicinal plants, and to encourage establishment of kitchen home gardens in one million households in Tamil Nadu. This project is integrated into the larger programme for promotion of local health traditions, which has reached over 40,000 households so far, and is directed at rural women and the local community organisations, the *sanghas*. Besides being a valuable aid to the household health situation, the possibility of growing certain herbs and medicinal plants for commercial purposes has been taken into account. At local level, the Women's Federation, a women's organisation covering all four states, has taken the responsibility for executing the kitchen gardens project.

The NGOs assist in technical aspects such as training and raising seedlings of the medicinal plants in nurseries. Monitoring is carried out by both the NGOs and the Federation. Local resource centres have been established where information and education on community health knowledge is provided. Moreover, citizens' support is sought for saving critically endangered species from extinction, by encouraging individuals, community centres, schools and other organisations to grow them in small numbers. Moreover, in order to lower the incidence of water-borne diseases in the household, the South Indian tradition of *choodo thaneer* - boiling water with specific herbs before it is used for drinking - has been revived.

Other field activities

Support to local healers. FRLHT seeks to give more recognition to outstanding folk healers, through combined efforts involving the healers, local NGOs and local sponsors. In the last three years nine awards have been given to native village-based healers, both men and women, in the states of Karnataka, Kerala and Tamil Nadu. The awards included 10,000 Rupees and a statue of Lord *Dhanwanthari,* the God of medicine.

Other activities of the 13 NGOs co-operating in this programme to promote local health traditions include the establishment of low-cost clinics to support local healers and accessibility of these facilities to the communities. A number of *nattu vaidya* meetings have been conducted and the proceedings have been documented.

People's Biodiversity Register. In regards to the intellectual property rights on medicinal plants, we believe that it is a common misconception that traditional knowledge, when documented and published, can be stolen and patented. Anything published cannot be patented, as it is 'prior art' and already accessible in published form. So, we believe that the best way to protect the oral knowledge in the local health traditions from theft, and subsequent patent claims, is to put it into published form and databases. A real problem can emerge, however, when a piece of traditional knowledge is 'modified', and a patent is then claimed on the modification, as if it were novel and new. Such modifications cannot be prevented in an open society. But, according to the Convention on Bio-Diversity, the owners of traditional knowledge can seek benefit-sharing from the commercialisation of this modification. Even if the published traditional knowledge has 'free access', it requires informed consent for use and this consent may be provided based on a benefit-sharing agreement.

A more serious problem is that the patenting authority experiences difficulties in recognising any modification carried out in an indigenous, non-western knowledge system as an 'innovation', because the evaluation of the patent claim has to comply with the rules of the western knowledge system. In traditional cultures, an intellectual contribution is recognised and rewarded in a very different way. Moreover, what may not be obvious in western culture may be very obvious in a traditional culture. We need 'intercultural councils' to settle disputes about the novelty of the modifications carried out on a piece of traditional knowledge. In order to prevent 'bio-piracy' - robbing of information from local communities for commercial purposes - there is a need for a sound information system on our biodiversity.

In addressing this challenge, the Centre for Ecological Sciences at the Indian Institute of Science and FRLHT have, in 1995, initiated a so-called People's Biodiversity Register. The objectives of this initiative are threefold: to respect and preserve the knowledge and practices of local communities; to promote the wider application of such practices with approval and involvement of the holders; and to encourage equitable sharing of the benefits arising from the use of these innovations and practices. Between 1996 and 1998 the Indian Institute of Sciences co-ordinated the People's Biodiversity Register at 52 sites in eight states. The register can be used to promote the sustainable management of biodiversity, while claims of communities and individuals to knowledge on these resources can be supported. Moreover, at local level, community health registers have been developed and released in public gatherings, as a first step towards protection of community intellectual property rights.

Lessons learned

The last four years of FRLHT's work in the Compas programme has shown the high contemporary relevance of local health traditions in achieving health security in the country. It is apparent, however, that these are eroding at a fast pace for a host of reasons such as want of successors, lack of confidence, lack of political and organisational support, and the influence of modernisation. Issues related to globalisation and social, economic and political marginalisation of traditional knowledge need to be addressed through appropriate interventions like assessment methods, sustainable utilisation of resources, policy advocacy and instilling of confidence in health traditions.

The documentation and assessment programme has been an experiment in understanding the local people's expertise and in codifying the health-related knowledge. The methodology for documentation and rapid assessment has been field-tested and is now ready for sharing with a wider audience, both government and other organisations working in the area of primary health care. A number of training programmes has already been conducted based on this methodology. Several valuable lessons have been learned during these workshops. One such lesson was the close attention needed in the selection and orientation of local healers and medical experts of different backgrounds, before embarking on the actual assessment exercise. Moreover, their experience in health care in the area and familiarity with the local language should be considered, as it helps to maximise interactions with the community members. It was also understood that each group involved in documentation should design formats for their specific locality. Teaching on how to develop documentation tools was therefore added on to the subsequent training programmes.

Difficulties and constraints in the programme also need to be mentioned, for example, the need of appropriate methodological tools for documenting and assessing the cosmovision aspects of the local health traditions. Moreover, processing and cross-checking the data is a time consuming task, and documenting can be hampered by discontinuity of some of the traditions. Areas like theory building related to these local health traditions, the dynamics of knowledge transfer through generations and from people to people, as well as the relationship between folk traditions and codified medical systems, still need in-depth studies to reveal the best strategies for revitalising them.

It is interesting to note that rural women pursue a major part of the household traditions in the 13 project locations: women are the carriers of household knowledge. During the documentation process with the local healers, the women's preference was reproductive health practices. They were especially interested in self-help methods that could reduce the health expenditure of the family, and therefore actively participated in the validation and assessment activities.

The methodologies developed by FRLHT to document and rapidly assess the most effective local health traditions have enhanced the self-confidence of the communities who use them. The workshops for rapid assessment have provided a platform for cross-cultural dialogue. This has resulted in additions to incomplete remedies, the removal of distorted practices, and the encouragement of positive ones. This methodology can now be replicated in other areas and in other fields. FRLHT will achieve this by stressing on wider dissemination of documentation and rapid assessment methodologies in the future, i.e. by initiating projects in medical schools for documenting and assessing local health traditions. Strategic networking with influential partners, including the government is another important aspect. So far, policy advocacy workshops have initiated the process of influencing the central government to recognise and support local health traditions. This promotional strategy may provide the basis for a national health system which incorporates support to local health traditions, thus ensuring effective and affordable care for all those who need it.

4.3 EMPOWERMENT OF THARU INDIGENOUS KNOWLEDGE

Maheswar Ghimire and Basanta Rana Bhat, ECOS, Nepal

The Tharu indigenous people live in the southern plains of Nepal and have been confronted with the western model of development over the last decades. In an attempt to revive the Tharu traditional culture, ECOS (Ecological Services Centre) has documented traditional knowledge and stimulated experimentation in the area of Dibya Nagar. Moreover, traditional institutions were supported and advocacy activities initiated, to stimulate recognition of Tharu rights in the local government.

The Tharu have lived for at least 600 years in Chitwan, the tropical plains of Nepal, at some 145 kilometres southwest of the capital, Kathmandu. Chitwan is regarded as the source of ancient Indian and Nepalese cultures. For example, Lumbini, on the south-western Chitwan plains, is considered the birthplace of Lord Buddha. In 1973 one thousand square kilometres of this jungle were declared Royal Chitwan National Park, which is now world famous for its bio-diversity and wildlife, and popular among tourists who want to observe the horned rhino, the Bengal tiger or the Ghadiyal crocodile.

Before 1960, the Rapti and Narayani rivers were the main mode of transport and trade in Chitwan, next to food trails. Oxen were used for ploughing, seeds were exchanged and there was a close relationship between biodiversity and the festivals celebrated by the Tharu people. Over the past 50 years, however, major changes have occurred. In 1956, a USAID supported malaria eradication programme decimated the mosquito population, which enabled the implementation of a resettlement scheme through which Hindus and Bhuddists migrated from the mid hills to the lowland plains. During 1960s, the agro-chemicals for agriculture were subsidised, favouring the more educated and rich migrant farmers. When the jungle was declared National Park, the Tharu people were deprived of utilising its natural resources, which formed part of their livelihoods. They were only permitted to enter the jungle a few times per year to collect herbs, grasses for thatch, or to utilise wood from specific trees for musical instruments.

Tharu cosmovision

By origin, the Tharu believe that supernatural beings residing in nature guide them in their daily life. They worship God in the form of natural forests, streams, rivers or a single tree, and can therefore be considered animists. Tharu have a totemic identity: the different ethnic groups have a specific plant or animal as their totem. Forests are protected by a Goddess, who is worshipped and asked for peace, prosperity and protection. For worshipping there are three types of temples: the first one is at the household level to worship the family deities, the second one is at the house of the *Gurau*, or spiritual leader. Here the Gurau meditates and performs rituals, for example to heal a person. The third type is the public temple, usually built close to a Pipal tree, or any other sacred tree, and it is here that public rituals take place. Astrological information is applied for several agriculture related activities, such as seed selection. *Mantras*, or ritual verses, are chanted to influence the environment, for example to stop heavy rains during beginning of monsoon. The Tharu also celebrate Hindu festivals.

Tharu women are the guardians of culture and tradition. For example, they do the majority of wall paintings before *Deepavali* - the festival of Lights and Cow in November. According to Tharu women, the major purpose of wall painting is to please the Goddess of wealth, called *Laxmi*. At the same time the cow is worshipped for good fortune in the house, as this animal is considered a major source of wealth. Sacred plants and trees, such as *Ficus religiosa* and *Ficus benjamina,* are often planted around the house.

Changing cultural identity. When the external influences based on the western model of development entered Chitwan, the traditional way of living of the Tharu people was seriously challenged. Over the years, the Tharu have adopted festivals and rituals of the migrant population and increasingly followed the modern monetary-based way of life. With this erosion of their cultural identity, even simple issues became complicated. For example, a dispute between people, which was earlier solved within the community, is now brought to the police and court. Extended families became nuclear families, allopathic medicine is replacing herbal medicine. The long tradition of cultural festivals related to agriculture and health, as well as indigenous thoughts and values, are gradually declining.

In Dibya Nagar farm sizes are small (0.5 ha) to medium (1.0 ha) and most Tharu farmers keep a buffalo and some goats. Major crops are rice, maize, wheat, finger millet and mustard. The majority of farmers use chemical inputs, though often not according to recommendations. There is quite some awareness, however, of the negative effects: poisoning, deterioration of soil life, increase of harmful insects and decrease of predators, such as the dragon fly, fire fly and tiger beetle. Older people recall that some 35 years ago, Chitwan was one of the best areas for paddy rice and mustard. But nowadays, even with high levels of external inputs, the former yields are hard to obtain. As Sikkha Gurau, the spiritual leader of the Tharu, states: *"Our people are trying to live the modern way without knowing its long term effect or consequences. Very little emphasis is given to revive the culture and indigenous value systems of the people. When the elderly people are gone, everything will be finished and our culture will disappear."*

Revitalising Tharu indigenous knowledge

Ecological Services Centre, or ECOS, is an NGO which started implementing field programmes since 1995 in Devghat, in the midhills of Nepal. It has 7 staff members, working on community development, with programmes such as literacy, local saving and credit schemes, as well as health and sanitation. It also includes technical assistance for small water supply systems, agroforestry, forest protection, organic and bio-dynamic agriculture, and kitchen vegetable gardening. The mission of ECOS is: 'to facilitate the empowerment of the rural poor in a way which involves them directly and actively to improve their social, economic and enviromental well-being.'

Dibya Nagar is the area with several scattered Tharu settlements, where ECOS started working in the context of the Compas programme in 1997. The main objectives were to recognise the importance of indigenous knowledge for sustainable development, to enhance the communication among farmers, and between farmers, ECOS staff and researchers, and to protect the property rights of the Tharu people. After discussions with farmers, Tharu leaders and school teachers it was decided to revive the indigenous system of agriculture, and to complement it with recently developed practices from organic agriculture, such as the use of Effective Micro-organisms (EM), bio-pesticides, and post harvest protection techniques. The methodology of ECOS includes experimenting with practices based on indigenous knowledge, empowerment of local institutions, and networking.

Revitalising spiritual and cultural practices. Several other activities were also implemented to revive Tharu culture. During a village fair, organised in December 2000, a Tharu house with traditional architecture and wall paintings was selected to exhibit traditional tools and equipment, costumes, ornaments and other art material. Some 3,000 people visited this site and the main interest of the visitors was to know how these traditions can enhance the environmental protection and health of the people today. Moreover, Tharu elders are sharing their indigenous knowledge on agriculture and health, the experiments, and their social ethics twice a year with school children. Community members have revitalised their songs, costumes, dance and musical instruments. This approach increased the interest of the children as well as their parents about the need for reviving indigenous knowledge and social organisation.

Experiments. In 1998 and 1999, experiments in paddy rice were set up with 18 farmers to compare chemical inputs, compost with Effective Micro-organisms, and compost with auspicious dates for sowing according to astrology. In February 2002, this fertilization experiment was continued with maize, comparing different treatments: only compost, compost with EM, and only EM. The type of information collected was the effect on plant growth, pest infestation, soil moisture content, soil friability and crop yield. ECOS has encountered considerable difficulty in developing a good methodological framework for these experiments, however, and so far no clear results have been achieved.

In 1999, a second experiment with a Tharu ritual to protect the crop from pests and diseases, called *Hari Hari Barna*, was started with paddy rice, which was replicated in 2000. The ritual is performed by the Sikkha Gurau in the period June-August, based on astrological calculations. The ritual consisted of putting a mud pot with sacred rice seeds in the centre of a rice plot, with coloured leaves and flowers as offerings around it, and combined with the chanting of specific mantras. This experiment was carried out at three places, again with three different treatments: the first crop was protected with this ritual and biopesticides, on the second plot only biopesticides were applied, and on a control plot, no ritual nor bio-pesticide was applied. The farmers monitored the progress through regular field visits, and information was collected about the number of harmful insects, the incidence of diseases and other physiological disorders. Clear effects of the different treatments could not be determined, however.

Discussion. ECOS is an organisation with a good track record in organic farming and rural development. However, skills are lacking to develop a systematic approach for experimentation and systematic research that includes cosmovision aspects. To improve this,

ECOS has now established formal linkages with the Kathmandu University to get more support on their experiments with indigenous practices.

Initially, it was difficult to motivate the ECOS staff and the farmers in the area into the topic of cosmovision. This was due to several factors, like the complexity of the local cultures in the area, with a mix of indigenous Tharu, Hindu and Buddhist communities. Also the fact that only the project leader speaks English inhibited the full participation and mutual learning of other staff in the discussions with other Compas members.

Mr Uttam Kumar Chaudhary, a Tharu farmer has worked intensively with the programme as a local promoter. According to him, ECOS should focus on deepening the understanding of the importance of rituals and share the findings, especially with youngsters. He suggests to continue the programme at the local schools and to establish a museum about Tharu culture, showing their tradition, agricultural tools and implements, as well as traditional varieties of paddy, maize, wheat and certain herbs that are beneficial for specific diseases.

Other Tharu farmer leaders and Sikkha Gurau also express their enthusiasm about the work, which has resulted enhanced recognition of the Tharu in the negotiations with the government on issues like bufferzones, indigenous rights and protected areas in the Royal Chitwan National Park. ECOS was also invited to assist in formulating the development plans for the Dibya Nagar and Meghauli area, based on culture, cosmovision and sustainable agriculture.

In order to strengthen the work on indigenous knowledge and cosmovision, ECOS plans to build a national network with universities and NGOs for information sharing, research and lobbying. In this way it is hoped to complement the modernisation trend and respond to the increasing demand from farmers to work on the basis of cultural heritage towards sustainable agriculture.

Mr Uttam Kumar Chaudhary, a Tharu farmer and ECOS' local promotor.

4.4 MODERN DILEMMAS AND TRADITIONAL INSIGHTS

A.V. Balasubramanian, K. Vijayalaksmi, Subhashini Sridhar and S. Arumugasamy
CIKS, India

What can be the role of traditional knowledge in India's quest to achieve 'food for all' in a sustainable way? The Centre for Indian Knowledge Systems, CIKS, has gained considerable experience in studying indigenous knowledge and its potential to meet today's challenges. In the context of the Compas programme, CIKS has experimented with traditional pest control techniques derived from the large number of ancient texts on Indian Plant Science, or Vrkshayurveda. The practical results are promising. The traditional practices and oral traditions can be strengthened with inputs from the Indian scientific traditions.

India today is facing a serious dilemma. Agricultural production has increased significantly over the past years: in fact, in the year 2001, India had large stocks of food grains, far exceeding the capacity of the warehouses of the Food Corporation. On the other hand, the per capita consumption of food remains quite low. In the year 1998-1999, India consumed 201 kilograms of food grains per person a year, compared to 314 in China and 1,272 in the USA. However, in terms of the productivity the amount of cultivated food grains (kg/hectare) are 1,600, 4,100 and 5,600. This exemplifies the kind of distorted development that has taken place. While we now have a technology that has increased agricultural production considerably, the cost of the inputs have risen so steeply that many food items have become too expensive for a large number of people.

Hidden behind the statistics of this larger tragedy are smaller tragedies, such as the ones indicated by nutritional studies. These studies show a disproportionate distribution of food amongst our population, with higher malnutrition rates amongst women and small children. According to official statistics on the past 50 years, there has been a significant improvement in the health of the people, when assessed in rates of mortality, morbidity, maternal and infant mortality, as well as life expectancy. At the same time, there is a strong feeling amongst the lower classes of the population that, in many ways, the quality of health has declined. There are several ways to explain this seemingly contradictory reality, for example the changes in life style, habits and food, as well as the very nature of the food being consumed. In terms of the quality of food, farmers say: *"Every year, we have to use more and more pesticides and chemical fertilisers to grow our crops. The soil has become like a drug addict who needs ever increasing dosages of the drugs to get a kick…when we eat this food, our health is obviously affected".*

Kancheepuram. The Kancheepuram district - where CIKS is working in the context of the Compas programme - is the northern most district in the state of Tamil Nadu. The majority of the people in the area are Naikers or Vaniyars, small land holders who have between half to one acre of land, where arable cropping is combined with cattle rearing. The major crop, paddy, is harvested in two seasons. Other important crops are groundnut, sugar cane, maize and sesame. The Kancheepuram district is close to the Chennai

(Madras) urban area and has been strongly impacted by modernisation and urbanisation. The percentage of the population involved in agricultural activities has dropped from 60% in 1961 to 50% in 1991, while the number of industrial units have increased nearly ten-fold over the past twenty years. It is also the district with the lowest forest cover in the state of Tamil Nadu. While the land use is gradually shifting from agriculture in favour of commerce and industry, the people are also moving away from agriculture to industry.

The Centre for Indian Knowledge Systems

CIKS, the Centre for Indian Knowledge Systems, is a non-governmental research and development organisation. Since 1986 we have been studying agriculture by looking at traditional agrarian knowledge as reflected, for example, in proverbs and folk sayings, and comparing this with classical texts. We soon discovered that there are not many active practitioners of traditional agriculture, unlike traditional medicine with an abundance of them. Since 1990 we started collecting material from the classical texts on Indian Plant Science, called *Vrkshayurveda*, and selected several practices described in these texts for testing. The aim of these tests was to verify their usefulness in developing sustainable farming techniques for farmers today. The work with Compas is mainly related to this process of understanding the current relevance of Vrkshayurveda for farmers in the Kancheepuram district. Another important area of work under the Compas programme is organic agriculture and indigenous seed conservation, through community seed banks. The work related to traditional agriculture includes material inputs, such as seeds and biofertiliser, as well as knowledge about pest control, certification, and market linkages. Presently CIKS works in about 35 villages with a network of around 1,200 farmers.

The Compas project acknowledges the 'spiritual' or 'metaphysical' elements in rural people's knowledge and practices. Thus far, the spiritual or metaphysical elements relating to agriculture and natural resource management have been studied mainly by sociologists and anthropologists, while technical studies and field projects have largely ignored these aspects. In spite of their relevance for farmers, these elements were often viewed as part of the problem, or as obstacles to 'progress', by the external agents.

Meanwhile, at CIKS we also have to be careful not to over-emphasise the spiritual, or to suggest that indigenous practices that do not have a spiritual element are not valid. It is our experience, however, that in trying to pinpoint the spiritual aspect of agricultural practice with groups of farmers, they are often unable to clearly state those practices they considered 'spiritual'. This is linked to the traditional worldview, where physical, mental and spiritual phenomena are not strictly separated, but considered 'woven together', like the threads in a piece of coloured cotton fabric. It is impossible to physically separate the cotton fibre from the thread and the colour.

Learning about Vrkshayurveda. India has one of the largest collections of ancient manuscripts in the world. While there has never been a precise count, estimates suggest that there may be as many as 300 million texts that pay considerable attention to philosophy, religion, health care, agriculture, livestock, rains and harvests. They include hymns, *mantras* or specific symbolic figures, and ancient prescriptions. Gaining special significance among them is the classical Indian health (*Ayurveda*) and plant science (Vrkshayurveda), which is highly advanced. Several types of Vrkshayurveda literature can be distinguished. There are the general texts with only specific sections devoted to traditional plant science, as well as texts that provide the theoretical framework to understand the Vrkshayurveda literature. Thirdly, there are those manuscripts devoted directly to plant science. These are of great interest and direct relevance for our work.

The subject matter of the Vrkshayurveda ancient texts is vast, detailed and varied. It includes subjects such as the collection and selection of seeds, germination, cultivation, sowing, planting, nursery techniques, soil, manuring, cultivation under unfavourable meteorological conditions, pest and disease management, as well as the traditional names and description of plants. Some of the prescriptions of Vrkshayurveda are of a general nature; other prescriptions relate to a particular species. Quite often the prescriptions list a set of ingredients without specifying the proportions to be used.

Even though there is considerable literature on plant life, much of it is not available in a readily accessible form. Vrkshayurveda texts are mainly written in Sanskrit, or other ancient Indian languages. Only a small fraction of these manuscripts have been published. There are no inventories of these manuscripts, location or contents, and although many of the prescriptions of Vrkshayurveda seem to be promising as pest control techniques, they need to be tested in the field. The conditions under which the prescriptions can be used need to be understood after which they should be standardised. Unless this is done, it will not be possible to propagate these techniques. Our preliminary experiments have shown that Vrkshayurveda is a potentially rich source of knowledge that can contribute to extending the knowledge base of sustainable agriculture. It also provides a theoretical framework for understanding farmers' practices.

Ayurvedic principles of health and disease. Prior to the introduction of chemical pesticides, farmers used a wide range of traditional pest control practices. These practices are rapidly disappearing in the process of adopting high-yielding varieties that require chemical inputs. The pest control techniques described in the original Vrkshayurveda texts include methods like irrigation with herbal solutions, smearing with pastes, and fumigation. It is remarkable that many of these ancient practices are still used by farmers. These practices also appear to be quite sound, when examined in the light of Ayurvedic theory and principles.

The Ayurvedic classification of plants is similar to that used for human beings: it distinguishes between *Vaatha, Pitta* and *Kapha* constitutions. Each of these characteristics exists in every living organism and, in good health, are well balanced. The Vaatha constitution, in both plants and humans, is slender and tall, light and dry. The Pitta constitution is medium in size, weight, colour and height, and is warm and dry. The Kapha constitution refers to plants or humans that are short, bulky, humid and cold. It is, however, common to find a plant or person of a combined type, like the Vaatha-Pitta type, Pitta-Kapha type, or Vaatha-Kapha. Plant diseases are also categorised in two types: exogenous and endogenous. Endogenous diseases are caused by a disturbance in the balance between Vaatha, Pitta and Kapha in the plant. Exogenous diseases are caused by external factors, such as pests, cold, hail, or lightning.

Project activities

Experimenting with ancient pest control practices. As we observe farmers' practices and gather prescriptions and procedures from Vrkshayurveda texts, we need to reflect on the methods used for experimenting with them. It has been our experience that technologies and practices that were tested, validated and verified by the western laboratory method, do not always suit traditional societies. Often the western method addresses only one aspect of a problem, isolating it from its linkages with other elements in nature. This is in contrast to the traditional method that looks at the world as a whole, trying to understand the multiple linkages. The solutions sought are those that can address problems without destroying this integrity. Methods drawn from Vrkshayurveda texts can be a valuable starting point in several ways. Techniques from the texts can be experimented with, in order to provide viable alternatives for the farmers that they are currently not aware of. Techniques that are already in use by farmers can be examined more rigorously in the field, as well as analysed in the light of Vrkshayurveda theory. And finally, using the principles and theories of Ayurveda, one can extend the use of currently available practices to new situations and problems.

At first glance, the prescriptions of Vrkshayurveda may look extravagant. The frequent mention of honey, milk and *ghee*, or clarified butter, might make one wonder if they are practical. However, many of these recipes are easy to work with. Even in cases where relatively expensive ingredients are specified, they are often used in quantities that make the effort very worthwhile. In some cases effective practices used by farmers are also found in the descriptions from Vrkshayurveda. One such practice or example is the *Ural Marundu*, literally meaning the 'brewed decoction'. In this practice, farmers fill up a pot with leaves from a wide variety of plants with known pesticidal properties, and add some cow's urine and water to it. This pot is covered, buried, and left to brew for at least two weeks. After uncovering the pot, the liquid is separated and diluted at least ten times with water. The resulting 'broad spectrum biopesticide' is then sprayed on the crops to prevent or control pests. CIKS encourages this practice rather widely, adding new components according to Vrkshayurveda.

Experiments on paddy. After 1997, we started experimenting with rice to study the effects of Vrkshayurveda recipes on improving germination, pest and disease resistance, and stimulation of plant growth. The recipes from the ancient texts were screened and selected based on the cost of ingredients, the ease of preparation, the possibility of replication, and the effort involved in carrying out the treatment. The experiments were conducted on *Kullakar*, a traditional rice variety.

Plant growth regulators

In the germination experiments, 1,000 grains of seed were subjected to four different treatments before being sown on a tray: soaked in water for 24 hours; soaked in a mixture of cow's urine and powdered vacha (*Acorus calamus*) for 24 hours; soaked in milk for 24 hours, then rinsed with water and coated and rubbed with cowdung, then dried in the shade for 6 hours, smeared with honey, and fumigated with powdered vidanga (*Embelia*

Paddy seedlings are dipped in different sollutions of plant growth regulators.

ribes); and soaked in cow dung mixed with water for 24 hours. The control seeds were given no treatment. The percentage of germination as well as plant height was measured after seven days. After being transplanted into pots on the 25th day, a plant growth regulator was sprayed, which contained a mixture of goat flesh extract, black gram powder and sesame seeds. We observed a remarkable impact of the growth stimulators on plant height and the number of tillers, as well as on the yield of grain. The yield of paddy nearly doubled when the growth regulator was applied.

In starting up our experiments, we encountered the problem that the treatments described in the ancient texts involve several steps and components. Because of these characteristics, we did not know exactly how to apply the prescriptions, or at what level we should look for results. For example, when we soaked the paddy seeds in milk, they curdled it. Later, when we washed the germinated seeds and transplanted them, the level of germination was quite low. We felt that this might be because the tips of the germinating seeds were injured when we washed them to remove the curdled milk. However, an anthropologist who had observed similar practices in a tribal area suggested that the objective of this exercise may be to ensure that the most robust seeds were selected, those that can survive this washing. We had to admit that this was an interesting possibility, but to test this would be quite a laborious process. We discussed the results of the experiments with a wide cross section of people and decided that in our next phase we would decrease the number of variables as well as the number of pots. We continued the experiments, both in farmers' fields and in our own fields, for two more cropping seasons. During this period we could confirm the positive results, especially with the use of plant growth regulators.

Other experiments. Subsequently, we carried out several other experiments. When paddy is soaked in diluted cow's urine before sowing, it considerably reduces the incidence of two diseases known as 'leaf spot' and 'rice blast'. We also found that soaking paddy seeds in milk stimulated resistance to certain viruses, especially the 'tungro' virus and 'stunt' virus. For this experiment paddy seeds were again allowed to germinate in a moist bag for two days. They were then soaked in milk mixed with water and sown immediately. We observed that seeds subjected to this treatment showed resistance to both the tungro and the stunt virus, even when plants in neighbouring fields were affected.

Introducing new prescriptions and methods is the most challenging task facing CIKS, and has proved to be very slow and time consuming. We need to study various aspects of a prescription, experiment with it for at least two or three cropping seasons and standardise it, before widely recommending it to farmers. Currently we have tested prescriptions to improve the germination of seeds, to treat rice crops during transplantation, and to secure the regulation and promotion of plant growth. We have moved our experiments from the laboratory to the farmers' fields. These joint activities are undertaken on the understanding that the farmer will be compensated for any unexpected loss as a result of the experiment.

Measuring plan height and tillers on the 45th day in an experiment with plant growth regulators.

Farmers are facing the impact of modernisation. The work of CIKS resulted in more confidence of farmers in traditional practices for pest control and traditional rice varieties.

Seed conservation. Another part of the action research with Compas focused on seed conservation. India is home to a great diversity of both wild and cultivated crops. In recent years, however, there has been a marked decline in the variety and diversity of the commonly cultivated crops, such as rice and cereals. With the advent of the green revolution, the emphasis has been primarily on the increase of yield; consequently a small number of paddy varieties were selected and promoted for their capacity to give high yields in response to the application of high doses of fertilizer. As a result the genetic base of paddy has narrowed down considerably. Yet, farmers in every part of the country have deep knowledge of their own rice varieties, which has enabled them to harvest a crop even under the most severe stress conditions. Farmers also possess high yielding varieties of their own, which are not included in the agricultural extension programmes.

The alarming ecological and biodiversity destruction, as well as the need for conservation, has been recognised at the level of farmers and the state. Farmers have experienced that high yielding varieties are not suited to all farming conditions; indigenous varieties are better adapted to alkaline soils or drought, have more resistance to pests, and require less farm inputs, such as chemical fertilisers and pesticides. They yield straw valued by farmers as cattle feed as well as roofing material, while many varieties fulfil specific nutritional and other dietary needs. Moreover, indigenous varieties provide the basic genetic material for developing other varieties in the future.

After conducting a detailed survey of traditional seed varieties of the state, CIKS embarked on a seed collection. The paddy seed collection counts over 130 varieties, each with a detailed documentation of its properties. A similar collection of vegetable seeds is being done with the involvement of more than 200 women. Meanwhile, a network of farmers has been organised, for exchange of seeds and information, and on-farm conservation of local crop varieties in different parts of Tamil Nadu. Farmers who put aside part of their land for conservation of indigenous grain varieties are provided with an initial supply of seeds, procured by CIKS from farmers who already grow it. These farmers are also supported in organic manuring of their fields and natural pest control methods. At the end of the season the farmers return twice the quantity of seeds taken from the seed bank. We maintain detailed records on every farmer involved.

In this connection, the CIKS farmer bulletin called 'News from our farmers' network' quoted a farmer's experience: *"Sri Ranganathan lives in Mangalam village of Kancheepuram district. His land is close to an irrigation lake and is prone to flooding. He has incurred heavy losses by cultivating high yielding varieties for the last several years. This year he cultivated an indigenous variety called Samba mosanam obtained from the CIKS seed bank. The rains were very heavy this year and his half-acre plot cultivated with Samba mosanam was flooded with 4½ feet of water. This did not affect his crop in any way. However, his neighbours who had cultivated other varieties, incurred heavy losses. The performance of Samba mosanam has convinced farmers in this area of the variety's excellent ability to withstand flooding."*

Supporting traditional Indian Veterinary Science. In 2001, CIKS commenced documentation and training in the area of *Mrgayurveda*, or traditional Indian veterinary sciences, in collaboration with another Compas partner, FRLHT based in Bangalore. Training programmes have been held by FRLHT for ethno-veterinary and veterinary practitioners, in collaboration with the Tamil Nadu Cooperative Milk Federation and the National Dairy Development Board. The approach builds on the large body of knowledgeable practitioners in veterinary traditions in many parts of India, combined with Ayurvedic principles, theories and literature.

Discussion

India has an extensive and rich knowledge base of farmers' practices and a scholarly tradition. It is essential that in our quest for sustainable agriculture, we also take note of the philosophical and theoretical foundation of this traditional knowledge. The experiments of CIKS with Vrkshayurveda are promising attempts in this direction.

Over the past years CIKS has developed an excellent overview of the literature and scope of Vrkshayurveda; both the primary sources in Sanskrit and the secondary sources in English have been surveyed. Certain traditional farmers' practices that were on the verge of disappearance have been revived, such as the *Ural pot*, a traditional 'broad spectrum' biopesticide. The training programmes on traditional agriculture have been very successful, and CIKS has now moved on to training trainers in selected target villages.

Some constraints. While we have created a more positive and confident outlook in farmers vis-à-vis traditional practices, their participation has been limited and slow to build up. Many initial trials have to be done before starting the experiments with farmers. The major interest of farmers is in the rice crop - a 4-6 months crop - which makes trials time consuming. CIKS has been very cautious in making recommendations to farmers, even at the level of small-scale experiments, in order to avoid any problem or loss if they take to a 'nascent' technology in a big way. Most often farmers seek solutions to immediate problems, an exploratory phase that is a foundation for future possibilities does not always interest them. For example, in testing the effect of a plant growth regulator, we had to experiment for 18 months before being able to start the farmer participation stage.

Educational and training material on Vrkshayurveda is lacking in the Tamil language. A Tamil version of a user's manual was published in November 2001. The recipes and specific growth promoters that have been recommended in it are based on field trials carried out by CIKS. Two publications on organic farming and organic vegetable gardening have also been translated into Tamil.

Training of field staff

Training programmes in many organisations tend to put field staff in a 'teacher-student' relationship with the local farmers, rather than foster a mutual learning situation. Meanwhile, our work on Vrkshayurveda revealed to us that the field staff also needed training and orientation on the basic principles and approach, since it is not an area in which they had received prior training. In fact, in this area the farmers and rural people have a distinct lead, as the technical terminology and worldview of Ayurveda is very much part of the living tradition of rural India. This aspect requires constant attention. In 2001, for example, a special session on Ayurvedic home remedies for minor ailments was conducted with CIKS staff, which provided a good introduction to the Ayurvedic way of thinking.

Interaction with universities. Scientists and field staff of CIKS have started interacting with agricultural universities and the State Department of Agriculture. We have also been interacting with scientists in several agricultural universities of Tamil Nadu, especially the Gandhigram Rural University, in the documentation and assessment of seed performance. We have also been in touch with the National Bureau of Plant Genetic Resources, which is the Apex body of the Government of India (functioning under ICAR - Indian Council of Agricultural Research) for the collection and preservation of seeds. Initially the Bureau took the position that its role is to interact only with other scientists and not with farmers and NGOs. Currently, the Head of the Conservation Division of the Bureau has agreed that samples of seeds deposited with them by NGOs or farmers can be taken from their collection for future use by the NGOs or farmers.

Networking. The numerous publications in English, Tamil and Hindi are used as educational and training material by a wide range of individuals and organisations. On the invitation of 'The Hindu', which is one of the leading daily newspapers of India, CIKS produced a supplement on Indian health traditions in October 2000 with special emphasis on traditional medicine. This gave rise to a lot of feedback and discussion about the value of traditional Indian sciences. CIKS has made a good beginning in the task of networking with other groups involved in traditional agriculture, by way of exchange of information, materials and visits.

We plan to hold a major national conference on the theme of Vrkshayurveda with the participation of some leading Ayurvedic practitioners. The purpose of this conference is to draw the attention of academics, researchers and policy makers to the potential and

Indian Compas partners discuss the effect of light traps in an organic cotton field.

possibilities of Traditional Indian Plant Science. And if such a cross-section of Indian society is impacted, traditional knowledge may eventually find its way into the mainstream programmes.

Looking forward. We are encouraged by the results obtained thus far with the experiments in the experimental centre and the farmer's fields, and feel that the prospects are bright. Our experience indicates that there are two major lines of work to be followed in the future. On the one hand, we need to continue conducting controlled experiments to test the applicability of ancient texts for present day agriculture. Meanwhile, there are many questions that need to be answered in this process, such as 'How can experiments based on ancient techniques be designed and interpreted?', 'Which parameters should be used?', and 'How can we incorporate the hymns and symbolic figures mentioned in the texts into our work?'

On the other hand, we need to look carefully at the living folk practices of farmers so as to understand and analyse them. The ancient Vrkshayurveda texts offer us many possibilities, especially in providing us a theoretical and practical basis for analysing and understanding farmers' practices. We are convinced that combining farmers' practices with the knowledge available in the ancient texts can revitalise present day agriculture.

4.5 SUPPORTING ENDOGENOUS DEVELOPMENT
OF THE ATONI

Marthen Duan and Yovita Meta, TIRD-p, Indonesia

On the island of West-Timor (Indonesia), threats to traditional land rights have triggered the development of peasant movements and the revival of indigenous cosmovisions. The experience of TIRD-p (Timor Integrated Rural Development programme) with the Atoni population over the past 5 years shows that working on the basis of indigenous cosmovisions make communities aware of their own strengths, limitations and potentials.

The Atoni are the original inhabitants of the western part of the island of Timor in Indonesia. They are mainly subsistence farmers and have some livestock kept under free-range conditions. Compared to the other Indonesian islands, Timor is dry. The average rainfall depends on the topography and the mountains receive significantly more, over 2,000 mm, than the surrounding flat lands (between 1,000-1,400 mm). Under Dutch colonial rule, and the early days of the Indonesian Republic in the 1950s, the 'self-ruling kingdoms' reigned on the island. Most Atoni practised traditional religions, but this changed after a leftist coup in Djakarta in 1965. Traditional religions were banned and the people were forced to become either protestant or catholic. Many *adat houses*, the ceremonial places of the Atoni, were burnt. The new political line also implied that the Atoni were no longer allowed to hold their ceremonies and sacrifice animals.

In the mid-seventies, the government formally abolished all indigenous self-governing structures. This led to a further destruction of indigenous institutions at village level. Everything related to *adat*, the traditional customs and the cosmovision, was looked upon as backward. Ceremonies, crucial for social coherence, declined in importance. People performing rituals were stigmatised as being uninterested in 'development', despite the specific function of rituals in strengthening the unity of the community, essential in surviving in the harsh climate of West-Timor. Many young people took up modern technologies, chemical pesticides and fertilizers, rather than sticking to age-old beliefs and practices. In spite of these developments, the Atoni traditional belief system could not be erased completely; some of the practices, traditional leadership structures and related cosmovision continued to exist 'underground'.

Atoni cosmovision

Traditionally, the Atoni lived in clans within their communities. The Adat elders and the *tobe*, the traditional clan leader with administrative and spiritual responsibility, decided on the timing of agricultural activities. *Dukuns,* or shamans, were consulted when people or animals were ill, or when pests attacked their crops. The tobes performed rituals to find solutions to these problems. The adat house was the place where elders met, a circular wooden structure with a thatched roof of a particular design. Sacred objects like swords, ceremonial maize and bones of ancestors were kept under this roof. Next to the adat house was the place where ceremonial sacrifices were performed. Some of these structures and traditions are still found today.

An important concept in the traditional cosmovision of the Atoni is *le'u* which means holy, sacred, something that provokes awe. It is a force that can be either dangerous or beneficial. Anything might become le'u as a result of a ceremonial act, or even a dream. The Atoni believe in three powers: *Uis Neno* - Lord of the sky, *Uis Pah* - Lord of the earth, and *Apinat Aklahat* - God Almighty, with their ancestors as go-betweens. The Atoni had, and to a certain extent still have, a harmonious relationship with nature, which is seen as a kind of extended family. Soil is considered the mother of life; food plants are thought to originate from one of the ancestors, hence crops are supposedly an incarnation of their

A feeling of pride of being Atoni was restored among the elders due to the revitalisation of indigenous knowledge.

ancestors. Therefore, a ritual ceremony to consult ancestors was undertaken before cultivating a piece of land. This is still done by some farmers today. On every garden plot the farmers build a small temple of stones, where they offer to the spirits, their ancestors and Uis Neno. The reasons for the ceremonies are multiple: to put the relationship with the Highest Being on a solid footing, to strengthen the social unity, to intensify the relationship with nature, and to assert shared commitment.

TIRD-p

TIRD-p is a consortium of four small NGOs working on rural development. One of the NGOs is called Justitia, a legal aid organization working on land ownership, human rights, and violence against women. The other three are Yayasan Timor Membangun, Yayasan Tafen Pah and Yayasan Haumeni, involved in activities related to agriculture, animal husbandry, traditional medicine and weaving. They are exchanging their learning experiences and joining forces to reach their main mission: realising a more just and democratic society in which there is a place for people to express their culture.

In 1998, TIRD started with an integrated crop management approach with farmer experimentation. All TIRD members are engaged in various activities related to endogenous development. Promoting organic and sustainable agricultural practices, such as intercropping, developing bio pesticides, conserving traditional seed varieties, and improving traditional storage facilities are a few examples. Another innovative activity is the process of strengthening traditional weaving practices with women's groups, and marketing their products through Fair Trade. Box 4d summarises these activities and their results so far.

The new adat house. The NGO Yayasan Haumeni works in the community of Laob, in the former Bijoba kingdom. When an industrial forestry project had succeeded in claiming 2,400 hectares of their land, the community acted upon their feeling of being treated unjustly. Their unity gave them a measure of success: 340 hectares were left out of the government concession to the company. One of the main claims of the community was their indigenous right to the land. During one of the meetings the farmers made a resource-flow diagram. The drawings showed the link between rain, sacred forests and rituals in ensuring sustainable livelihoods. In this process the village leaders gradually recognised the importance of adat. A general feeling that revitalisation of adat was needed to succeed in their struggle against the industrial forestry project grew. As a result, they decided to rebuild their adat house, or *Ume Le'U*, where rituals could be performed.

The adat house they had in mind would not only have a ritual function: it would also become a place to teach their children about indigenous knowledge, the cosmovision and their ancestors. A group of young adults strongly influenced this decision, because, unlike their parents, they had never experienced any of these rituals. They felt it was now their turn. Luckily there were some old people who were still practising rituals. Gradually their reluctance to talk about their *mantras*, or ritual prayers, and to perform them in public, changed. During the meetings the elders presented their experience with rituals related to agricultural practices. The Laob people also decided to experiment with spiritual practices in pest management. For this purpose the area around the adat house was planted with medicinal plants, as well as plants that produce natural pesticides and dyes. Part of the area was also used for experiments with different cropping methods.

Revitalising ceremonies. Taekas is one of the villages where the NGO Yayasan Timor Membangun, or YTM, works. During a participatory rural appraisal activity in 1997, YTM became aware of a conflict in relation to a sacred forest and its natural cave, Popnam, from which the village got its drinking water. Trees had been cut, plants harvested, and birds' nests

Weaving is developed and maintained by women and has high symbolic meaning. Yayasan Tafan Pah, one of the NGOs in TIRD, facilitates fair trade marketing to Australia.

Box 4d   Results of the Compas related TIRD activities

Elements of endogenous development	Activities carried out in 9 villages	Results
Building on local iniatives to use resources	Regreening of Holy places Revitalising traditional rice and wheat varieties. Organic agriculture and biopesticides. Banul - revitalising traditional banning ceremony to protect Popnam cave.	Mutual co-operation achieved. Trees, the drinking water well and wild animals at Popnam cave are protected.
Building on local needs	Promoting sustainable agriculture through intercropping practices in maize, groundnuts and legumes.	Poorer community members have access to food in hungry season.
Improving local knowledge and practices	Laying out pilot vegetable garden in Oinlasi; value of traditional medicine; effectiveness of biopesticides; organic wheat cultivation.	Vegetable gardens have increased farmers' income and improved nutritional status; 12,000 litres of biopesticides produced (in 2000).
Local control of development options	Discussing conflict of adat land ownership between parties; Developing a critical attitude of farmers on legal and political rights for ancestral lands.	Adat houses restored in 3 villages; traditional ceremonies performed in greater number; farmers regained their pride in being Atoni instead of feeling backward.
Identification of development niches	Marketing of traditional weaving to empower women. Developing Fair Trade co-operative for trading bio pesticides within traditional adat context Exploring eco-tourism potential of the natural caves of Popnam.	Income generated for 300 women in 12 villages. Farmers sold 5000 litres of biopesticides . Government interest for eco-toruism mobilised.
Selective use of external resources	Enhancing knowledge on bio pesticides; introducing hand tractors and hand sprayers according to adat regulations.	When purified and cooled through adat, equipment becomes part of the community; better land preparation, higher yields, more co-operation and more sensitivity to adat.
Retention of benefits in the local area	Revitalising dry season granaries for seed storage of maize and paddy for food security in 3 villages.	Stronger linkages between community members established; women's role recognised (because they are only allowed to collect food).
Exchange and learning between local cultures	Exchanging traditional varieties of seeds between villages.	Genetic erosion reverted and stronger linkages between communities established.
Networking and strategic partnerships	Publishing on traditional varieties; Making calendar about Atoni adapt. Doing campaign (with stickers) to bring back the traditional name of the area: Biinmalo.	Other NGOs are positive about the results and co-operate with TIRD; local politicians lobbied for Biinmalo; schools give attention to Atoni culture.
Understanding systems of knowing and learning	Meetings and workshops to reflect and agree on the value of adat rites and ceremonies; restoring adat house and elders' authority.	Ceremonies revived in agriculture; altars established in vegetable gardens; rites performed to restore the relationship with the ancestors; more unity between clans.
Other activities: Adat and state law	Reflecting on land rights and traditional rights.	Farmers are more informed about their rights; self-confidence is raised; outside agencies are more careful in claiming resources from the people.

had been stolen from the cave, as people no longer respected the traditional adat rules and taboos, known as *banul*. Different clans claimed ownership of the sacred forest. YTM and the village representatives decided to explore the meaning of banul and see if it could be used to resolve the conflict.

Within adat, a banul or taboo can be put on soil, water, animals, plants, forests, and even humans. A symbol, for example an animal bone or head with specific leaves, is put in a strategic place so that everybody can see it. Violation of the banul can lead to a sanction, such as a fine, or misfortune befalling the violator. There was clarity on the fines (50 kg of rice and 1 pig) and YTM helped to establish a code of conduct on dealing with the fines. The first banul ceremony in Taekas was held in 1998, establishing the Popnam cave and its immediate vicinity of some 10 hectares, as a sacred area. This was the basis for resolving the conflict. The area, now protected through adat, provides clean drinking water for the villagers, who need permission from the adat elders to enter it. There have, however, been violations of banul. In such cases the violators have experienced illnesses that could not be cured by medical means, and which required honest confession of their violation to the traditional elders and a ceremony of making amends. To the villagers these examples demonstrated that the power of traditional rites is still strong and reliable. The role of YTM was not only to settle the conflict, but also to involve the community in a discussion on the sustainable use of natural resources.

Discussion

Activities like rebuilding the new adat house symbolises the pride of the Atoni people in their culture - a culture that had nearly disappeared. It is interesting that farmers could regain awareness on the importance of their traditional knowledge after a long period of suppression. In a way, the pressure put on them by the government made the people more aware of the potential of the knowledge that resided with their elders. This included elements of both natural resources management and spirituality. Through this re-encounter with their cosmovision and spiritual resources, the farmers working with TIRD were encouraged to experiment with it.

Constraints encountered by TIRD in implementing the programme were threefold. Firstly, in the initial phases, the field staff lacked skills to work with and analyse the still existing adat institutions. Secondly, not all adat groups found the courage to hold their adat activities openly, still entrenched by the fear of suppression of these institutions after 1965. And finally, engaging young people on a larger scale was difficult as many of them consider adat customs ancient and lacking potential for the future. The work of TIRD shows, however, that cosmovisions can make communities aware of their own strength. This creates a path towards endogenous development that includes advocacy, nature conservation and agricultural development.

4.6 THE PATH OF REDISCOVERY

Vanaja Ramprasad, G. Krishnaprasad and Manasi S., Green Foundation, India

Today in India, rural people are struggling to make ends meet in a fast changing environment. It is not only their ecological resource base that is threatened; also national and international legislation are not addressing their major concerns. Green Foundation, a NGO, situated in the dryland region of South India, is working to enhance biodiversity as a means of sustaining the livelihoods of the rural people. Innovative methodologies have been developed to recover traditional crop varieties, medicinal plants, and sustainable ways of producing food, within the cultural context of the people.

The very foundations of traditional agriculture have been given hard blows over the past decades. The introduction of monocultures and high yielding varieties, and the associated application of external inputs, have increased the economic dependence of farmers and eroded the rich and diverse bio-genetic base. More recently, the removal of subsidies by the government has made farming a less viable option for many rural people. Increased contacts with the 'modern' world of towns and cities, as well as exposure to mass media and the influence of outsiders have had an impact, especially on the younger population. While the older members of rural communities are often independent and rich in skills and knowledge, the young people are at cross roads, still seeking their values. As lifestyles, values and knowledge change rapidly in the rural context, the need to conserve the fast shrinking natural resource base assumes paramount importance, so as to secure the livelihoods of the people who rely on these resources for their survival.

Development, including the perception of poverty, hitherto has been determined on criteria based on the western concept of economic growth. Governments that took over from the colonial rulers adopted this model of development, without realising the consequences on their people. This development process can be called 'exogenous', because it is initiated by external influence, is rooted in the market economy based on cash transactions, and includes unsustainable use of resources, often alien to the local cultural ethos. In a market-oriented economy, development means to increase people's purchasing power and participation in the consumer market. Peoples' non participation in the market economy is therefore often misconstrued as poverty. During an informal dialogue between a Green Foundation fieldworker and village elders, the latter explained their perception of welfare as '*sowbagya*'. This concept of welfare includes 16 aspects, amongst others, having good children, good health, wealth, bravery, adequate food throughout the year, long life, good neighbours and friends, a healthy environment, a good family, communal harmony, as well as a good administrator who takes care of the people.

The location and its people

The communities that Green Foundation works with are located in a highly complex rural environment not far from Bangalore, a major city. Around 90% of the farmers depend on rainfed agriculture. This area with a predominantly Hindu population is dynamic and driven by the urban market. As a result, a plurality of strategies and a diminishing sense of identity as farmers can be observed. A third of the total population of 148,000, however, lives either inside or adjacent to the forest. The remoteness of their location has to a large extent kept their traditional culture and lifestyles intact. These remote villages, often with tribal populations, have been neglected as far as infrastructure and services such as approach roads, education, health centres, transport and communication, are concerned.

Sowing finger millet, the major food crop, with other intercrops, using two types of seed drills simultaneously.

The people still resort to the forest for their food crops and income-generating resources off-season or in summer. Bamboo shoots, tubers, gooseberries and special tender leaves are the most preferred food supplements. Due to increasing population and migration, deforestation is a common feature. The farmers have maintained crop diversity, the level of which depends on the influence of modernisation. In most areas a basic mixed cropping system still exists, while indigenous seeds have been replaced by high yielding varieties in varied measure. *Ragi*, or finger millet, minor millets, pulses and oil seeds are the main crops.

The caste system and gender biases. Traditional societies in India have certain deep-rooted caste differences and gender biases that need to be analysed and questioned in a constructive way. The caste system has divided the communities, and is very apparent in how the benefits of development are shared. People of the lower castes have for long been deprived of the opportunities, though the government in its political manifesto has attempted to reverse this through various interventions. Despite people like Mahatma Gandhi and other leaders, who have pursued the cause of educating the masses, many parts of interior India still retains the ugly face of the caste system. Women's development has also been denied over generations. Therefore, any attempts to bring about change through endogenous development have to give prominence to the poor and deprived.

Caste groups like Lingayat and Vokkaligas dominate the area. Other castes such as Vanniyar, Gounder, Vadda, Kumbai, Golla, Besta, Harijans, as well as Muslims, also live in the villages. Farmers belonging to the lower castes and tribes live apart, in separate colonies with own water sources and poor conditions. Even today their involvement in day-to-day affairs and social occasions are taboo.

Though diverse in caste, people normally follow the common values, rules, customs and beliefs of their community. Along with the major festivals they also celebrate local festivals associated with the village deities to give thanks, to evoke blessings for good harvests, and to secure the welfare of the entire village community.

Cosmovision and traditional agriculture. Traditional agriculture in India is one of the oldest, yet one of the most advanced forms of food production. Traditional practices are a result of farmers choosing crop types or varieties depending on soil depths, water holding capacity, slope and drainage, and by observing their interactions with each other. The combinations of different agroclimatic conditions, such as low rainfall, high temperatures and different soils, gave rise to various crop combinations and crop rotations. The limitation of household labour further determined the type of crops and cropping patterns. Traditional agriculture generally ensured food security and preserved genetic diversity.

Influence of the planets
Some of the traditional beliefs about farming are linked to the influence of the planets. The sun is addressed in the *Vedas*, the ancient Hindu texts, as the soul of the universe. The texts describe the planets, and how the planetary positions of the sun and moon affect the sea, causing tides. They also affect the stores of fluid on the surface of the earth and its vegetation. It is an old belief in traditional agriculture that trees should not be cut close to the time of the new moon, for the sap dries quickly. It has been shown through experiments that the maximum growth of wheat corresponds with the period of the increasing moon and that maize was found to grow best when planted two days before the full moon.

Women, seeds and rituals
Gender and biodiversity are linked symbolically as well as in the material domain. Women play a major role in conserving seed at the farm level: they decide on the amount of seeds to be preserved, the variety, and the preservation methods. Because women share the sacred power of *Shakti*, the female power of reproduction, they are vested with the responsibility of selection, conservation and propagation of seed. These activities include a variety of ceremonies and festivals.

A few days before sowing, the seeds are taken out of storage. They are dried and those damaged by pests are discarded. Directly before sowing, the women take the seeds to the house deity for a blessing. Women also worship the draft animals and the farming implements that will be used for sowing. None of these rituals are followed for the seeds of high-yielding varieties bought at the market. While the local varieties are considered sacred, the high-yielding varieties are regarded as impure. Seeds of the latter kind are sent directly to the field and are sown only by men.

Coinciding with the appearance of mustard, the first flower to bloom in the field, a festival called *Gowri Pooja* is celebrated, in which the relationships between the plant and the soil, water and other crops are maintained. The Goddess Gowri is identified as the Goddess of water, essential for crop growth, as well as with the fertility of the flower for good grain formation. Working in the fields, women continually observe the plants and decide which seeds to select. They identify plants of good quality on the basis of size, grain formation and resistance to pests and insects. To cover the risk of drought, women select enough seed to see them through two seasons.

When the selected heads of grain are brought into the threshing yard, women welcome the first cartload with a ritual. On the last day of threshing women worship the mounds of grain and a portion of each mound is given to the poor. A gift of grain is also present-ed to the families who have helped with the harvest. Before the seeds are carried away for storage, women ritually invoke the forces essential for a good crop in the next growing season. This ritual is also an important part of seed preservation as some of the leaves used in the ceremony have insecticidal properties.

Each region has its own way of testing the quality of the seeds. *Negilu pooja* is an impor-tant ritual performed as a test of germination before sowing. Two new ploughs are placed in a north-eastern position and tied together. A sheath of areca palm leaves is attached and a mixture of manure and cow dung deposited inside it. Nine varieties of seeds are then placed in this mixture to germinate - sorghum, finger millet, niger, field beans, red gram, horse gram, mustard, paddy and castor - and water is sprinkled. A symbolic deity made of mud is placed on top of the leaves and worshipped with flowers and fruits. After nine days the seedlings are examined. The varieties with the best germination results are chosen for cultivation. Healthy germination is crucial to cultivation, and the ritual marks the celebration of diversity.

Family members examine the results of Negilu Pooja, a germination test of different seed varieties.

Green Foundation

Green Foundation is a grassroots organisation working with marginal farmers based in the dryland region of Thalli, some 70 km from the Bangalore metropolis in Tamil Nadu, South India. The main objective of this NGO is to restore faith in the indigenous farming system and re-establish valuable practices that are on the verge of extinction, so as to ensure rural livelihoods on a sustainable basis. In the activities directed towards conserving, promoting, and reviving genetic diversity, seed and soil conservation are its major concerns. Though the main conservation activities focus on traditional agricultural crops, they also include bio-pesticide plants, green manure crops, medicinal plants for humans and animals, agroforestry, and wild plant species.

Green Foundation considers cosmovision as a basic element in its development strategy. Animators and knowledgeable people like spiritual leaders and local healers, who know the local language and culture, form an essential link between the staff and the farmers. Therefore, in 1998, before engaging in field activities and group formation, a survey to assess the prevalence of traditional healers, spiritual leaders, existing wild flora and fauna, and resourceful people was done. It also allowed for the identification of potential animators and volunteers. The survey brought to light the existence of traditional practices in agriculture and health in most villages. It also allowed the mapping of biodiversity at village and ecosystem level.

Green Foundation is aware of the cultural difficulties related to the caste system and gender biases, and this concern cuts across all its interventions. In rural India women play a central role in agriculture as well as in all other walks of life. When it comes to decision making and social positioning, however, they are often marginalised. We have observed an increasing awareness among women about the need to conserve biodiversity and the local knowledge base, and women are thus central in the activities.

Biodiversity conservation and training centre. Green Foundation has established a biodiversity conservation centre in Thalli. On this demo-farm seed varieties from various eco-regions have been collected and are experimented with, to determine their viability and acceptability in the farmers' fields. Germination is tested; crops are monitored on the effects of drought, as well as pest and disease resistance; grain and fodder yields are determined. Presently the seed bank consists of: 41 varieties of dry land paddy, 36 varieties of wetland paddy, 70 varieties of finger millet, 10 varieties of little millet, 6 varieties of pearl millet, 10 varieties of sorghum, and 6 varieties of foxtail millet. The centre has a herbarium and many photographs and slides on traditional crop varieties. Activities of the centre include food processing, annual seed fairs, documentation, publications like seed catalogues and strengthening indigenous knowledge and related practices.

The centre also provides training programmes for farmers, women's groups, and school children in the areas of seed, soil, water and biodiversity conservation. For example, youngsters have been trained as 'barefoot taxonomists' who then analyse the local biodiversity. Green Foundation has also hosted two meetings of spiritual leaders at its training centre. On both occasions spiritual leaders chose to display their skills in communicating with the supernatural powers, and a forum where traditional healers and spiritual leaders could share their experiences was initiated. Among them were Goravas, a singing nomadic sect; Kanikara of the Irula tribes; and Dasas, a religious sect, who are also story tellers and traditional healers. Having identified a select number of spiritual leaders, we will work closely with them to explore the use of spiritual powers in conserving biological diversity and promoting the well-being of the community.

Training and attitude of field staff. Green Foundation staff is involved in various activities with the villagers to get a better understanding of their cosmovison and indigenous practices. Village fairs, festivals, village agricultural rituals and ceremonies are some of them. Interactions with village elders and informal discussions with prominent persons are also important in this respect. The meetings with the spiritual leaders have given insights into many traditional practices. The leaders have also stressed the need for reviving the traditional rituals and boosting the morale of villagers in continuing with these practices. The need to cross caste barriers and gender differences was obvious, though not always easy. The field staff would sometimes come across practices about which they would question the rural people. In one case they were able to discourage a particularly barbaric sacrifice ritual of buffaloes; in another village the sacrifice of goats during a Karibanta ritual was replaced by vermin mixed with water.

Field methodology. Our Compas field programme, which was implemented 4 years ago, aims at enhancing endogenous development by linking biodiversity with culture. Against the backdrop of the hybrid culture in the rural area where Green Foundation is working, a two-pronged strategy was adopted, according to the level of modernisation of the different areas: 'in- situ' and 'on-farm' conservation. There is a subtle difference between these two conservation approaches. In the areas where the agricultural societies remain relatively untouched by market forces, and modern crop varieties have not been introduced vigorously, the farmers have conserved traditional varieties for generations. Green Foundation's strategy here has been to encourage farmers to be aware of the importance of this 'in-situ' conservation. In areas where a plurality of cultures exists, for example, near large urban centres, Green Foundation is stimulating the farmers to make informed choices by conserving traditional seed varieties on a small portion of their land and by evaluating them. This 'on-farm' conservation has been extended with seeds from similar climatic regions, which has added to the genetic pool in the area.

"What methodology did Green Foundation use to revive the cultural and biogenetic diversity?" is a logical question at this point. Here, we present the five major aspects of the methodology Green Foundation has followed in the past few years: creating awareness, documenting indigenous knowledge, experimentation, creating institutional structures, and networking.

Creating awareness
One of the major concerns, and the first step in the methodology, was to create awareness about the importance of biodiversity and culture, and foster bonds with and amongst the rural people. Over the years we have developed several ways to create awareness, such as organising regional and local seed fairs. These fairs bring together farmers from vari-

The annual seed fair provides a forum for exchange of indigenous seed varieties, knowledge and practices.

ous states and provide opportunities for the collection and exchange of indigenous seed varieties. The regional seed fairs are held annually at the Green Foundation farm since 1993. Over the years the seed fairs have extended to the villages and are usually held after the harvest. With the start of the Compas programme in 1998, a new dimension was added on. The event now starts with a traditional ritual, thereby testifying its importance in Indian agriculture. Traditional seed varieties are displayed, as well as 'cosmovision charts'. Folk songs and dances, that were threatened by extinction, are presented during these seed fairs. Local groups of folk artists, local health healers, school children, and women who go from village to village telling stories of the flora and fauna, are honoured for their contribution to promoting genetic and cultural diversity.

Documenting indigenous knowledge and practices
Documentation of indigenous knowledge and practices related to crop diversity is the next step in the Green Foundation methodology. This is an ongoing and integral component of the programme. Besides specific data related to the traditional crop varieties, the documentation includes more general aspects, such as technologies to increase disease and pest resistance, pest management, agricultural rituals, weather forecasting, community fairs/festivals, health care systems, plant genetic resource conservation practices, food security practices, spiritual perceptions, folk tales, and tribal culture and traditions. Most of the documented techniques are simple and often quite effective. For example, a mixture of sand with cow's urine functions as an organic nitrogen supplement to the soil; controlling rats with mint leaves has been successful.

To document indigenous knowledge and record oral culture, a combination of methods like observation, participatory rural appraisal, guided field walks and interviewing the elders in the villages is used. Many times we found that the information is incomplete as far as form, content, language, and a host of other factors are concerned. Eroded cultural values may explain this problem in part. The fact that indigenous knowledge has a strong practical base, but a weak theoretical foundation, is another reason. We have concluded that, unless a concerted effort is made to document oral knowledge, the next generation will have very little of it in written form.

Experimentation

Though well aware of the advantages of traditional crops, farmers are often hesitant to switch back to them all at once. Instead they follow a very cautious and step-by-step approach that enables them to withstand risks. Therefore, if practices and rituals are to be revived, it is necessary to experiment with them, to understand their nuances and give them more scientific validation. Traditional seed treatments for withstanding stress and ensuring early germination are important practices that we have documented and experimented with. In this process a participatory breeding programme of finger millet and rice has been initiated, which involves farmers in the selection process. Farmers determine their selection criteria and after suitable material is identified, on-farm trials are carried out to test acceptability in farmers' fields. Other experiments include rituals and ethnoveterinary methods to treat and prevent livestock diseases. An example is the experiment with the *maddina madike*, or 'medicinal pot', which includes soaking 16 medicinal plants in a pot for several days and using the water for treating various livestock ailments.

It is not only in reviving and strengthening lost practices that Green Foundation intervenes, but also in adding elements of external knowledge. An example is biodynamic farming, which has influenced our farming practices in the cultivation of rice. The biodynamic concept (see chapter 7.2) is quite similar to those that rule Indian traditional science and folk knowledge. A group of farmers in 8 villages has experimented with so-called 'preparations', herbal medicines prepared according to the biodynamic methods, on their paddy crop. Farmers have found the results to be positive with improvement of yield, grain colour, tillering, pest and disease tolerance, and lodging resistance, in both millet and paddy crops.

Creating institutional structures

Strengthening village-level organisations is another central element of the Green Foundation methodology. Distribution of seeds was first conducted from the centre in Thalli. Later on, the aim was to strengthen and promote decentralised systems of seed distribution. The villagers opted to revive or start farmers and local artisan *sanghas*. The general membership of these groups is between 15 and 25. These village-level organisations, which include a large number of women, take their own initiatives. They identify seed requirements for the following year, and select and purchase their stock from the savings of sangha members. In each of the sanghas a central storage room has been set apart, and seeds are being conserved by using traditional methods.

Networking

Networking is the fifth and final important element in the methodology used, and is taking place at various levels. Networking between the different villages and farmers' groups within the project area is stimulated, for example, by the dissemination of the quarterly newsletter 'Pairu Pacche' in the local language. Other publications in the local language include the agricultural calendar, with details of auspicious days for agricultural activities, and posters on specific themes. The national and international level of exchange is stimulated by the publication of the GREEN Update in English. Three books and two CD-roms have been produced. Networking also takes place with other organisations in Karnataka state, and at national and international level, also with Compas partner organisations.

Examples of field activities in cosmovision perspective

Enhancing biodiversity and related cosmovision. On-farm conservation of traditional crops and marketing of the surplus of their seed to fellow farmers is being re-established in the villages. The objective of this exercise is the continuous improvement of crops and the conservation of sustainable livelihood systems. Apart from seed conservation by individual farmers, the highlights of these seed conservation efforts include community seed distribution, training of farmers as seed keepers and an association of farmers who will take the movement forward. The revival of appropriate traditional seed storage facilities has brought down the costs of inputs.

The impact of this work is quite impressive. For instance, in the year 1997, only one farmer in Yerandapanahalli was growing 'Godivari', a wetland paddy variety. By the year 1999, 25 farmers from his and surrounding villages had begun to multiply seed of this unique wetland paddy. Between the year 1994 and 2001, the number of farmers who participated in seed conservation has increased from 10 to 794, and the number of villages has increased from 2 to 113. Many other farmers have informally acquired seeds from the conservation centre. Through seed fairs and awareness campaigns, there has been a consistent increase in the varieties that have been conserved by farmers, in the case of ragi, from 21 in 1998 to 52 in 2000. Dryland paddy varieties grown on-farm have increased in the same period from 14 to 37 and wetland paddy varieties from 11 to 32. This shows that farmers have broadened the genetic base of ragi and paddy varieties. The traditional crop varieties revived cover a range of food-crops, like finger millet, dry land paddy, wet land paddy, pearl millet, sorghum, maize, little millet, foxtail millet, kodo millet and proso millet. Also traditional varieties of beans, peas, greens, brinjal, tomato, red gram, green gram, black gram, horse gram, chilli, gourds, oil seeds and other vegetables have been revived. Traditional village organisations that have been revived in 31 villages now manage seed diversity. Community seed banks (8 at present) have also contributed to a broader genetic resource base and provided seed and food security to the farmers.

Involving school children. School contests in biodiversity conservation are used as a means of involving school children, the first of which was held in August 1995. Our first step is to establish contact with the head of the school and explain Green Foundation's

Enthusiastic children at the government high school show the medicinal plants they have identified in the wild.

philosophy and the relevance of indigenous knowledge. This is followed by a slide show on traditional practices and agricultural biodiversity, and stories and songs reflecting the need to preserve culture are shared. For the school competition, children are requested to collect information from (grand)parents or often knowledgeable people. So far five schools have organised such a contest, which has resulted in information on several topics. 'Traditional health care for humans and cattle' attracted the most entries; the other subjects were wild flora and fauna species, agricultural tools, indigenous varieties, riddles, folk tales, village fairs, agricultural rituals, religious ceremonies and traditional recipes. Two prizes and eight consolation prizes were awarded to successful entries. Parents were encouraged to attend the prize giving ceremony. With the encouraging response, school competitions have been extended to include several primary schools, twelve high schools, three pre-university colleges and a university.

Our experience is that establishing contact at the school level has been an effective way of disseminating information. Children from different villages attend the same school. Thus the school is important for gathering information that might not otherwise be found. School competitions have made it easier to involve children at village level meetings. Through these contests teachers have also been sensitised. Villagers are often reluctant about sharing hidden knowledge, particularly with outsiders, whereas they share it readily with children and other family members. Elders were happy to see their children being involved in reviving knowledge, customs and traditions and have therefore significantly contributed to the effort. Other initiatives with school children involved 'demonstration plots', in which groups of high school children tended various finger millet varieties and observed their performance.

Village-level biodiversity registers. A more recent effort was to document indigenous knowledge related to natural resources. Patenting and intellectual property rights have become crucial issues in recent times and awareness on these issues seldom reaches the grassroots level, where the major custodians of the natural resources are found. In order to create people's awareness and ownership of these resources, and avoid any bio-piracy, the concept of 'biodiversity registers' was introduced in 32 villages of Achubalam Panchayati. A central 'biodiversity conservation committee' was formed, together with village sub-committees consisting of local health practitioners, farmers, cattle grazers, forest guards, school teachers, village elders and other resourceful people.

The initial work of the village-level committees was to draw a resource map of sacred groves, rivers, fields and forests. Thematic concerns, such as renewable energy resources, traditional healing, traditional artisan skills, medical plants and their uses, and traditional farming practices were also documented. The data was consolidated through field visits under the leadership of local resource people. At the end of a six-month period the village level biodiversity registers were drafted. Updating and protecting the natural resources in the area is easier now, because this biodiversity document serves as a frame of reference.

Reviving agricultural rituals. Two agriculture related rituals, *Negilu pooja* and *Karibanta*, have been revived in different project villages. Karibanta was once an important ritual related to pest and disease control, performed before the harvest in drought prone regions. It has now ceased in popularity and is on the verge of extinction. Farmers have expressed a desire to revive this ritual as part of their cultural practices. Karibanta is a community ritual performed with the advent of the rains, when the ears of grain begin to mature or when crops are especially prone to pest attacks. A platform is constructed in the plot with branches and leaves of the Karibanta tree. A big branch is fixed in the middle of the platform, and a turmeric soaked cloth containing 5 varieties of grain (ragi, horsegram, little millet, paddy and field bean) is tied to the pole indicating the commonly grown varieties of crop. Three uncut stones are placed in front of the platform and worshipped by applying vermilion and turmeric. Villagers worship the Karibanta branch and request that their crops be protected against disease and pest attack. Karibanta is believed to protect crops from pest attacks or diseases, e.g. Leaf Blast or Leaf Spot in millet.

Farmers assess the impact of Karibanta by looking at the size of the area in which crops are protected, the level of aphid attack, the degree to which ears of grain wilt, and the presence of red spots (Kembatti disease) or neck blast on the crop.

Bio-cultural seed villages. The concept of the 'bio-cultural seed village' as a single market area, and centre for endogenous development, has been developed over the years. Laxmipura, a village located approximately 20 kilometres from Thalli, was identified as an ideal location, being in the midst of indigenous communities and tribal groups. Initiatives undertaken in this village include community organisation, seed conservation, strengthening health traditions, promoting kitchen gardens, reviving the cultural heritage, children's activities and marketing. The local sangha organisation is now promoting on-farm conservation and multiplication of traditional crops, such as paddy, foxtail millet, areca, chillies, and red gram.

A community hall was restored and painted for the sangha meetings. A children's group is growing traditional crop varieties of paddy, finger millet and vegetables on community lands. Composting using earthworms has been adopted by some of the farmers in the area. Village-level mapping of Laxmipura and surrounding villages was undertaken and the village level biodiversity registers were completed and subsequently handed over to the headman of the village at a village gathering. A herbarium of medicinal plants has also been developed, to cater to the growing health requirements of the farming communities.

Next to sanghas, other village-based groups of resource people, spiritual leaders and local health practitioners are being built up in four villages. At Laxmipura, twelve spiritual leaders were brought together, while at Mastapanadoddi the tribal Irula cultural revival is a major undertaking. In Bellalam village, knowledgeable persons, spiritual leaders and health practitioners as well as the youth are actively involved. At Aralagadakalu, village experiments with traditional farming are being carried out. All these groups are engaged in the finalisation of agricultural calendars.

Marketing of organic products. Farmers, who grow food crops like ragi, rice and minor millets organically, keep what they require for household consumption; the rest is collected and sold to consumers of organic food in the city Bangalore. Women at different sanghas have also been encouraged to add value by making organic food products, which are also marketed. Examples are ragi and rice pappads, ragi flour mixed with edible spices and jaggery, ragi and pulses fried and flavoured with edible spices. Products like honey, chilli powder, tamarind and pickles are also included. Though the demand for organic products remains inadequate, the sale of organic food has generated an income for farmers and improved the economic and social status of women.

Reflections on endogenous development

Diversity in agriculture is the heart of sustainability. The approach adopted by Green Foundation has enabled farmers to control the choice of crops adapted to local conditions. Critically evaluating the relative merits of a wide range of cultivars allows farmers to have confidence in the varieties they choose. This makes them less dependent on the market. Marketing of seeds and grains may have great potential in the future. The increased demand for local seeds from different regions is supporting economic security. We have found that the alternative seed systems need to be enhanced by an alternative marketing system, both for seeds and grains. In this sense, endogenous development involves supporting strong farmers' networks, which can continue with developing sustainable practices for better yields and enhancing the marketing infrastructure.

Rural people are enthusiastic to reveal information on indigenous knowledge and culture. The majority of the farmers mentioned that it was the first time that anyone inquired about their traditional practices. With awareness spreading about the significance of reviving their culture and crop varieties, the farmers are positive and are interested in retaining many practices. The local healers are feeling encouraged and are showing keen interest in recovering local herbs that are becoming extinct. The role of the local spiritual leaders has been strengthened by reviving agricultural festivals and rituals.

At the same time, several constraints need to be tackled. It has been observed, for example, that many indigenous practices and rituals cannot be tested by simply using standardized tools or techniques. Since they are not laboratory-based experiments, it is difficult to control the environment and observe consistently and make analyses. Experiments which involve beliefs, spirituality and other non-quantifiable components are difficult to measure. The

The local concept of welfare includes having good children, good health, wealth, bravery, adequate food throughout the year, long life, good neighbours and friends, a healthy environment, a good family, communal harmony, as well as a good administrator who takes care of the people.

methodology for implementing these experiments needs to be worked on.

An external evaluation in April 2000 concluded that the efforts of Green Foundation have contributed to an appreciable increase in seed diversity in the project region. The creation of sanghas, village-level seed management committees and farmer seed conservation networks leads to decentralising and strengthening activities at the grassroots level. But, the rapid globalisation process makes the task of genetic diversity conservation a difficult one. Therefore, policy advocacy, through strategic alliances, at all levels is important. Moreover, in-house resourcefulness among staff is needed to address overall development issues within a rapidly changing internal and external environment. Maintaining the enthusiasm of the farmers to reinvent the good elements of traditional practices will also depend on the ability of Green Foundation to facilitate a wider movement. This up-scaling needs to be done at several levels: at the village level, by strengthening the village level organisations, at the NGO level, by networking and experience sharing with other institutions, and at the general policy level.

Culture and indigenous knowledge generated by resource users are under constant threat by external forces. It is our belief that crucial aspects of endogenous development such as the local economy, livelihood and culture can be protected from total erosion. Small initiatives to protect culture and indigenous knowledge, such as these, facilitate the conservation effort and thereby the kind of agriculture that stands at the basis of the livelihood of millions of farmers.

4.7 REVITALISING TRADITIONAL AGRICULTURE

G.K. Upawansa and James Handawela, ECO and COMPAS Network, Sri Lanka

Traditional agriculture in Sri Lanka was an integrated system based on ecological principles that included trees, crops, livestock and fish. Astrology and beliefs about supernatural beings played an important role. Though under threat, many of these traditions are still practiced today. In this chapter we share how various organisations in Sri Lanka have established a system of field experimentation to understand, test and improve indigenous farming practices.

Sri Lanka is a small pear-shaped island to the south of the Indian sub-continent. Altitudes up to 3,500 meter above sea level give rise to a varied pattern of rainfall and several agro-ecological zones. In the dry land areas, the ancient peoples made constructions in the undulating topography to reduce erosion, control floods, and to improve water availability during the dry season. In the highlands and tropical lowlands forest-based swidden farming was practiced with supplementary irrigation from reservoirs.

In spite of the recent renovation of most of these ancient irrigation systems, and the construction of new ones, heavy imports of rice and wheat are needed to meet the national requirements. This contrasts sharply with the past when the country produced all its food, which consisted of a wide variety of grains, yams, vegetables and fruits.

Sri Lankan agricultural cosmovision

Most (70%) Sri Lankans are Buddhists and 15% are Hindus. These formal religions generally merge with a range of traditional beliefs and practices. Many rural people and farmers make decisions according to traditional cosmovision, and the different local spiritual leaders often play an important role in village-level agriculture and health practices. The *daiwatnya* deals with astrology, the *kattandirale* with yantras and mantras, the *kapua* with Gods and spirits, and the *vedemahataya* is the traditional healer, both for humans and animals.

Indigenous knowledge, and the traditional practices of agriculture and irrigation, survived for over 2000 years due to the unique institutional system that supported it. This institutional system was made up of many components and organised as a hierarchy. At the base was the village with a village council and a village chief. Villages were grouped in larger divisions, and at the apex of this pyramid was the king. Any problem that could not be resolved at local level was referred to the higher levels. While religion was taught by Buddhist priests, other sections of the indigenous knowledge system were taught by masters, or *gurus*. In passing down this knowledge from master to pupil, some important sections were deliberately withheld from the pupil, and only revealed when the master died. In many instances knowledge so retained by masters was lost. This knowledge system is written in *ola* scripts, using a writing surface made of palm leaves. These writings can be categorised into four main fields: medicine, *dhamma*, which includes agricultural practices, astrology, and the category dealing with spirits and the symbols related to it.

Traditionally, Sri Lankan people believe in Gods and deities, and it is customary to invoke their blessings. They believe that the help and blessings of the Gods protect them from danger, ill-health and hardship. The Gods inhabit trees, and the Bo tree (*Ficus religiosa*) is held in special regard, because Buddha attained Buddhahood under it. Therefore, people construct temples and make offerings alongside Bo trees. It is also believed that certain Gods and Goddesses guard rivers, forests and mountains. On the other hand, people believe in the existence of demons that haunt cemeteries, funeral houses, empty buildings and unclean places. Spirits that are neither Gods nor demons, *bahirawas*, are believed to live underground or within air space, and are able to appropriate part of the harvest and cause loss to the farmers.

Buddhism. There are three major sections to Buddha's teachings. One deals with the discipline of monks or priests; a second refers to the understanding of thoughts, and the process of thinking; and a third section is known as the *Suthara Pitakaya*, which describes 'good ways of living'. This section consists of many *suthras*, or sermons preached by Lord Buddha. Reciting suthras, which is done to get rid of evil spirits and to invoke blessings, is called *pirith*. Farmers often chant pirith to prevent or obtain relief from crop diseases, animal epidemics and evil effects. There is nothing secret about these methods. One important requirement is that the chanting has to be done by a devout person, who leads a pious and righteous life. Fortunately, such people are available in our villages today. They are familiar with traditional religious practices, such as charming sand and water for protection against pests. Many farmers in the villages obtain their services to protect their crops against pests and diseases.

Box 4e   Buddhist interpretation of reality

Mabima, a Buddhist priest from Kataragama, explained his understanding of reality: *"In classical knowledge, upon which both Hinduism and Buddhism are based, reality is understood to function through a multitude of powers and forces. Besides the powers are of matter and energy, Sri Lankan Buddhism recognises at least eight other forces and powers: the power of the moment (each moment has its special quality, which explains the importance of astrology), the power of a certain location (sacred places), the power of sound (mantras), the power of symbols (yantras), the mental powers of certain persons (enhanced by training and a pious lifestyle), the power of plants (beyond the nutritional or pharmaceutical values), the power of place and space (induced by certain events that have taken place there), and supernatural powers, that have their origin in spirits or divine beings. It is important to understand all these powers, know how to relate to them and understand their balance and synergy. This understanding cannot be achieved through mental efforts only: spiritual perception, feelings, intuition, ordinary and extra-ordinary senses, dreams and visions are also necessary. Therefore, personal spiritual development that helps overcome personal prejudices and biases is required. A different language is necessary: the language of metaphors, art and rituals. The traditional practices related to health, construction and agriculture are firmly based on the existence of these forces.*

Mantras, yantras and kems. In Sri Lankan Buddhism, it is considered evil to kill any form of life. Although in traditional practices related to hunting, farming and fishing this basic principle is not always observed, it implies that the use of chemical pesticides, which kills insects and other living organisms, is not approved. Instead, practices that relate to the spirits of the different living organisms have been developed. A *mantra* is a certain type of verse, a combination of sounds that together create a nucleus of spiritual energy. According to the *Upanishads,* ancient writings from India, mantras have their origin in the eternal substrate of the creation. The words, the sounds, the rhythm and timing of the recitation is important. In agriculture, certain mantras are used for obtaining higher yields, others for protection of crops from pests and wild animals. The spiritual leaders know which mantras are required to achieve specific effects.

Yantras are specific symbols, which have been empowered by a sacred person through a mantra or pirith chanting. It can have the form of a drawing, an idol, or inscriptions on a thin strip of copper or palm leaf. Certain yantras are used for protection from enemies, from the anger of the Gods and evil spirits, or from the ill effects of forces of nature, envy and the evil eye. Other yantras are used for crop protection: against flies, rats, and for animal health. In Sri Lankan agriculture, the use of yantras is widespread. For example, a specific yantra is often placed in the centre of the rice threshing floor.. Moreover during the threshing operations no item is referred to by its real name. The idea is to mislead the spirits so they will not know that a threshing operation is going on.

The practice of *kems* is quite widespread in rural Sri Lanka: it is a kind of practice, technique or custom that is followed in order to obtain some favourable effect. This may include relief from a specific illness, damage or problem. For example, the following kem is used for protection against the paddy fly: *"Go to the paddy field early in the morning, catch a fly at the entrance of the field, chant a specific mantra seven times, and then release the fly."* Some kems combine astrology with the use of certain plants. Other kems depend on the use of specific plants and mantras. These traditional practices have survived because they are believed to be effective. There are also kems that do not involve any belief in spiritual beings, as they are based on a careful observation of natural phenomena. For example, a kem practised to destroy the paddy caterpillar. In this kem, milk rice is prepared very early in the morning, before the crows leave their nests, and put on circular slices of banana leaves. These are placed on tree stumps located in those parts of the field where caterpillars have infested the crop. When the crows perch on the banana discs to eat the milk rice, the milk rice falls to the ground. When the crows pick up the fallen milk rice, they see the caterpillars and eat them instead of the milk rice.

It is believed that various conditions have to be met to make kems successful. For example, the farmer should not visit the treated field for a specific period. With other kems, women are prohibited from entering the field. The effectiveness of a kem can be nullified if the person is exposed to an impurity caused by eating certain foods, especially meat. Attending a funeral or women's menstruation may also cause impurities. Other kems have to be performed by women only, or by pregnant women.

Astrology. Astrology plays a significant role in the cosmovision of Sri Lankan people, who often consult astrologers before embarking on any significant undertaking in their personal, educational or professional life. Astrology is also dominant in agricultural practices, especially in the cultivation of rice. Most farmers follow the astrological calendar to ensure success and avoid bad luck. This calendar provides information on 'good' and 'bad' days due to the position of the moon in relation to the earth. Twenty-seven such positions, or *nekathas*, are known of which twelve are believed to be appropriate for different undertakings. For example, usually a Sunday is chosen to initiate work related to paddy cultivation.

There are also auspicious *horas*, or one-hour periods. Seven horas are identified and each hora is divided into five *panchamakala hora*, or 12 minutes. Each of the latter is divided into three *shookshama horas* of 4 minutes, and further sub-divided into periods of 36 seconds each. The astrological calendar also gives information on the evil period, also called *rahukalaya*, during which one should not start any important activities. It lasts for an hour and a half, and every day there are two such periods. It is also believed that one should face certain directions on certain days. For example it is believed to be inauspicious to begin any important enterprise while facing the north on a Sunday.

Changing agricultural practices. Traditional agriculture used to be a communal activity, in which individual decisions had to fall in line with communal decisions. The *gamarala*, or village chief, saw to it that all collective decisions were adhered to. Cultivation was initiated by the village leader in each area at an auspicious time, and started with a vow to the Gods to ensure the success of cultivation. These activities were followed by several agricultural practices, which we would now call eco-friendly, including minimal tillage of the land, mixed cropping, and fencing activities at auspicious times. Traditional crop protection included the cultivation of a small portion of land to attract birds, performing kems and rituals, supplemented when necessary by the use of certain plants or plant extracts as bio-pesticides. After threshing the harvest, a small portion was separated for the *Mangalya*, the first eating ceremony.

Despite the impact of the green revolution, many of these traditional practices exist in Sri Lanka even today, though their meaning is often not fully understood by the younger farmers. Frequently they are practiced away from the eyes and ears of outsiders. People have learned not to express their spiritual practices openly as they are often ridiculed by outsiders with a technical focus, who are looking for rational explanations.

The indigenous systems began to disappear with the advent of the British colonial regime. The *gamsabha*, or village council structure, was abolished in 1832. The gamarala was replaced by an officer called the *velvidane* in the 1860s, who dealt with the cultivation of paddy only, neglecting the other components of the farming system, such as highland and livestock farming. The Waste Lands Ordinance enabled buying up land at very low prices, to establish coffee plantations and later on tea and cocoa. This caused natives to loose access to the land, further destroying village agriculture. The institutional arrangements favoured individual activity rather than communal or co-operative efforts, and paid labour was introduced into village agriculture, which until then had depended on the mutual exchange of labour. Agriculture became an economic pursuit, and no longer a way of life. As a result, values such as respect for nature and cultural considerations began to disappear.

Moreover, Christian missionaries could not appreciate the value of indigenous practices and often deliberately suppressed and ridiculed them to introduce their own beliefs and practices.

The introduction of science-based education accelerated this process further. Modern

science has not seriously studied indigenous knowledge, and, instead of subjecting it to scientific study to test its validity, most scientists tend to dismiss it as a backwardness. Almost all farmers use fertilisers and agro-chemicals, though often in combination with traditional methods such as making a vow to the Gods when starting cultivation. At present, one can observe an increased interest of agricultural scientists in traditional practices, however, including their spiritual aspects.

Different age groups take part in rituals to prevent or remedy field problems.

ECO and the Compas Network Sri Lanka

The activities related to ecological agriculture were initiated in 1990 by ECO the Ecological Conservation centre, who joined Compas in 1997. ECO is experimenting with farmers on eco-friendly practices, including the use of kems, rituals and offering or *poojas*.

Eco works with volunteer farmers who carry out tests on their own fields, to verify the effectiveness of cosmovision-based methods and techniques, and those found to be effective are introduced by them to other interested farmers. During seminars and workshops for farmers, NGO officials and government officials, the experiences are discussed. Successful case studies are given publicity through the mass media. The small plots selected for testing traditional practices include Buddhist temples, as priests carry out indigenous practices such as charming of water and sand. The close relationship that exists between the rural people and the Buddhist temples are a great help in popularising indigenous knowledge. Buddhist priests have close contact with farmers and moreover they command respect in the farming community.

In 1999, four NGOs decided to join ECO, to jointly establish the Compas Network Sri Lanka: Negampaha Agro-producers Society, Dambulla Community Resources Development Centre, Janodaya, and Future in Our Hands. The objective of this network is to increase the effectiveness of their activities related to agriculture with the farmers.

Since 1999 considerable efforts were put into understanding the concepts of endogenous development and indigenous knowledge. During the initial discussions within the network it became clear that endogenous development is more than just a way of escaping from the economic crisis caused by passively submitting to market forces. The challenge is not just to resist these external forces, but to enhance development based on indigenous resources and knowledge. In this process, indigenous knowledge is not to be romanticised or proclaimed as the ultimate truth, neither is to be rejected as primitive or inferior.

Methodology for fieldwork. The network decided to start their activities by document-ing the indigenous knowledge and practices in the field work areas of the respective organisations. First, the custodians of indigenous knowledge, who had been holding on to it despite powerful external pressure, had to be recognised. During village meetings with interested and experienced farmers the objectives of endogenous development were presented, and the field workers expressed their desire to learn about farmers' indigenous knowledge, the concepts behind them, and the cultural and spiritual aspects involved. After these discussions the process of sharing, discussing and analysing the indigenous practices and knowledge began. The findings were documented with the farmers' consent, and presented and clarified during follow-up meetings. This information was used to draw up a baseline document on indigenous knowledge in Sri Lanka. It indicated the extent of indigenous knowledge and practices, which included many ecological aspects, such as water management, landscape, climate, and seasonal differences. Traditional agricultural practices encountered included mixed cropping, the association between trees and crops, soil identification practices, game management, and the use of plants for crop protection, medicines and natural fertiliser. The findings also confirmed that indigenous knowledge systems in Sri Lanka have three main components: the ecological, the spiritual, and the astrological.

During one of our field visits we discussed the use of yantras with the farmers. One of the farmers remembered that his father made use of these, and that he should have a booklet with the designs of the yantras in the attic of his house. He found the book, which contained some 20 abstract geometric figures, each referring to a specific plague or pest. We copied the booklet and showed it to several other farmers. In many instances they were recognised by traditional leaders as consistent with their own knowledge. Other farmers were eager to copy the drawings to test them in their fields.

Testing indigenous knowledge. Subsequently, a novel methodology was needed to cre-ate opportunities for testing, revitalising, and improving the selected traditional practices. In the village meetings it had become clear that it would be impossible to select individ-ual practices for testing, as most practices consist of a mixture of indigenous elements that are seemingly inseparable, and with varying degrees of interaction and synergy. One practice, for example, could include ecological concepts and materials, astrological timing, spiritual influences, and social norms. Moreover, farmers often apply a variety of indige-nous practices, and these too are interrelated and complementary. Testing indigenous practices at field level with so many variables, some of which could not be quantified, would produce results that would be extremely difficult to interpret.

Mr Upawansa (left) meets with a spiritual leader and a Buddhist monk. The effect of yantras, or ancient symbolic drawings, to control pests in rice is tested in the farmers' fields.

Therefore, rather than focusing on testing individual indigenous practices, it was decided to compare farmers who were using indigenous knowledge (IK) practices with those following modern, or non-IK methods. Every network partner agreed to select 12 so-called IK farmers, and 12 non-IK farmers, who would be comparable in crops grown, social status, and economic standing. Arrangements were made to record their base-line status and to monitor their farming operations, costs, yields, and income. However at an early stage in the monitoring process it became clear that it was impossible to differentiate farmers into IK and non-IK categories. All farmers practiced a mixture of IK and non-IK applications, though in different proportions.

It was then decided to change the focus of the testing towards assessing the level and intensity of IK application of each farmer, and to express this in terms of the 'degree of indigenousness'. Farm performance could then be compared in relation to the degree of indigenousness of their farming practices. This idea was also discussed with agronomists at the Peradeniya University, who agreed that it might be a sound way of expressing the effect of indigenous practices on farming performance. After this endorsement each partner organisation reassessed the same 24 farmers according to their indigenousness. In this assessment the number and type of the IK practices adopted by each farmer were determined. This was based on the farmers' own assessment, the opinion of neighbouring farmers and the impressions of the field worker. As the testing progressed, the farmers and partner organisations suggested that instead of giving negative marks for the use modern farming methods, the assessment could be based solely on the extent to which specific IK practices were followed. A provisional checklist of IK practices for this assessment was proposed (see box 4f).

Box 4f   Indicators for 'degree of indigenousness'

- Mixed cropping
- Crop rotation, including fallowing for long periods
- Indigenous methods of crop processing and storage
- Enterprise diversity and the degree of integration of crops, livestock and trees
- Adherence to auspicious times for performing farming operations
- Adherence to accepted seasons
- Minimum tillage, avoiding inversion of surface soil
- Application of organic manure
- Labour sharing and village level co-operation
- Farm-level breeding and seed improvement
- Weed management by indigenous means
- Measures for rain harvesting or for improving rainfall efficiency
- Making vows to spirits at the beginning of the season, and honouring the vows at the end of the season
- Repetitive chanting of Pirith (poetic Buddhist texts) against pests and evil forces
- Application of yantra/mantra to ward off pests, disease, evil effects, and to invite spiritual blessings
- Application of kem (customary action) to prevent or remedy field problems
- Application of Vrkshayurveda (traditional treatments) against plant pests and diseases

---

In the assessment all 17 practices had equal importance. Marks were allotted as follows: on a scale of zero to six the highest score - 6 - was awarded for maximum use; 4 signified moderate use; 2 low use and 0 no IK used at all. Each farmer's total degree of indigenousness was determined by adding up the number of marks he or she had scored. After this more refined method was accepted, the level of indigenousness was determined in consultation with the farmer while drawing on the results of their own field observations, and the farmer's own data.

Some results and constraints
Initially the idea was to collect accurate information on costs, labour, yields, and farm income, and compare this with the level of indigenousness. This task proved difficult, however, because it was the first time the field workers and the farmers tried to monitor farming operations at some level of clarity and detail. Activities were also affected by a lack of literature on this subject. The following general conclusions emerged, however, after qualitative data was combined with the ideas and judgements provided by farmers and field workers. First of all, farmers with a high level of indigenousness - with high IK rating - spend less cash on inputs. At the same time their returns per unit of cash invested were higher than those of farmers with low IK ratings. Also, according to the farmers, the quality and taste of the produce tended to be better with increasing levels of indigenousness.

Another striking difference was the hardiness of crops under circumstances of environmental constraint. When there were no constraints, the low-IK (modern) farmers obtained higher yields and higher monetary incomes than the farmers with higher IK levels. This did not always result in higher profits, however, because of the high cost of external inputs. Where the external environment was unstable, however, crops on high IK plots proved hardier and better able to withstand water scarcity than crops in low IK fields. This could be due to their deeper root system and the lower moisture content in body tissue. These elements are still to be studied and measured. The higher risk of the low IK farmers is not only due to the decreased hardiness of the crops they use, but also to poor input management, as farmers tend to concentrate on nitrogen fertiliser at the expense of other fertilisers. And, the application of insecticides is often after the damage has already been done. We must state here, though, that at this stage the results of the experiments are still preliminary and incomplete. During the next cropping seasons more accurate information on costs, labour, yields and farm income will be collected, and the results between different degrees of indigenousness will be compared. Field staff and farmers will also receive more training in collecting accurate quantitative data.

When we took up this study of IK, the fieldworkers of the Compas Network Sri-Lanka were unfamiliar with the concepts of endogenous development and indigenous knowledge. Moreover, they lacked field experience in testing agricultural practices, keeping relevant field records, and making reliable comparisons. During the first year of network operations they have grown to understand the concept of endogenous development and to grasp the relevance of indigenous knowledge. The field workers' capacity to make field observations and record them, and their ability to explore the effects of indigenous practices together with the farmers, have improved considerably. They have established good relationships with the IK resource persons and have been able to bring these otherwise isolated individuals closer to each other, so they are better able to interact, share and improve their knowledge and practices. In this way an informal 'forum for endogenous development' has been established at all four locations.

Improving traditional rice growing practices. The long tradition of irrigation in Sri Lanka has led to monocultures in paddy cultivation, in which insects, birds, rodents, as well as large animals and micro-organisms cause damage to the crop. Under mono-culture conditions, pests and diseases can be considered a natural reaction of nature to restore the biodiversity. Traditional Sri Lankan agriculture has developed solutions to these attacks, while still respecting the universal law of compassion and inner connection, combining insights in the natural processes with astrology and spiritual practices. ECO has worked on a mix of indigenous knowledge and new insights, which gives way to new practices. A good example is the *Nava-kekulama*, an adaptation of the traditional paddy cultivation system called *kekulama*, which includes minimum tillage and direct seeding. The adaptation is based on the use of rice straw as a mulch, and no weeding of the bunds. The mulch reduces the evaporation of water, protects the roots and reduces weed growth. Because of the high temperatures, the mulch decomposes easily, and when it rains, the nutrients of the mulch reach the ground water. The natural plants that grow on the bunds harbour a variety of insects and birds which act as the natural enemies of paddy pests.

Indigenous communication in extension

In promoting this nava-kekulama system in rural communities, we found that the processes used in conventional extension are not suitable. The common framework in conventional extension is: creating awareness of a problem; rousing interest for a new method; providing information and giving a demonstration; carrying out small-scale tests with interested farmers; and finally the adoption of the innovation. Experience has taught that in Sri Lanka, efforts to introduce innovations that build on indigenous knowledge cannot use demonstrations as an essential part of the extension methodology. This is due to the common notion of 'evil eye' and 'evil mouth' in folk stories. People who own demonstration plots do not want others to see them, because they feel that the comments of the observers could have a negative effect on their crops and families. Therefore, ECO had to find a suitable communication system to use in spreading innovative practices in these rural societies. Analysis of the situation in the past as well as in the present provided an answer: communication about testing of innovations takes place during village meetings and during ceremonies associated to the agricultural cycle. This indigenous form of communication is now an important methodological basis for ECO to enhance in situ IK conservation.

With modern agriculture taking over, the practice of ceremonies in the cropping season has diminished over the past decades in Sri Lanka. ECO has found however, that it is relatively easy to bring back these practices into the rural communities. Suggestions from ECO staff to revive these traditional ceremonies, as part of their extension work on organic cropping practices, were received positively by community members. They were quick in organising the events.

In the traditional societies, at least three stages of the cropping season are used to carry out special ceremonies. The first is undertaken before commencing work in the field, the second when the paddy is in full growth and vulnerable to pests, and the third ceremony takes place after the harvest. The village astrologers determine the auspicious times of these ceremonies. It was found that the discussions between farmers about specific agricultural practices during these ceremonial gatherings led to decisions at an individual level to engage in field experiments. Based on these insights we consider the village-based ceremonies as the most appropriate way to draw attention to possible innovations based on IK practices and to stimulate the villagers to experiment with them. Field staff of ECO work together with the spiritual leaders and participates in the rituals. ECO also supplies some financial support for the ceremonial activities.

During the one-day ceremony at the start of the cropping season, the community makes an offering to the Buddhist temple, and to the local and regional Gods. During this occasion the people share their plans about the work to be undertaken in agriculture. A case in point was the use of rice straw as a mulch in the paddy field: some people used thick layers, others thin ones; some covered the whole field while others left the channels open; some used an auspicious day and others used any day available. These individual variations led to a comparison of experiences. In subsequent village rituals these different experiences were compared and assessed.

The second village ritual takes place when the rice is full grown and vulnerable to pest attacks. A *pooja,* or offering, is carried out in the field. For example, in the south of Sri

Lanka a bowl of rice, of which the participants of the ritual have eaten some, is thrown over the field. This attracts predatory animals of paddy insects such as birds. This meeting also allows an exchange of observations about the differences in crop performance, as well as the incidence of pests and diseases, and to discuss the need for and effects of specific spiritual practices to counteract them. The third ceremony takes place after the harvest. In some villages there are certain taboos associated with harvest and it is common that no grain from the new crop is eaten unless this 'thanksgiving' ritual has taken place. All villagers are expected to take part in the ritual and everybody makes a contribution either in kind or cash. Even those who for good reasons cannot be present are taken into account during the ceremony, and are presented with some of the food that was ceremonially eaten by the community. This ceremony lasts between 6 - 12 hours, and it is obvious that during this time the process of reciprocal learning takes place.

Further probing into village-based experimentation indicates that the purpose of this activity is not limited to the rational interpretation of cause-effects in the biological and physical world. The aims of the experiments are not in the first place to maximise material gain through domination or manipulation of natural processes. The use of offerings, astrology and meditation techniques, in combination with an interpretation of the natural phenomena, indicates that these experiments are tied up with a comprehensive set of moral principles and inner knowledge. Therefore, the village-based agricultural experi-

Village based rituals can be an opportunity to discuss farming experiments.

ments include various social, ecological and spiritual aspects.

The results of this process are encouraging. Many organisations and farmers are now enthusiastically involved in the experiments with organic paddy production. The results of a comparative study between conventional farming and this kind of organic farming has greatly surprised the researchers involved. Yield-wise, the results are comparable. Other aspects show the greater advantage of the latter, especially the economic and ecological sustainability and the improved soil fertility. But the most striking accomplishments of introducing IK innovations in paddy farming has been the production of sufficient quantities of tasty food, that is of good quality and free of poisonous pesticide residues, as well as a noticeable increase in biodiversity - wild plants, insects, birds and other organisms - in the paddy fields.

Involving universities. In co-operation with universities in Sri Lanka, field tests have been carried out, in which conventional research methods are combined with the traditional ones. For example, the University of Peradeniya has studied the impact of ecological farming on the population of predators of paddy pests. These tests confirmed the effectivity of the neva kukulam method and appreciated the methods used. Yet, a theory to explain the possible effects of the astrological and spiritual practices in traditional Sri Lankan agriculture is hard to find in these scientific institutions. Therefore, a dialogue with traditional spiritual leaders has been initiated to learn from their interpretation of the life processes. Buddhist as well as shamanistic leaders are consulted and their knowledge is taken as complementary to that of the university scientists. Eventually the Peradeniya University will incorporate the lessons learned from these experiences in their research programme and the curriculum.

Lessons learned

Although often not openly shown, in Sri Lanka there is still a great wealth of traditional knowledge related to agriculture. The selection of indigenous practices to be experimented with is important: it must be advantageous in relation to conventional practices, in terms of income, environment, or taste, for example. The choice for improvement of paddy production responds to the felt needs of the farmers, as it is a major crop, while the economics and environmental issues related to it are problematic. The revived traditional practice of mulching and zero-weeding of the bunds proved positive, as it enhances biodiversity and reduces the need for costly external inputs, such as fertilisers and pesticides. Moreover, the quality and taste of the paddy food products was enhanced.

Over the years we have experienced that it is much easier to work on the basis of indigenous communication systems, than to adhere to conventional extension methodologies, such as the use of demonstration plots. Working with IK practices, in this sense, requires more than only promoting effective traditional practices such as mulching, minimal tillage, and no weeding on bunds to improve paddy production. It implies a combination of these practices with traditional communication systems, such as those taking place during the various ceremonies related to agriculture. Other important aspects of the traditional belief systems, such as auspicious timing of the agricultural practices, and spiritu-

Traditional crop protection combines the use of herbs with meditative practices.

al practices like mantra, yantra, pirith and kem, all need to find their place in this methodology. Building on these practices and involving the village shamans during rituals, ensures local ownership of the experimental processes and enhances the experimental capacity of the rural communities without breaking with the traditions. The theoretical background of the effect of these spiritual practices and astrology is a difficult aspect to grasp.

Therefore an agreement has been made with a consortium of universities in the country to do research, not only on the effectiveness of traditional practices, but also on their conceptual frameworks and spiritual background.

We believe that genuine traditional practices should stand up to testing, and their effectiveness should be explained by a theory. The NGOs in the Compas Network Sri Lanka want to avoid romanticising traditional practices, and distinguish between effective knowledge and superstition. Assessment of the degree of indigenousness of local farmers, and how this correlates with farm performance, appears to be a useful method for testing the relevance of indigenous practices. By involving farmers with a wide range of IK levels, and by keeping proper records on them, it may be possible to compare their performance and the effects of certain spiritual and astrological practices as well. In terms of institutional development, the NGOs have made considerable progress, while more and more farmers have expressed the desire to join the activities and improve their farming operations. Interest in astrology and spiritual practices is increasing, and government extension workers, who are now considering this methodology as a serious alternative, are keen to see further results.

Active networking has resulted in an increase interest of government agencies and scientists in the approach for endogenous development. A number of mass meeting have been held, agreements were established with government organisations, and articles and books on the subject have been distributed. The application of the approach is no longer limited to a few villages, but is spreading over the island, and is now welcomed by many in the mainstream. A point that requires constant priority is the training of field staff in the participatory methods of experimenting in the cultural context. By involving students in this work, and a future modification of the university curriculum, new professionals may become better equipped to enhance endogenous development in Sri Lanka.

4.8 BUILDING ON TRIBAL RESOURCES
Endogenous development in the North Eastern Ghats

Gowtham Shankar, IDEA, India

The non-governmental development organisation IDEA (Integrated Development through Environmental Awakening) has supported endogenous development in the tribal areas of the Eastern Ghats in southern India since 1985. A central element in its activities was documenting the agro-ecological practices and cosmovisions of 10 tribal ethnic groups, emphasising the role of gender. An attempt was made to understand the linkage between tribal and modern knowledge in the process of endogenous development. Subsequently, during the five years of implementing the Compas programme, IDEA has systematically worked in developing approaches to test and improve local knowledge systems, and supported the 'Network of Tribal Leaders'.

The Eastern Ghats is one of the major natural resources of India. It is home to about 60 tribal communities with a population of nearly 10 million. The majority of these people live in hilly and forested areas. Well-known groups among them are the Konda Reddy, Koya, Pulikonda and the Konda Dora. Each tribal group has a distinct lifestyle based on the belief that nature, mankind and the spiritual world are inter-related. The tribes of the Eastern Ghats practice different types of agriculture, depending on the location of the land. In the hills, shifting cultivation is practised as the major component of the subsistence economy in all communities. It involves a mixed agriculture with a variety of cereals and millets, pulses, beans, tubers, medicinal plants, fuel, fodder and roofing material. Short duration crops produce a harvest in a relatively brief period of time and can enhance economic stability and food security in times of drought and floods. The harvest is sequential, which enables the farmer to use part of the crop for food grain, part for investment and festivals part to pay off debts. Terraces to control soil erosion are combined with the application of farmyard manure and bio-fertilisers. Cultivation in the plains includes wetland and dryland agriculture, with a variety of mixed crops such as dry paddy, millets, pulses, beans, vegetables and fruits. These agricultural lands are either community property entrusted to different clans by traditional village institutions, or property owned by individual families.

Tribal cosmovision

The tribal people in the Eastern Ghats believe in the existence of a wide range of divine beings and ancestral spiritual forces with benevolent and malevolent characters, who inhabit houses, villages, agricultural fields, burial grounds and surrounding forests. The Pulikonda, for example, have more than 100 Gods, Goddesses and spirits. The tribals believe that these divine beings are beyond human control and able to help or harm nature and human beings. The tribal people also believe that the good and bad ancestral spirits always watch over them and may help them in times of danger and distress. Therefore, the tribal people perform certain rites and rituals to appease the divine beings and ancestral spirits so as to protect themselves and to get rid of evil influences. They do not start constructing a house, distributing land, felling trees, performing a marriage, or going hunting until they have performed the appropriate rites.

The tribal people believe they are the children of Mother Nature and that she protects and guides them. Some trees, such as tamarind and mango, and wild animals such as the Indian bison, tiger, common langur (monkey), peacock and dove are considered to be holy. Besides this, they also have sacred hills, forests, streams and mountains, which are inhabited by divine beings. Hence, they are worshipped through rituals, ceremonies and fairs.

The majority of cosmovisions in this region contain beliefs that are related to their agro-ecological and health practices. The tribal people from the Konda Reddy, Koya and the Konda Dora, believe that certain crops, such as the major and minor millets, hill paddy and red gram, are not only important food crops, but also sacred gifts from their ancestors and the Goddess of nature and earth. Hence any ritual connected to their festivals would not be complete without offering these grains to the divine beings and ancestral spirits both good and bad.

Traditional leaders. The physical and material well-being of the tribal people is supported by traditional institutions and functionaries. The *naik* is the village headman, responsible for village administration, law and order, and co-ordination of festivals. The *kotpaik* is the sacerdotal head, who is responsible for ensuring the functioning of various social, cultural, religious and agricultural norms. The *disari* is responsible for traditional medicine, including the use of magico-religious and herbal remedies. The *poojari* is the priest who controls the religious protocols of the village and performs rituals associated with agriculture. There are the priestesses or shamans, called *gurumayi, guniya* and *sutrani*, who are also the traditional birth attendants. *Kattela disari* and *sirla disari* are the specialists on magico religious medical and agricultural practices of the region. A group of eight to ten or more villages constitute a *muta*, headed by a *mutadar*. This person plays a vital role in maintaining the cohesion, stability and social identity of the communities.

Indigenous knowledge. Though the traditional 'dormitories' have disappeared physically from the villages studied, we found that tribal people have retained their knowledge systems in different forms. The knowledge related to cosmovision is mainly vested in the four important functionaries of the village: the disari, poojari, guniya and gurumayi. The community has clearly visible knowledge of soil conservation and land management. The disari, and the kattela and sirla disaries, are able to test soils by colour, weight, and taste, and assess the degradation of the land. They know about specific floral species for improving soil fertility, and understand how to use green manure and growth hormones for the benefit of the plants. They celebrate the festivals related to grain conservation, and ensure that all villagers follow the principles of conservation of food grains and other natural resources. Touching, eating or selling grains, vegetables, wild vegetables and medicinal plants without celebrating the necessary 'first eating ceremonies' is taboo.

Mutte is the name given to the body of the tribal science, written on palm leafs. These are possessed by disari, poojari and guniya and include subjects like astronomy, herbal medicine, *chakras/gondas* (symbols), eco-agricultural ethics and knowledge, and ways to influence the divine beings and evil spirits. Their mythological histories, clan totemic relations, agro-ecological and health knowledge are also preserved in the form of folk songs, dances and music, mostly retained by the tribal women and elders. For example, the *kandul Baza* is a combination of music and song that explains the origin of red gram and its cultivation practices as well as the need to protect its germ plasm. *Gondas*, or specific chalk marks, are the symbols of communication with supernatural beings, which have the powers to absorb and release the most sensitive cosmic information and supernatural powers. The gondas are used to propitiate or to appease evil spirits and to protect crops from pests, animals and witch craft.

Rituals and ceremonies. To appease the benevolent divine beings, the tribal people carry out acts of propitiation with a number of rituals and ceremonies. The disari fixes the auspicious dates for festivals or rituals on the basis of his astrological calculations and the lunar calendar. The poojari performs the ritual for the community. There are different costs for performing the major festivals. The individual families also celebrate the same festivals in their homes with the head of the family as family priest. Prosperity always depends on the proper functioning of the disari and his accurate astrological calculations. If he miscalculates the dates of festivals, it would disturb all agricultural practices, upset the benevolent divine beings and spirits, and result in serious consequences for the community. This can include crop failure, cattle death and even sickness and death to humans.

Gender. During community rituals and ceremonies, the male functionaries play a major role. The female gurumayi is only allowed to officiate in rituals and ceremonies relating to the family Goddesses or spirits. In some villages, she is even limited to spiritual healing of women and child diseases. Their ritual status is not equivalent to that of men, and they are subject to several taboos. Although the majority of divine beings are Goddesses, communities do not allow women priests to directly or

IDEA staff is watching how tribal people make gondas, or chalk marks, to communicate with the spiritual world.

indirectly serve or communicate with them during the communal ceremonies. No woman is allowed to touch the sacred sword, axe or spear belonging to the divine beings. Women are limited to the role of preparing food and offerings, merry making, dancing and singing during most of the festivals, except during the first eating ceremonies for mango and pumpkin, where they are allowed to worship *Bondurga* - the Goddess of forests.

External influences

The forests of the Eastern Ghats have remained largely undisturbed until the middle of the 18th century, when fuelwood and coal were needed for industries and transport, and timber logs for construction purposes. Bamboo harvesting for the paper factories is another reason for the ecological destruction. The growing food and economic needs of the tribal population also forced the tribals to exploit considerable parts of the natural resources for traditional shifting cultivation practices. In more recent years this process of deforestation has further accelerated, due to loss of their lands to non-tribals, and to several forest-based industries. Following this ecological destruction, rainfall in the area as well as soil fertility has decreased considerably, resulting in further exploitation of the natural resources. This process includes the loss of social control regulatory mechanisms, cultural identity, agro-ecological as well as health-related practices.

The tribal elders and traditional institutional functionaries have developed a strong sense of insecurity, as a reaction to this loss of culture, indigenous knowledge, worldviews and bio-diversity. As K. Pothanna, a tribal traditional leader explains: *"As the richness of our forests disappears, the richness of our community worldviews, the knowledge and our ethics also get lost. What is left is barren hills and barren minds like my bald head. You see, the water is now lifeless and is not carrying any juice of the leaf litter of the forests on the mountains. Soils are dead, since there is no life and taste in it. These are the two things we lost due to deforestation. We are groups with rich diversity of bio-cultural practices, but our worldviews, totemic clan concepts and knowledge systems are similar. Hence, we call ourselves the children of mother nature - the eco-people - and our world is the eco-world..."*

Modernisation has entered into this remote area in many other ways too, like the introduction of formal education based on western knowledge systems. When attending the local primary schools, or the secondary schools in the larger towns, the tribal children have to adapt their dress and language as well as their ways of thinking, reasoning and seeking answers to questions. Traditional ways of learning are largely, or totally, ignored in this process. Similarly, formal efforts of the state and the communities to improve tribal livelihoods have not taken into account the relevance of indigenous knowledge systems and the role of traditional leaders. The government-supported community health workers did not take into account the local health systems nor the experience of the herbal medicine men, snakebite specialists and midwives. In agriculture, the policy based on subsidies and modern development inputs have ignored the existing agro-ecological practices, which are the lifelines of these tribal communities.

Moreover, population growth, external socio-economic pressures and tribal land alienations are also forcing them to intensify the use of forest resources, including land for cultivation and collection of minor forest products. In time, there may not be enough food for people to survive and individual families may decide to take up hunting and shifting cultivation practices again. At the same time, a process of tribal migration to new areas where the forests had been cleared, usually to the 'settlement villages' in Orissa, resulted in the displacement of millions of tribal youth. The elderly people and priests were left behind in the original villages, and with them the best part of their knowledge and world-views.

Other effects of modernisation. Modernisation has resulted in many changes in tribal lifestyles. For example, new food habits have been adopted, changing from the mixed and highly nutritious traditional dietary habits and staple foods, to modern rural and urban breakfasts, snacks, beverages and drinks. Deforestation, the change from mixed crops to cash crops, and the availability of exotic vegetables and tubers in the markets, has reduced the consumption of local foods, such as wild leafy vegetables, meat products, edible tubers, fruits, nuts and berries. The trends of the cash economy are attracting the youth, and hitherto well knit social systems are eroding, replaced by inter-elitism, personal violence, inequality, socio-economic differentiation, gender discrimination, and political elitism. Traditional musical instruments such as the *dompu, kiridi, tomuku* and *bousi* have been replaced by the harmonium, clarinet and guitar. The *oili* and *sankidi* songs are now dominated by songs from the film world and from christianity.

Besides this, community ownership, as well as traditional leaders with their norms, taboos and customary practices related to natural sustainability and cultural identity, are breaking down. The functions of disari, naiks, kattela disari and sirla disari in relation to agriculture have weakened. Their decision-making role in terms of land, crop management and traditional agricultural practices has eroded under the influence and impact of modern agricultural policies, such as watershed development, water harvesting technologies, hybrid seed and cash cropping. This has resulted in further exploitation of natural resources, as well as the deterioration of soils, water resources and bio-diversity in this fragile natural environment. The change in agricultural practices under the influence of a high-tech approach to agriculture has not taken into consideration the possibility of judiciously combining traditional tribal agricultural and land management practices with elements of modern agricultural technologies.

In this process, the cosmovision beliefs, festivals, crop calendars, and traditional agricultural practices of the tribal population are changing rapidly. Frequent contacts with neighbouring non-tribal communities, settled landlords, merchants and the coming of christian groups have also contributed to this acculturation process. The adoption of alien religions and practices can create disharmony. Many of the christian missions openly advise the tribal people to change their religion and rid themselves of the wrath of traditional deities, whom they cannot please because of the high cost of performing the necessary rites are too expensive for poor people.

At the same time, we have found that there are also forces within the communities, which aim at maintaining their identity, traditional system and practices. Though changing trends are affecting tribal life, the well-knit social systems have resisted the influx of alien cultures to a certain extent. It was also observed that in several tribal villages the traditional functionaries themselves realised that there were negative elements in their practices, and slowly began to change their attitudes, strengthening their positive practices and looking for selective support from outside. For example, in the villages of the Konda Reddies, women are now allowed to participate in religious ceremonies and worship the Goddess at communal ceremonies. And in some villages, the *guniya* and *sutrani* - the traditional birth attendants - are interacting with governmental health workers. These trends indicate the attitude of these functionaries, and their intention to interact with modern development approaches whilst keeping their identity and community functions intact.

IDEA

IDEA, or Integrated Development through Environmental Awakening, is facilitating a process to halt degradation of cultural identity of the tribal people and their natural resources in the North Eastern Ghats in southern India since 1985. Currently, IDEA is working in 300 villages covering about one hundred thousand tribal people in the states of Andhra Pradesh and Orissa. IDEA started its development projects by organising the tribals into environmental protection and developmental groups. In the '90s the traditional leaders continued to discuss their experiences with natural resource practices during a series of eco-cultural meetings. They concluded that the deforestation and rapid depletion of floral and faunal species was due to human interference, especially to the violation of traditional regulations in the communities due to the weakening relationships between the traditional leaders and the community. Therefore, resolutions were passed to conserve natural resources by reviving traditional conservation practices.

IDEA was one of the founder members of the Compas programme in 1997, who started conducting experiments to test and improve local knowledge systems, systematic networking and intercultural dialogue. The following are a few examples of its methodology over the past 5 years.

Documentation and action research. Different aspects of the tribal cosmovision have been documented and experiments have been conducted to test and substantiate their effectiveness. Themes include: totemic clan concepts, the use of natural pesticides, organic and green manures, biological pest control, indigenous poultry breeds, weed management, medicinal plants, regulatory norms for natural resources, first eating ceremonies, traditional soil and seed testing, and traditional nutritional practices. Several of these indigenous practices and genetic resources have been successfully revived, using a combination of traditional practices and elements of modern knowledge systems. Several pictorial representations of tribal cosmovisions have been prepared, and agro-ecological songs and dances have been documented, analysed and reconstructed, and are now being revived successfully. The development significance of different festivals has also been analysed, especially its impact on agro-ecology, health and animal husbandry. Several endogenous development related educational materials have been prepared, such as stickers, cosmo-world pictorials, posters, booklets, calendars, audio & video material, and newsletters in local languages.

Tribal networks and support divisions. Traditional leaders, such as disari, poojari, guniya, gurumayi and gowdas, have initiated their Naik Gotna network, with about 5,000 members. Through this network they have intensified their efforts to further document and experiment with tribal knowledge, practices and worldviews. A similar initiative has been taken by nearly 7,250 mountain agricultural farmers, who have started their own federation. IDEA has also set up several technical support divisions for indigenous knowledge and resource conservation (IKRC), and for development interaction and natural resource conservation services (DINARCS). Other technical support and research centres have been strengthened to further facilitate the tribal communities in conducting experimentation to validate their endogenous development activities, such as FRUS, the Farmers Research Unit/Stations. Several traditional conservation units have been set up, such as BION, the conservation unit of traditional seeds (with a collection of about 285 traditional seed varieties), KOILARI (with about 243 wild vegetables, edible tubers, berries and nuts), KASTURI (with about 500 species of medicinal plants), and ASEEL (with about 32 traditional poultry breeds). IDEA also interacts with other NGOs, government tribal development agencies and universities, who wished to interact, share and learn from their experiences with endogenous development.

Training programmes. A dormitory education training programme has been initiated among tribal youth and women. About 500 tribal youth have been trained, so far, on a variety of subjects related to agriculture, ecological protection, nutrition and health. Groups of tribal women have participated in several training and participatory exercises, enabling them to participate in the revival of various traditional agroecological, health, and nutritional practices. Documentation, experimentation, and the revival of traditional tribal practices and networks has proved to be a practical and feasible development model. It is a good strategy to link the past - worldviews, indigenous knowledge and institutions - with the present in the quest for sustainable development options for the tribal communities.

Women of the tribal population in Orissa, India, identify the different weeds of their paddy fields to determine and test their use for food, fodder, medicine and soil improvement.

Three field examples of endogenous development

From hunting to ecological protection. The growing pressure on the forests in the Eastern Ghats has severely affected the living standards of the tribal peoples. The capacity of the ecosystem to replenish itself has been affected and tribal traditions are undergoing a process of degeneration. Hunting is one of these traditions. To address this issue, IDEA has considered hunting in its bio-cultural context and, together with the traditional leaders, found a way to modify hunting and turn it into a festival for ecological protection.

Tribal peoples believe that their ancestors originated from nature. Each clan, therefore, is the direct descendent of a bird, an animal or a tree. This totem is a supernatural power that protects them. Thus, in each community, people identify themselves as belonging to clans such as the Barking Deer, Peacock and Jungle fowl. Each clan has a strong affinity for the particular species they have adopted. There are many different totemic clans in each community. They will never harm this animal or plant and will protect it as much as possible. This cultural practice was found to be an important starting point for IDEA for peoples-based biodiversity conservation. IDEA found that a similar festival is being celebrated by different tribals in India and elsewhere under different names.

A hunting ceremony transformed

The tribals traditionally conduct a festival called *Itukala Panduga*, which includes a ceremonial hunt. In the past, this festival included an informal natural resource survey during the ceremonial hunting. During this exercise communities would take stock of the surrounding natural resources to make their future plans under the guidance of the traditional village institutions. Whilst this informal survey was being carried out, the people would eat what the hunters had caught. However, due to several reasons, the major significance and objective of this festival was lost, and the image that prevailed was one of destroying forest resources and indiscriminate killing of wild animals during the ceremonial hunting time.

In the early 1990s IDEA had started an eco-development project, and promoted tribal Environmental Protection and Development Groups (EPDG) in these villages. During a series of meetings the tribal elders expressed their concern about the changing environment and ecology in the area, as well as their insecurity about the attitude of younger generations towards mother nature. These discussions led to the development of a dialogue between the younger generations and traditional institutional functionaries in the villages, which resulted in a collective decision to revive and re-transform the Chaitra Parob concept for the conservation of natural resources. Courses were organised to exchange views on the traditional environmental protection system. The practice of ceremonial hunting was then completely stopped and transformed into an exercise for conducting a natural resource survey, which would pass resolutions related to natural resource conservation. This exercise was initiated in 40 villages in 1998, and has since then spread to some 450 villages.

During the Itukala Panduga festival, the villagers divide themselves into four groups based on age, sex and vocation and spend two to three days in the natural resource survey. Children of 10-15 years old take stock of the fruit bearing trees, birds' calls and animal footprints. The intention of this exercise is to prepare them for the complex environmental issues they are likely to meet in the future. Youth in the age group of 16-35 survey tree species, grasses, wild life, water sources and wastelands. Adults above the age of 36 survey the pattern of shifting cultivation and various trees of fruit, economic and timber value. The fourth group consisting of traditional leaders surveys the medicinal plants and other ingredients for their practices. The findings of each group are discussed and recorded systematically.

On the third day, all groups assemble in the village and perform a ritual to Goddess Sanku Devatha. Each group presents their findings. Together, they analyse the status and identify various floral and faunal species that are disappearing. They further analyse the reasons and factors responsible for this disappearance and decide on a course of action to conserve these species. This exercise of a people's survey is better than the modern surveys. It assesses the exact strength of natural resources, the state of biosphere and tribal knowledge regarding the natural resources.

Revival of Adivasi Dharbar

Adivasi Dharbar, or the tribal eco-cultural meeting, is another ancient practice revived by IDEA to address contemporary issues related to natural resources. Traditionally, group leaders and active members from hundreds of villages would come together to share their experiences. Now, the leaders discuss the outcome of the observation and protection activities taking place in their villages during the festival of Itukala Panduga. They discuss the strategies used to stop wildlife and ecological deterioration. They also discuss the experiences of the previous year in improving their ecology and punishing those who disobey the code of behaviour. The Adivasi Dharbar meeting helps the villagers to understand the ecological situation on a regional scale.

To enforce the rules determined during the Adivasi Dharbar, the communities have set up a coordinating committee that closely interacts with the traditional village heads and clan heads. Violations of the Adivasi Dharbar resolutions are viewed seriously. IDEA's trainings, the totemic concepts, the festivals, traditional songs and the experience of the elders all play a role in implementing these resolutions successfully. As a result of these resolutions, families are dissuaded from practising shifting cultivation. This has prevented approximately 250,000 acres of forestland from being reduced to barren patches. The existing cultivated patches are being rehabilitated with sustainable agriculture and agroforestry using local species. Some 50 floral and faunal species are being protected through clan totemic concepts.

The Naik-Gotna network. In 1998 the co-ordination between the tribal leaders and IDEA resulted in the establishment of the Naik Gotna network, the 'Network of Tribal Leaders'. The major objective of the network is to form a strong group of tribal leaders to support the endogenous development process of their communities. Though the starting point of IDEA's activities in the Eastern Ghats has been natural resources management, it has also facilitated the traditional leaders in the Naik Gotna to address many other aspects such as agricultural innovations, herbal medicine, and wild leafy vegetables for improved nutrition. These practices are being experimented with in the communities; the results are documented by IDEA together with the Naik Gotna members, and exchanged during meetings and training sessions. In order to support endogenous development of the tribal communities and prevent further destruction of local natural resources, the tribal leaders aim for integration of their local knowledge, practices and structures with modern tribal development institutions and knowledge systems. With the help of IDEA, the Naik Gotna has initiated several activities, ranging from exchange meetings to training sessions, bio-cultural expeditions, and workshops. This has resulted in increased communication between the different tribes and communities in the area.

Indigenous Knowledge Fair

In September 2001, the Naik Gotna organised its first four-day indigenous knowledge fair (mela) at IDEA's indigenous knowledge resource conservation centre. Hundreds of representatives of all ages and from different tribal communities gathered at the fair. The major objective of this event was to provide a platform for the tribal communities to exchange and demonstrate their knowledge, practices and experiments. A wide range of practices related to agriculture and soil conservation, natural resources, traditional medicine for humans and animals, as well as folklore, bio-cultural practices and development-related rituals, were exhibited. Far from giving the feel of a museum, this activity showed the importance of letting these practices remain in the hands of the people themselves. By sharing the results of their experiments with representatives of other tribal communities during the numerous workshops, the experiences were analysed and deepened. In this way the IK mela provided another opportunity for in situ conservation of indigenous

The Indigenous Knowledge Fair presided by Naik Gotna traditional leaders and attended by Compas members from different countries.

practices. The event created a platform for inter-cultural dialogue and strengthened the networking between different tribal communities. Moreover, it provided an opportunity to demonstrate the relevance of tribal indigenous knowledge to local policy makers, universities and administrators.

The increasing strength of the Naik Gotna has not gone unnoticed. The traditional leaders themselves experience great satisfaction. Gollori Sadu, one of the leaders of the Naik Gotna network explains: *"We started 3 or 4 years ago; it was our own idea based on our own experiences. Now we are very big, some 5,000 traditional leaders from 400 villages! Now we are here from many communities in Andhra Pradesh and Orissa, see how far it has spread.......... The IK Mela is the best thing we have done so far. Look how many of us have come! Here we can show what we know and who we are in regards to our agriculture, our medical practices, food practices, and our rituals and beliefs. See how the representatives of the government have come, and how they are impressed with what they have seen and heard. The government has never been able to fully stop the problems with the environment. Now they are impressed with what they hear from us and how we are integrating our indigenous knowledge, worldviews and institutions with modern knowledge systems for meaningful tribal development."*

The Naik Gotna, as a new organisation of tribal traditional leaders, cannot lean on similar experiences from the past. The organisation will have to face major challenges in a fast changing world, as its pride and successes grow. Efforts are being made to support the forum to work in the direction of strengthening the tribal cultural identity, while co-ordinating with modern knowledge systems and institutions.

Tribal women in endogenous development. Tribal women possess a vast knowledge on agro-ecological and health practices. Several training programmes on tribal women's indigenous knowledge and worldviews have been conducted by young tribal women and women farmers. With the support of IDEA, groups of tribal women have focussed their attention on the documentation and revival of indigenous agro-ecological and health practices. They have done several revival experimentations and validation studies on various ceremonies: first eating ceremonies, which ensure that only ripe products are harvested, seed and soil testing ceremonies, and batbiba - a health related ceremony. About 800 women have been supported for conducting experimentation on different agro-ecological practices.

Groups of women have started documenting and classifying weeds into various subgroups: edible, medicinal, green manure and fodder weeds, and have conducted more than 100 village activities to train other women in the practices of weed management. So far, this has resulted in the increase of crop production by 30%-35% in about 200 villages. The women farmers, moreover, have identified about 243 wild vegetables and edible tubers, berries and nuts, and started a unit by the name KOILARI (the wild leafy vegetables research unit) to conduct research and experimentation on this subject. They have brought out posters, calendars and stickers on these subjects and distributed them. As a result, the nutritional status of the population has improved. Women's groups have also successfully documented, analysed, re-constructed and revived some of the eco-agricultural songs, dance and music such as *Sankidi, Oli, Dhimsa, Pathorthola, Ninjani, Baag dhimsa*.

IDEA has identified about 300 *gurumayies*, medical women or shamans, and *sutranis*, or traditional birth attendants, who possess knowledge on traditional reproductive and magical religious herbal practices for gynaecological diseases, childcare and nutrition. Several re-orientation trainings have been provided to enhance their knowledge systems with the integration of modern knowledge systems, such as hygiene, use of aspirin as painkillers and bandaging.

Analysis of results for endogenous development

Box 4g indicates that the model of endogenous development could effectively be applied in the tribal areas. Respect for the culture and collaboration with local experts and spiritual leaders has led to enthusiasm of the people, of both sexes and all ages, to test and improve traditional practices. As these people are highly dependent on the local resources, it was not difficult to make a joint assessment of the risks involved in traditional land management systems. By building on the traditional leadership and belief systems, such as totem concepts, it was possible to transform hunting into ecological protection. Ethnoveterinary practices could be improved by involving the traditional experts in a network to exchange experiences. Women were interested in taking part in several activities to test and improve nutrition and agriculture. This is evident from the massive participation of women in activities such as the IK mela organised by the Naik Gotna network.

Marketing of organic products and eco-tourism mark a beginning to improve income, though these activities need more attention. A major factor contributing to the effectiveness of IDEA's work has been the exchange of experiences between development staff and rural people, and the eagerness to test and improve adaptations to the existing system in co-operation with traditional experts and spiritual leaders. The extension and training activities involve many local experts, which is a good way of ensuring local ownership and capacity building, but also implies problems with continuity of available field staff. It is our experience that field staff well trained in participatory methodologies and cosmovisions often move to higher-paid jobs with government institutions. Networking with government agencies, other NGOs and Compas partners has been important in the sensitive activity of working with tribal people in India.

Discussion and future plans

Over the past 10 years, IDEA has achieved notable results. At the same time, a rapid transition and erosion of tribal indigenous knowledge systems and their institutions, due to acculturation and modernisation, is taking place. Hence, there is a need to expand the present endogenous development programmes in other selected areas and communities, to revive and enhance the endogenous development of tribal communities along sustainable lines. Moreover, there is a need to further strengthen the network of traditional leaders to enhance their cross-cultural dialogues and lobbying, as well as their interaction with local research organisations, universities, agriculture and forest departments, and NGOs.

The present natural resource management policy of the state does address the needs of the tribal communities in the North Eastern Ghats in an insufficient way. Tribal natural resource management practices and regulations, such as the clan regulatory mecha-

Box 4g   Results of endogenous development of activities supported by IDEA

Endogenous development activity	Field activity implemented	Results Qualitative	Results Quantitative
Building on local iniatiatives to use resources	Ethno-veterinary practices	Traditional veterinary practices revived and integrated with modern practices.	About 750 tribal ethno-veterinarians joined network.
	Bio-pesticides	Indigenous knowledge revived, on-farm experimentation.	Cultivation costs reduced four times
Building on local needs	Transformation of traditions to eco-friendly practices.	The ceremonial hunting transformed into natural resource study and conservation exercise.	76 Totemic clan concepts revived and totem species are being protected
Improving local knowledge and practices	Indigenous poultry breeds	Women's economy improved	32 traditional breeds conserved
	Traditional weed management	Weed management practices revived	Food production increased by 33%
	Traditional nutritional management	Health and nutritional status improved	243 wild leafy vegetables etc. are conserved and revived.
	Programmes for women	Women participation in indigenous knowledge revival increased	Agro-eco-cultural and health practices
Local control of development options	Strengthening traditional leaders.	Clan regulatory mechanisms for shifting cultivation revived	5,000 Traditional institutional functionaries joined network.
	Tribal identity	Tribal cultural identity revived and enhanced.	The symbols Gonda & Chakras classified and relevant symbols revived.
Identification of development niches	Organic markets	Farmers get fair prices for their eco-friendly products.	Women groups produce more eco-friendly products
	Eco-tourism	Positive to show cultural identity	Income generation.
Selective use of external resources	Modern health practices combined with local practices	Positive attitudes to integrate local health practices with modern practices	Traditional medical men and women actively integrating modern practices.
Retention of benefits in the local area	Local economy strengthened	Organic products and ecotourism	Women's income improved
Exchange and learning between local cultures	Exchange fair for seed and ethno-veterinary medicines.	Open to exchange their knowledge provided it is acknowledged properly.	Exchanged seeds and medicinal plants with Compas partners and other tribal communities.
Networking and strategic partnerships	Lobbying with NGOs, forest department, tribal development agencies and agriculture and health departments	Interactions with forest department on nature resource management.Interaction with tribal development agencies improved and knowledges are being integrated	Traditional seeds, medicinal plants and agro-ecological experiments exchanged with government agencies and conducted combined trainings
Understanding systems of knowing and learning	Interactions with Universities	Positive attitude to develop scientific theories of tribal worldviews and indigenous knowledge.	Interacted with local universities on theory building, action research methodology and training.
	Tribal cosmovision belief documentation and classification	Significances of festivals and ceremonies analysed and being understood	Classified the worldview with diagrammatic representations

nisms to control deforestation, the totemic clan concepts, and the environment related festivals, are not recognised as means for sustainable development. The government's 'integrated tribal development programmes', therefore, need to integrate the indigenous knowledge, worldview and institutions into a more meaningful and sustainable tribal endogenous development programme. The same is true for the case of agriculture and health.

Tribal indigenous knowledge systems and related practices with a significance for development need to be further highlighted and projected with proper theory building exercises at various micro and macro levels. Moreover, youth organisations need to be strengthened further with the concept of endogenous development in the region. There is also a need to further develop dialogues, lobbying and networking on cross cultural exchanges of experiences and knowledge systems, between IDEA and other NGOs, research organisations, policy makers, and funding communities. IDEA's present educational material such as newsletters, brochures, pamphlets, posters and video films, are catering to the needs of target communities, NGOs and other research organisations at various levels. Hence, we need to further develop this activity.

The sustainability of endogenous development depends on its integration with modern development components. Many of the NGOs, research organisations, research scholars and government development agency personnel need to know more about tribal indigenous knowledge systems, world views in relation to sustainable development. Hence, we need to encourage them by conducting workshops, seminars, trainings and certificate courses and offering research scholarships. All these exercises require economic inputs, professionalism and stability of field staff, and strong commitment.

Cultures and development. Through globalisation, modern media have reached many homes, even in the remotest villages, enabling information sharing and networking. Globalisation has also shed light on the differences between the rich and poor economies. However, most rural people throughout the world still depend on their traditions, local knowledge and resources for their livelihood.

A rural woman in Zhongdian, South China, receives visitors during a field visit of the Congress on Cultures and Biodiversity in Yunnan (July 2000). She is churning yak milk, as her ancestors have done for centuries, while being exposed to the outside world through modern media.

Endogenous development builds on locally available resources: human, natural, produced, social, economical and cultural. Compas supports rural people in their search for complementarity between different sources of knowledge.

Left In order to find their contemporary relevance and potential for dissemination, indigenous practices are tested in field experiments. Tribals in Orissa, India, supported by IDEA, experiment with organic fertilisers.

Below Spirit medium in Iganga, Uganda, explains how local flora and fauna influence healing and farming during a meeting of African organisations involved in endogenous development in May 2000.

Intricate forms of solidarity are central in the strategies of the indigenous peoples in Bolivia. At many fairs products are exchanged without the involvement of cash. AGRUCO supports the annual fair of Sipe-Sipe, where farmers from the higlands and the valleys exchange their products and celebrate their kinship.

Indian traditional cultures centre around 'Universal Consciousness'. Though many traditions are still alive today, a revitalisation programme is required to avert the ongoing process of erosion of these cultures and the related knowledge.

Right In Sri Lanka a traditional pest control ritual, involving mantras and chanted water, is revived and tested by ECO. Universities are engaged in the research process.

Below Pulse diagnosis is an important tool in the Indian health traditions, which takes years to master. FRLHT documents, assesses and promotes effective local health practices to avoid their further erosion.

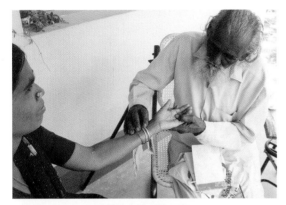

The *Sankranthi* ritual is celebrated by tribals in Lingapatna village in southern India, and symbolises victory over difficulties. Jumping over the fire brings to mind the story of a cow rescued from the clutches of a tiger (Green Foundation).

The **African belief system** is complex and highly diverse, with its own concepts of time, matter, life, and death. Ancestral support is crucial, and the advice of ancestors is sought in all aspects of life through dreams, sacrifices and spiritual specialists.

The *Tendana*, or earth priest, during a village harvest festival in Bongo, northern Ghana. CECIK has concluded that it is possible to identify real development needs only when a relationship of confidence has been built up between the community and the field workers, which may imply the consultation of ancestral spirits.

Today, many rural people in **Latin America** are combining their faith in ancient knowledge and their aspirations to become 'modern people'. Endogenous development has to take both aspects into account, as intimate parts of their existence.

Right A child is blessed during a ceremony on the Tojil sacred hill during a workshop on endogenous development in Guatemala, organised by Oxlajuj Ajpop.

Below A child suffering from a cold is rubbed with leaves of a medicinal plant in Chorojo, Bolivia. Later on the child will be wrapped in warm cloths with the rest of the leaves. Half of the wild plants in the area have medicinal properties.

Exchange of ideas and seeds between Colombian and Bolivian farmers during the Compas regional workshop in Cochabamba, hosted by AGRUCO, February 2001.

Endogenous development in **Europe** focuses on regional diversity. Farmers' initiatives include organic farming, regional products and environmental co-operatives. Benefits include environmental improvements, increased social cohesion and cost reduction..

Left A biodynamic farmer in the Netherlands who participates in farmers' groups to explore the value of 'eco-therapy' for healthy crop growth.

Below University professors and Compas members discuss the traditonal practice of managing hedges in east Fryslân, the Netherlands. Farmers negotiate with the State about compensation for their nature management.

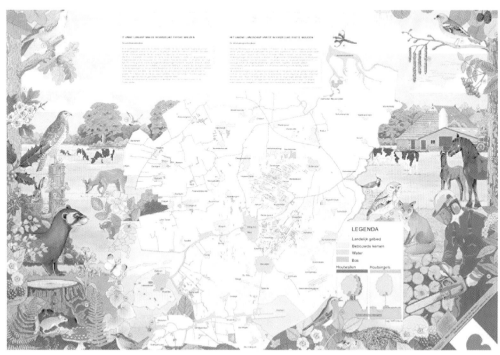

The management of hedges and related biodiversity by the farmers in Fryslân, the Netherlands, is explained to tourists by means of large information panels located in various places in the area.

The **results** of the first phase of the Compas programme can be summarised as 'in situ conservation and development of local knowledge'. Endogenous development is made tangible in the practical results gained by the communities and organisations involved.

Right Compas members from three continents visit the CIKS farm in India to observe the experiments with traditional rice varieties and compare it to their own experimental methodology.

Below Building on rural people's worldviews: village-based learning and dialogue in northern Ghana is the basis for innovative development initiatives, improved nutrition and incomes.

School children in southern India exhibit earheads of different seed varieties from their demo plots. Green Foundation also promotes school competitions, for which children collect information on local flora and fauna, agricultural practices, folk tales, indigenous medicine and recipes, as well as agricultural rituals.

A **co-evolution of cultures** implies various aspects, such as the in situ development of local knowledge, the ability to share the knowledge generated, an intercultural dialogue based on mutual respect, as well as a diversity of sciences.

Right Tribals in Orissa, India, have elaborated a poster to share their cultural heritage with other local communities within the Compas network.

Below The Tanzanian Maasai representative (on the left) hands over the resolutions of the Pan-African workshop on endogenous development, organised by AZTREC, to the Zimbabwean Minister for Environment.

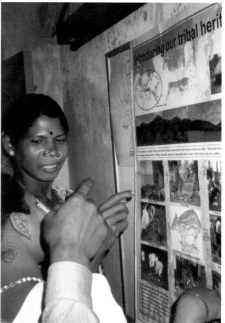

Buddhists have assisted local farmers and fishermen in their struggle against the Pak Moon Dam in Thailand which threatens to shatter the local lifestyle. The strengthened interaction between spirituality and activisim is based on the foundations of organic agriculture and the concept of 'Culture of Peace'.

5. KNOWLEDGE AND BELIEF SYSTEMS IN SUB-SAHARAN AFRICA

Bertus Haverkort, David Millar and Cosmas Gonese
Compas, the Netherlands, CECIK, Ghana and AZTREC, Zimbabwe

This chapter explores the indigenous knowledge, practices and belief systems in sub-Saharan Africa, with special reference to agriculture. Despite obvious differences between the regions and ethnic groups on this vast continent, one can identify common elements in traditional cosmovisions of its peoples: their religions, worldviews, relationships to land and nature, their notion of time, respect for elders and ancestors, leadership, and ethnic organisations. In contemporary Africa, traditional knowledge and values still are an important driving force in peoples' decisions making, which can be seen as a point of articulation for development activities.

The authors of this chapter have worked many years in community based development work in different parts of Africa. As is the case with many professionals, we started our activities with programmes to increase agricultural production. Gradually, our attention was drawn to environmental issues and the use of local knowledge and resources, opening our eyes to the relevance of indigenous knowledge. We learned that indigenous knowledge is more than a compilation of traditional practices, and started to explore the cultural dimension of it. We soon found that in our quest to gain a better understanding about these aspects, our dialogues with traditional leaders and communities were enriched, and the effect of our work with them was enhanced beyond compare.

Africa's past and present

The first anatomically modern human emerged in the southern part of Africa. The first African people hunted a wide range of animals, and learned the use of fire to control vegetation. During the last glacial period Africa was not covered with ice, but, as much of the earth's water reserve was frozen, it endured drought. Evidence exists that around 9,000 years ago, sorghum, millet, rice, yam, oil palm, as well as cattle were domesticated, while barley was introduced from western Asia. The first domestication took place in the territory between the Sahara and the equator. The spread of farming and herding south of the equator was a long and gradual process, impeded by the dense forests and parasites, especially the tse-tse fly.

The introduction of iron tools made way for the development of sophisticated settlements in West Africa and the construction of monumental centres such as Great Zimbabwe. Bantu speaking people moved from west Africa to east and southern Africa, claiming more fertile regions and integrating or displacing earlier occupants. From the 8th century onwards Arab trading penetrated sub-Saharan Africa, bringing oil, lamps, pottery and cowry shells in exchange for ivory, ebony, gold, as well as slaves. Islam spread and impressive mosques were built in Djenné and Timbuktu (Mali). Several kingdoms with important cultures emerged: Ghana, Benin and Akan. The Portuguese were the first

Europeans who got involved in (slave) trade, bringing Christianity with them. In the 19th century the Portuguese lost their monopoly and the British, French, Belgians and Germans colonised and christianised the continent, except Ethiopia. These colonies lasted till around the second part of the 20th century, when the independent nation states were formed.

Sub-saharan Africa today. It is obvious that there are many different cultures, and many differences within cultures in sub-Saharan Africa. Historic developments, demographic and ecological differences, as well as economic opportunities, colonial impact and religious missionary activities, to mention but a few factors, have resulted in a diversity of lifestyles, professional practices, values, religions and knowledge systems. Africa has a diversity of ecosystems, ranging from extensive mountain areas, savannah and dry land areas, to lowlands, coastal plains and tropical forests. Nomadic peoples often compete for land and water resources with sedentary peoples. The urban population is increasing and a considerable number of large cities exist. Traditional religions have common elements, but there is also a great variation in rituals, traditional institutions and leadership structures. They are often combined with, or have been replaced by Christianity or Islam. As a result, a great number of different religious denominations can be observed.

Yet, sub-Saharan Africa has a lot in common, as its peoples have known a great number of migrations across the continent. Although there are more than a thousand ethnic groups, many of them have similar origins or historic relationships. The population has a predominantly rural background, and even today agriculture remains to be the main occupation. Many African soils are aged and tend to be quite poor, which, combined with a harsh climate, makes agriculture a difficult and low productive activity.

The colonial past has had a strong impact on the indigenous cultures and peoples, limiting their capacity to solve their own problems and develop technologies and skills that serve their own needs. Colonisation left the continent with a low level of literacy, few educated people, and with poor physical and institutional infrastructure. The most productive agricultural lands, forestry and mineral resources have been, and often still are, exploited by entrepreneurs with a colonial background. Most of the present nations, those that exist less than 50 years, still reflect major aspects of the colonial system rather than the precolonial indigenous systems of governance. The same holds for the legal system and the education system. The religions of the colonisers and missionaries over the past centuries, though they introduced alien concepts and rituals, have not been able to suppress the value attached to ancestors, funerals, and a host of other traditional practices. Most health practices in rural Africa today are based on traditional healers and knowledge, using a wide range of herbs and rituals.

Africa is changing fast and there exists a mix of dominantly traditional, dominantly modern and more hybrid subcultures. Some aspects of indigenous knowledge are expressed openly, whilst other aspects are secretive and hidden from outsiders. This chapter describes the elements of the past, which still play an important role in the values and decision-making processes of African rural peoples, and somehow also in the modernised African mind. Obviously, the degree and relevance vary per location, ethnic group and person. Many studies about African worldviews and indigenous knowledge either stress the positive aspects, or strive to show the limitations and negative aspects. The first written anthropological studies on Africa often included biases and Eurocentric prejudices, which, in part, have been corrected later. Romanticising indigenous knowledge, however, is not a good basis for endogenous development either. Phenomena such as taboos against planting trees, gross inequalities between men and women, land use practices that have detrimental ecological effects, and misuse of their position and knowledge by local leaders, are aspects which need to be observed and brought into the intercultural dialogue.

African technical knowledge and practices

Most of the attention of development professionals to indigenous knowledge has a technical focus. Here, we give a brief summary of the literature on African indigenous technical knowledge divided into three sub themes: soil and water management, crops and trees, and animal production.

Soil and water management. One of the common characteristics of the sub-Saharan African cultures is the perception that the earth is associated with the concept of the mother, or womb. It is often considered to be a deity, the property of the Gods, and the founders of a clan or tribe who were the first settlers in the area. Traditional functionaries, such as the earth priests, exercise spiritual control over the land. A wealth of information exists about agricultural traditional knowledge, especially on soil classification and practices of soil and water management. Mulching, use of water pockets in plant holes, soil and water conservation, traditional erosion control, and irrigation are all examples of effective traditional practices.

Experiences on how traditional African soil and water conservation concepts can be matched with participatory approaches are accumulating. They are resulting in increased understanding of farmer livelihoods, and more and more programmes today put farmers in the centre of their activities [Reij and Waters-Bayer, 2001]. However, many of these programmes hardly address the African worldviews, beliefs systems and the traditional systems of land tenure on which these practices are based. In the development literature reviewed for this chapter, a general lack of information about the spiritual dimension of soil and water has been observed. Traditional functionaries, such as the earth priests, the spirit media and rainmakers, who are traditionally consulted for issues related to land and water management by rural people, are hardly involved in rural development projects. In practice, the divide between anthropologists and development workers with a technical focus is quite deep.

Crops and trees. The literature on traditional African management of crops and trees reveals that the subjects most frequently dealt with are sacred groves, agro-forestry, plant breeding, and crop cultivation. Again, the literature gives more information about the biophysical aspects of traditional use of trees and crops, than about the cultural and spiritual dimensions, with exception of the studies on sacred groves. Several studies stress the importance of sacred groves in relation to the efforts of the rural people to appease the spirits related to rainmaking, good crops or health. Traditional spiritual leaders play an important role in the management of these important patches of high biodiversity. Several authors also indicate [Fairhead, 1993; Millar, 1999] that sacred groves can be an important starting point for development and rehabilitation of savannah areas, forests and wetlands.

Indigenous agro-forestry is widespread and several systems are described in literature. Farmers know the qualities of trees, what they can be used for, and the possibilities and limitations of combining trees with crops. Some tree species have a spiritual significance, which is reflected in taboos and rituals associated with them. Many studies on the traditional cultivation practices of crops, including traditional food crops and wild plants, can be found.

Livestock keeping. Livestock systems in Africa are extremely complex. In a broad sense we can distinguish between two major livestock systems, which are the extremes of a continuum: livestock systems associated with settled farmers and pastoral husbandry systems. The role of animals in the spiritual life of African rural people is quite unique and has been the subject of several studies. Literature describes beliefs and practices related to livestock on aspects like feeding, breeding, animal health, small stock and wild animals.

Literature also shows the immense changes that African livestock productions systems are undergoing currently, especially the pastoral systems, due to modernisation, population growth and government policies. It is necessary to look at indigenous knowledge related to livestock in the context of the culture of the people involved. In many ethno-veterinary and animal husbandry studies, this aspect has been overlooked, focusing mainly on the use of medicinal plants for curing diseases. There is much potential in activities that combine ethno-veterinary aspects with village based animal health care. There is an imbalance in the extent to which the different animal species are studied, and the use and importance of the species in rural peoples' lives. For example, most literature on fowl deals with chicken, though many families use a combination of species including guinea fowls, ducks, turkeys and pigeons.

The role of women related to livestock is subject to many changes. In some cases they become more involved in livestock, in others less; the effect on their social position and status also shows a wide variation. In the last decades there has been a decline in 'conventional' livestock projects, due to disappointing results, especially the range development projects, and the projects based on the import of exogenous breeds. Meanwhile, the number of participatory projects, for example on ethno-veterinary medicine and village-based animal health care, has increased. There is a sharp decline in the number of traditional breeds in Africa, which are adapted to the local culture, ecological circumstances and social structures. It is necessary to look at these breeds, taking into account not only the conventional productive role of livestock (like meat, milk and traction) but also the importance of manure, the role of livestock as a factor in risk-management, transport and in social and cultural life.

Indigenous knowledge and development. During the colonial period and after, the main models of formal agricultural development and health care efforts have been based on the introduction of western technologies, not to complement, but to substitute traditional practices. Emeagwali [1997] states that one of the major effects of colonialism was the subordination of science and education to the logic of the colonial production systems and class structures. Science and development ceased to emanate from the womb of African civilisation, indigenous problem solving and experimentation. The colonial system was exploitative, geared towards export of a surplus from the continent. Also after independence, the focus of research, education, extension and services to agriculture and health professionals continued on the basis of knowledge transfer from the west to Africa. In recent decades, the efforts to introduce the green revolution, cash crops and to train farmers to become entrepreneurs have not resulted in the expected outcome. This is mainly due to the fact that they were not rooted in African knowledge systems, and did not take into account the specific ecological and socio-economic conditions.

In sub-Saharan Africa, various blends between completely western and completely traditional practices exist. This is more true for health than for agriculture. The World Health Organisation (WHO) estimates that up to 80% of the people in Africa use traditional medicine as a major source of health care. People go for modern health services or high-input agricultural technologies when they can afford it. Most people opt for combining both systems, however, or limit themselves to the traditional practices.

African worldviews and belief systems

Traditional sub-Saharan African ways of thinking and reasoning differ in many respects from the dominant international approach. Despite generations of western influence, the decisions about agriculture, health and nature management are still heavily based on the concepts of African traditions. Nowadays, thinking amongst Africans ranges from traditional to modern, but in many cases both systems of thinking can be observed parallel to each other. Traditional worldviews and traditional leaders play an important role.

Religions. According to Reverend Mbiti [1969], Kenyan professor in comparative religion, existence for Africans is a religious phenomenon; man is a deeply religious being living in a religious universe. Mbiti points out five categories that are consistently mentioned in the various African religious practices: God as the ultimate explanation of the genesis and sustenance of man and all things; spirits, made up of superhuman beings and spirits of ancestors; man, including human beings alive and those not yet born; animals and plants or the remainders of biological life; and phenomena and objects without biological life.

In addition to these five categories, a vital force, power or energy permeates the whole universe. For the Africans, every plant, animal and natural phenomenon is a carrier of the divine. God is the source and the ultimate controller of these vital forces, and the spirits have access to some of them. Selected human beings, such as medicine men, witches, priests and rainmakers, have the knowledge and ability to tap, manipulate and use these forces, Some use it for the good and others for the ill of their communities. In order to appease the gods, people have to perform rituals and make sacrifices. There are numerous rituals such as those for the fertility of humans, crops and animals; for birth, initiation, marriage and death; for rainmaking, planting and harvesting [Mbiti, 1969].

Cosmovisions. Religious and philosophical concepts have their place within traditional worldviews. Cosmovision, to a large extent, dictates the way land, water, plants and animals are to be used, how decisions are taken, problems are solved, experimentation takes place and how rural people organise themselves [Haverkort and Hiemstra, 1999].

Obviously Christianity, Islam and western education have influenced the cosmovision of the Africans especially those with formal education.

For the Shona, the human world, the natural world and the spiritual world are linked. The natural world provides the habitat for the spirits and sends messages from the spiritual world to the human world. The spiritual world provides guidance, punishment and blessing to the human world. People therefore have to relate to both the natural and the spiritual world.

Box 5a   Shona cosmovision in Zimbabwe

Also for the traditional people in northern Ghana the spiritual world (Gods, spirits, ancestors), the human world (including spiritual and political leaders), and the natural world (sacred groves, ritual crops and animals, food items and cash crops) are interrelated. Often a hierarchy between divine beings, spiritual beings, men and women, and natural forces is indicated (see box 5b). These cosmovisions give rise to several rituals in which elders, priests, soothsayers and spiritual leaders play a prominent role.

From these examples of traditional cosmovisions in two countries as far apart as Ghana and Zimbabwe, it becomes clear that in the general traditional African worldview, land, water, animals and plants are not just a production factor with economic significance. They have their place within the sanctity of nature. Moreover, certain places have a special spiritual significance and are used as locations for rituals and sacrifices, for example

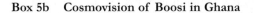

Box 5b   Cosmovision of Boosi in Ghana

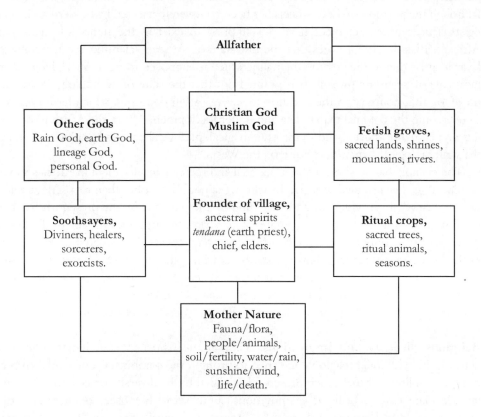

sacred groves, shrines, mountains and rivers [Millar, 1999; Gonese, 1999]. Fig trees and baobabs are often treated as sacred trees. The sun, moon and stars feature in myths and beliefs. Certain animal species have a spiritual significance too. Cattle, sheep, goats and chicken are often used for sacrifices and other religious purposes. Snakes, lizards, chameleons and certain birds are considered to be messengers of the spiritual world.

Eurocentric bias. The way Africans think and reason has been the subject of several studies. The first studies on this subject were carried out by anthropologists in the colonial period and reflect the Eurocentric bias characteristic of that era. These reflections often made distinctions in terms such as savage and civilised, prelogic and logic, oral and written, magic and scientific, and perception and conception. The anthropologist Levy-Bruhl [1910], for example, concluded that African reasoning was essentially 'prelogic'. *"They do not have a logical character in the western sense. The law of non-contradiction and reasoning about applicability of certain general principles, that form part and parcel of western philosophy since Aristotle, is not adhered to. Yet, they may see things of which we are unconscious."*

Levi-Strauss [1966] concluded that scientific thought is based on concepts, while mythical thought is based on perceptions. Scientific and mythical thought is not unique to any given culture, and can therefore not exclusively be attributed to western or African cultures. Although the position of Levi Strauss has been completely rejected by modern anthropologists, Eurocentric prejudices have not stopped to exist in the minds of many non-Africans. Biakolo [1998] notes that the low state of African scientific and technological knowledge is due to the African mentality, which is supposed to be mystical, illogical and incapable of scientific pursuit. It is pointed out that the state of technology in Africa is proof of this, contrary to the situation in several Asian countries, which have been able to overcome the colonial experience and underdevelopment. Thus, for Africa to develop it is argued that it must abandon the oral, magical, prelogical past and gradually assimilate the written, logical, scientific culture of the West.

The fashionable pessimism about material and societal development in Africa seems to be related to the sustained western doctrine of superiority, rather than to a serious reflection of history. It provides no understanding of the past nor of the present. It has been used in great measure to colonise and exploit Africa, but provides no key to the knowledge about this continent. On the contrary, it merely repeats the outdated myth of Africa as the 'white man's burden'. This frustration is widely felt in Africa. During a workshop on African knowledge systems, one participant stated: *"They have taken our land, our mineral resources and forests, our language, our laws and jurisdiction, our religions and our system of governance and leadership. And then they blame us that we do not develop in accordance with their criteria!"*

Religious diversity and innovations. Though the Christian church has often condemned the traditional religions, and tried to prohibit the combination of Christian practices and traditional rituals, their presence has added to the diversity of cosmovision practices. In many cases a duality in cosmovisions can therefore be observed: the same people or person observe both western and African visions. According to van Beek and Blakeley [1994], there is great variability and flexibility in the different African religions. Divination techniques move widely across the borders, cults spread from region to region, magical techniques are borrowed. Even at the local village level, this results in multiple options for the individual, which co-exist without conflict. The oral transmission and the non-dogmatic character of indigenous religions enhance this plurality and the absence of conflicts. This is also in line with the idea that religion is not an abstract theoretical reflection on beliefs, but one that implies action. Religion means performing or doing something: consulting a diviner, offering a sacrifice, praying, talking about a problem, enthroning a chief, falling into a trance, making magic and dancing at a funeral. Indigenous African religions often also are a means to an end. They aim at health, fertility, rain, protection, and harmony in relations. Religion is thus part of a survival strategy and serves practical ends, immediate or remote, social or individual.

Time concept

Past, present and future. According to Mbiti [1969], the linear concept of time in western thought, with an indefinite past, a present and an infinite future, is practically unknown in African traditional thinking. For Africans, time has two dimensions: a long past and a present. In the African languages, terms and verbs that refer to the future are practically absent because events that lie in it have not taken place and cannot therefore constitute time. At best they are in potential time, not actual time. Time moves from the present to the past. Events move from the present into the past, the ocean of time in which everything becomes absorbed into a reality, that is neither after nor before.

Box 5c   An African (circular) concept of time

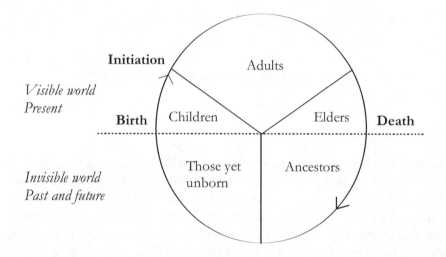

Mbiti's analysis has encountered considerable criticism. Opata [1998] explores the idea of future in the Igbo worldview. He concludes that at each critical point of existential action, the person must ensure that everything is well in the spiritual world related to the intended action. This is why at the beginning of the planting season, before a marriage, burials, initiations, child naming ceremonies, or title taking ceremonies, there is always much concern to learn whether the action may imply potential dangers, and if so, how these can be averted. According to Opata, prayers are petitional in nature, and are said in order to avert the fulfilment of these events lined up for one in future time.

Destiny. In this context, the African notion of a human being is important. Swanson [1980] studied the belief system of the Gourma in Burkina Faso, and found that in their cosmovision each person enters life with certain basic possessions, that qualify and define him or her as human. They are: the ancestral soul, the personal soul, the guiding spirit, the physical body, a God consciousness, and a destiny. The notion of destiny has great implications for development. This notion of destiny is in contrast to the western concept, in which the future can be influenced by special human efforts and nature can be controlled by human intervention.

In the Gourma cosmovision everything a person receives, good or bad, is part of destiny; success and failure in agriculture or health are interpreted as the result of one's personal destiny. Especially when a failure is encountered for the second or third time, it is interpreted as the result of metaphysical reasoning, and not from direct material causes. Swanson describes experiences of failure in rabbit keeping and tree planting programmes. The interpretation of the farmers was *"rabbits are not for me, they are not part of my destiny"*. A similar destiny is ascribed to land, when the failure in fruit tree planting was explained by *"my land did not like this particular tree"*. Van der Breemer [1984] found that the Aouan in Ivory Coast have a taboo on rice cultivation with the explanation: *"Our soil does not like rice"*.

Artistic expressions

Proverbs. Gyekye [1996] has compiled more than 150 proverbs and explained their meaning. These proverbs represent different values related to religion, immortality, survival, brotherhood, communal and individual values, morality, responsibility, marriage and family life, work ethic, chieftaincy, aesthetic values, knowledge and wisdom, human rights and ancestors. Gyekye argues that by listening to the proverbs, and trying to understand their deeper meaning, much can be learned about the values and motivation of the people that use them.

Colours and numbers. Colours and numbers have religious meanings in many traditional cosmovisions. A number of peoples have black and white as their sacred colour, and black and white animals are used for ritual sacrifice. Bartle [1983] describes the Akan cosmovision and mentions three colours: red the sign of danger, black the sign of power and white the sign of purity. Black clothes are worn at funerals, but contrary to its meaning in western societies, this colour does not indicate sadness. It is the recognition of the changes in life: death, reincarnation and ancestral power, stool power, history, tradition and memories. The colours red, white and black are frequently used in African sculptures, paintings and architecture. Tribes like the Abaluyia, Baganda, Watumbatu and Gofa only use white animals for their religious rites [Mbiti, 1969]. In northern Ghana the colours of the fowl determine their use in sacrifices [Millar, 1999].

Numbers can have a religious meaning too. As documented by Mbiti [1969] counting people and livestock is forbidden in many African societies, partly for fear that misfortune would befall those who are numbered, partly because people are not individuals but corporate members of a society that cannot be defined numerically. For the Nandi, the number 'four' seems to be sacred. The number 'six' is sacred to the Shona and Jie, who sacrifice six animals. The Akamba and Vugusu have taboos attached to number 'seven'. The number 'nine' is sacred for the Baganda and all their gifts, sacrifices and sacred vessels must number nine or its multiples.

African art. African art and artefacts such as masks, clothes, music, body painting, architecture and sculptures have often emerged in the function of religion, rites and rituals, and are undoubtedly expressions of African emotions and identity. These expressions of art have reached high levels of aesthetics and can be divided into different styles and techniques. During colonial times many masks and sculptures were taken to the capitals of the colonisers, and many of these pieces are now exhibited in prestigious museums. Internationally reputed artists like Picasso, Moore and Giacometti have found great inspiration in African sculptures and paintings. Music such as jazz, blues and reggae also find their roots in Africa.

Wilkinson [1998] states that *"at the risk of generalisation and oversimplification of the complexities of the continent, African society - being communitarian and collective instead of embracing individualism - builds itself around the community and extended family. Hence, acts of individual creation, which can be found in western cultures, in Africa are replaced by co-operative ventures between the maker and the client. Since the client often dictates the look and even the shape of the work, the maker assumes the status of what to western eyes is considered to be that of an artisan rather than of an artist".*

Angela Fisher has produced a few beautiful books with many photos from African wall painting, body painting and ceremonies. These books leave no doubt about the high artistic value of African culture, while also pointing at the erosion taking place in these traditions. African Americans feel proud and moved to discover the tremendous beauty and power of their African roots (International Herald Tribune, 26 October 1999). What is often not observed by the contemporary art analysts is the spiritual function and symbolic messages expressed in these pieces of art. Music has the function of strengthening rituals and helping people to get in a trance, thus enabling them to communicate with ancestral spirits. Mural paintings may contain messages about the social identity or the spiritual status of the inhabitants of a building, while sculptures and masks are frequently used to represent a spirit, or to strengthen the effect of a ritual. Among the Mijikenda of East

Sirigu women (Ghana) are famous for their artistic wall decorations. The motives used here refer to cattle (top) and broken calebash (bottom).

Africa, the mediation role of sculpture is most noticeable in the natural process of sickness and death. Sickness is often associated with spirit possession and its cure may require
elaborate exorcism, in which a sculpture plays a crucial role [Orchardson-Mazrui, 1993].
In Ghana idols are often considered to be the real spirit - and not just a representation -
and supernatural powers are ascribed to them, with whom humorous relationships can be
established

Cultural erosion and revival. Many of the traditional artistic expressions are subject to
erosion. Traditional architecture, wall painting and sculpture are being replaced by modern practices, in which the cultural and spiritual values are marginalized. The number of
museums in Africa is quite limited, and their exhibitions can often not be compared with
those in Europe. Many African artists live outside the continent, adjusting their expression
to suit potential buyers. At the same time, one can observe some significant artistic innovations. For example, Zimbabwean villagers have started to make stone sculptures for the
western buyers, the unique architecture in Djenné, Mali, is being restored, and a number
of African musicians have developed their own styles and international reputation.

Traditional leadership

Most traditional communities have a variety of traditional leaders, specialists and spirit
mediums, who play an important role in village life. Below we describe the different spiritual specialists, according to Mbiti [1969].

Medicine (wo)man, healers, herbalists (or sometimes called witch doctors) are present
in almost all villages and towns in Africa. They can be men or women, have undergone
formal or informal training, and are influential. Their professional quality may vary, but
they are expected to be trustworthy, morally upright, friendly, willing to serve, able to dis-
cern peoples' needs and be reasonable in their charges. They are to be concerned with
sickness, disease, misfortune, which in African societies, are often attributed to negative
action such as witchcraft or magic, of one person against another. The medicine (wo)man,
therefore, has to find the cause of the disease, find out who the criminal is, diagnose the
nature of the disease, apply the right treatment, and supply means to prevent the misfortune from occurring again. Thus the healers apply both physical and spiritual, or psychological, treatments.

Rainmakers are engaged in the art of rainmaking or rain stopping. The entire livelihood
of people, either farmers or pastoralists, depends on good rains. The seasons control the
rhythm of community life, and in many societies the change of the seasons is marked by
ritual activities. There are rites to mark occasions like the onset of the rains, the first planting, the first fruits, the harvest, the beginning of the hunting season. Rainmaking is one
such a rite, and rainmakers are amongst the most important spiritual leaders. Their work
is not only to 'make' rain, but also to 'stop' rain when too much comes at a certain time,
or when it is not welcome at a given moment. Rainmakers are well versed in weather matters, and may spend long periods acquiring their knowledge: learn from other rainmakers,

observing the sky, study the habits of trees, insects, animals, study astronomy and use common sense. Rain is a deeply religious theme, and those who 'deal' in it should be of high religious calibre. Rainmakers not only solicit physical rain, but also symbolise man's contact with the blessing of time and eternity.

Kings, queens and rulers do not exist in every African society. These rulers are not simply political heads, they are also the mystical and religious guides, the divine symbol of their people's health and welfare. The weakening of the office of traditional rulers is leading to tensions between their supporters and African politicians, who think in terms of nationhood rather than in terms of local kingdoms.

Priests, soothsayers and religious founders. The priest is the chief intermediary between the divine and the human. Just as the king is the political symbol of God's presence, the priest is the religious symbol of God amongst his people. His of her duties are mainly religious, but as Africans do not disassociate religion from other spheres of life, he or she may also have other functions. Earthpriests play an important role in land tenure. They are considered the sons of the earth God, and regulate the ownership, tenure and use of land. They perform important roles in rituals related to soil fertility [Millar, 1999]. Soothsayers and diviners are persons with special skills to interpret the messages of the divine world. They can read the signs given through animals, or objects, and are often consulted by earthpriests.

Mbiti [1969] states that, to his knowledge, there is no African society that does not hold beliefs in some type of mystical power. There is mystical power in words, especially those of a senior person. Words of parents can cause good fortune, curse, success, peace, sorrows or blessing, especially when spoken in situations of crisis. The words of a medicine man work through the medicine he gives to his patients. Curses and blessings are considered extremely potent, and many African people consult experts to counteract evil effects or to obtain powerfully charged objects, like charms and medicine. Magic can be either good or evil. Good magic is used by medicine men, diviners and rainmakers, and combined with their knowledge and skills for the welfare of the community. Evil magic is used to harm human beings or their property. Sorcerers, or evil magicians, are believed to send flies, bats, birds, animals, spirits and magical objects to achieve their goals. Experiences of misfortune are often blamed on the misuse of mystical power. The subject of mystical power has religious as well as social, psychological and economic dimensions.

Traditional organisation and governments

Although Africa at present consists of nation states, the traditional organisation of its peoples is mainly based on ethnic lines. African social relations are often tribal, involving communal resource management patterns and group decision making [Izugbara, 1999], though a system of indirect rule was introduced in many places during the colonial period. Tengan [1991] gives a description of the people's perception of this process for the Sisala in northern Ghana. 'Indirect rule' meant the institution of chiefs in stateless societies, in combination with district and provincial councils directly responsible to the central administration. This whole implied a major transformation of the political scene. Villages, which had been relatively autonomous, suddenly found themselves part of an extensive nation with a structured government. In most cases this process was not comprehensible to the villagers. The government imposed taxes, initiated forced labour for the construction of roads, and drafted young men to the army. Hence the government was identified with forced levies, forced labour and forced conscription. The chiefs who had to enforce these laws were considered part of the government, and regarded as harsh people in contrast to the more humane traditional rulers.

The independence of Ghana did not bring about any drastic changes in this system, as far as the Sisala were concerned. The Ghanian government took over and granted constitutional backing to much of the political machinery set up by the British [Tengan, 1991]. For Zimbabwe, AZTREC has reported that the war of liberalisation was not fought just to replace colonial regimes but to revive, restore and resuscitate an African system of governance. Yet, in many cases African politicians took over the governments, and actually consolidated what the colonialists had imported into the African continent.

Government is identified with the execution of law through the police force and the levy of taxes, and is disliked for both. Tengan [1991] reported that the Sissala subsistence farmers in Ghana have the idea that the literate and the government workers serve an impersonal entity, with an inexhaustible source of money. In their view, the government can never run out of money; it only needs to print more. Hence, government employees who have access to this wealth should not suffer any want, and, since government cash belongs to no person, it is not really immoral to 'chop' or steal some of it. The nation state has thus become an anonymous body, which attracts corruption, and it is common in Africa to talk about the 'national cake' from which everyone can take a slice. Those who try to be honest are seen as abnormal or foolish.

It is important to resist both romanticicing and rejecting traditional practices. Hamar woman, Ethiopia, preparing ritual coffee for an initiation ceremony.

The role of traditional leaders. Traditional authorities, and the traditionally ascribed social obligations, do not suffer the same fate, however. When an offence takes place, it is considered criminal, and there is no such thing as a 'tribal cake'. This tribal loyalty transcends even national boundaries, as national borders have been established irrespective of ethnic lines of division. This makes national leadership ofte more problematic than traditional leadership, as the latter is more easily identifiable and seen as part of people's cultural identity.

At the same time, the role of traditional leaders in Africa is often debated within the context of endogenous development. Good and bad examples exist of their influence on the well being of the people. An example of the latter is put forward by Sheila Oparaocha in the Compas Magazine no. 4 (March 2001), as a reaction from readers: "...*More criticism could be included on the role of traditional leaders in Africa. For example, throughout the African continent, leaders are being criticised for their role in spreading HIV/AIDS and victimising young girls and women. Traditional leaders in various countries advocate sex with virgins as a cure for AIDS, or are proponents of cleansing rituals of widows through sexual intercourse with a male relative of the deceased. These kind of traditional practices need to be critically looked at....*"

Conclusions

In this chapter, the diverse and complex sub-Saharan African belief system and world vision is presented. It has been indicated that many differences exist between African and western concepts of matter, nature, religion, time, art, agriculture, nature conservation, local governance, community leadership, and decision making. Contacts with non-African cultures have certainly brought about intercultural exchanges and substitutions. But, in many respects, the traditional belief systems still form the roots and branches of the knowledge systems of rural people in Africa.

During the last decades there has been a renewed interest in African indigenous knowledge. This is partly due to the influences of African culture on some European scholars and cultures, and partly due to a new positioning of Africans themselves. This renewed interest, however, is more concentrated on technologies rather than on systems, structures, and processes. It often has the intention of validating traditional technologies from a western scientific perspective. As local knowledge and values still form the main driving force for rural people's decisions on land use, food production, community management, health practices, religious practices, teaching, learning and experimenting, these should be seen as the main point of articulation for development activities. Programmes for health, agriculture, and the management of natural resources, should and can be built on African religious concepts, institutions and practices.

Strengthening traditional cultures implies supporting the internal dialogue. Baganda woman, Uganda, combines traditional and modern elements in her clothing.

Endogenous development. It is becoming increasingly clear that for most traditional Africans, adoption of a new technology does not imply abandoning what they have been already doing or believing. Adoption means, therefore, doing both things side by side. For the African it is a question of survival in a diverse and risk-prone environment. Strategies for modernisation, by means of stimulating introduction of new innovations from outside, could be replaced by strategies of endogenous development, 'development from within'. Outsiders can build up relationships with traditional leaders and discuss the possibilities of experimenting with forms of agriculture, health, or management of natural resources, according to the interest to the population in a given community. Rural appraisal exercises can include co-operation of spiritual leaders, and take notice of the worldview and religious concepts of the people involved. On-farm experiments and tree planting activities can be successfully planned together with the traditional leaders, and rituals can be held to initiate these activities and to discuss the traditional criteria to be used in evaluating the outcomes.

For this, the field workers need to establish a relationship with the community based on respect. And, in this process, awareness is required to resist two temptations: the temptation to condemn and reject local knowledge and practices, and the temptation to justify and idealise them. Hountondji [2001], a philosopher from Benin, rightly emphasises the need for an internal debate within traditional cultures in order to develop new alternatives for negative traditional, as well as modernisation practices. He states: *"It is not enough to develop a new reading of the past, a new comprehension of tradition. Once it has been recognised that tradition is plural, the practical question is how to promote the internal debate inside our cultures in such a way, that it may itself develop the best possible new alternatives. We need to rebuild the traditional cultures with elements provided by debate."*

Since 1998, two African Compas partners, CECIK in northern Ghana and AZTREC in Zimbabwe, are systematically building up experiences with endogenous development. They have consciously chosen to predispose themselves to learning from the traditional systems, and to question and redefine their professionalism, which until now had been western-biased. They also seek co-operation with other organisations and persons in Africa in order to exchange experiences. The ENEDA (Enhancing Endogenous Development in Africa) Network is now spreading the approach in East Africa, Southern Africa and West Africa.

5.1 IMPROVING FARMING WITH ANCESTRAL SUPPORT

David Millar, CECIK, Ghana

During the last four years the Centre for Cosmovision and Indigenous Knowledge (CECIK) has carried out field experiments with endogenous development in the area of Bongo, northern Ghana. It is a rural area caught up in a vicious cycle of poverty. This chapter presents various new methodologies developed by CECIK, which take into account the worldview of the people in these communities, as well as the way they want to combine traditional with modern practices in agriculture, natural resource management and income-generating activities.

Savannah landscape in northern Ghana.

Northern Ghana is located in the Savannah Grassland belt. This belt is characterised by low vegetative growth of mainly grasses, low shrubs and dispersed trees. Rainfall in the region is unevenly distributed, erratic in start, duration and intensity, and ranges between 900 mm and 1000 mm. The temperature ranges from 22 to 40 degrees centigrade. Agriculture is rain-fed. Most farmers practise mixed cropping of trees, grain crops such as sorghum, millet, maize, groundnuts, and root crops such as yam. They also keep live-stock in the form of poultry, goats, sheep and cattle. In the dry season there is virtually no cropping, except for small gardens along the riverbeds and dams.

The immediate impression one gets on entering the region is that the bio-physical environment is seriously degraded. One observes many gullies and sheet erosion due to water and wind. The major causes of this are deforestation for fuel wood, and inappropriate methods of traditional farming, such as uncontrolled bush fires and overgrazing. The annual population growth rate in the area is 6.8%, leading to serious pressure on the land, with estimates of about 300 people per square kilometre. The average land holding of a farm family is three acres, including rocky outcrops, and is continuously under cultivation. All these aspects have contributed to low crop yields - the average cereal yield is estimated at 300 kgs per acre. Inadequate food results in malnutrition of pregnant women and children. About 70% of the population are illiterate, and shortage of drinking water affects about 25% of the population. To supplement the little income from agriculture, local crafts and cottage industries have found a special place in the lives of the people.

The people

The people combine patrilineal and matrilineal forms of inheritance, with patrilineal being the most prominent. Access to land by women is limited. The primary source of labour is family labour; surplus labour can be purchased directly with cash or in exchange for an animal, or food and drinks. Various organised labour-sale groups exist in nearly all communities. Women groups dominate followed by youth groups. Reciprocal farming arrangements are common among the various groups. The traditional organisation of the household continues to be an aspect of identity, authority, and regulatory arrangement. The head of every extended household is its oldest male member. Female-headed families are common but female-headed households are rare. There are distinct gender roles in farm operations, access to land and other resources. The overall head of extended household presides over matters general in nature. Critical decisions about mobilisation and investments, offence and defence, disposals, opportunities and risks, are better managed at the level of the household.

Income from the livestock is more evenly spread over the year than from crops. Pigs, goats, and poultry are the most common sources of cash. Cattle are sold rarely, and only as a last resort. Income generated from handicrafts (hats and basket weaving) is considerable, especially during the dry season. Dry season gardening in the area is also quite common due to the proximity of the irrigation dams. Trickles of donations from family members living outside the community, and wage labour during seasonal migration of the labour force, are recognised sources of income. Women's income sources can be distinguished as crop sources, livestock sources, and commercial activities. There is marginal income support to women from their husbands. Nonetheless, women provide an income buffer to the household. They contribute to health and school expenses, procure most of the protein and vegetable requirements of the family, buy most of their own clothes, and respond to some social demands for cash.

Perceptions of poverty. Traditional lifestyles are continuously being challenged with calls for renewal. Perceptions about the future and the way to get there differ according to one's cultural background, age, sex, the country one lives in, and economic position. During a traditional festival called *Ndaam Koya,* Adongo Nso, an elder in the Gowrie-Kunkwa community in northern Ghana, played an ancient musical instrument with strange and beautiful rhythms, to herald the occasion. This was the first time David Millar, director of CECIK, had seen this instrument or heard its music, in spite of several years of working with the community. In a discussion the elder revealed his ideas about poverty.

David: *"How old is this instrument and how long have you been playing it? I have never seen it or heard you play."*

Elder Nso: *"It is an ancient instrument used by our ancestors to sing praise, or for burial songs. Only my family have the skill to craft this instrument and use it. You cannot find it elsewhere."*

David: *"I imagine you have quite a large family. How many of you play this instrument and how many of the young ones are learning it from you?"*

Elder Nso: *"Only two of us use it - me and my twin brother. Our sons and grandsons refuse to pick it up because they say it is for poor men and it will make them perpetually poor. You see! Our people experience poverty in many ways. In addition to not having material things, we also see poverty in terms of spirituality, knowledge and skills."*

Ghanaian elder: "Poverty is not only referring to material things. We also see poverty in terms of knowledge and skills about community and spirituality".

David: *"Can you explain these other dimensions of poverty a bit more?"*

Elder Nso: *"The missionaries were the first to tell us about our spiritual poverty. They thought it poverty to worship our ancestors. They also made sure we got even poorer by doing everything to destroy our religion. Then the government workers came with their knowledge about food production and again we were told that our own knowledge and skills were poor. They also made us poorer by trying to destroy our knowledge and replace it with theirs. Today there is large-scale poverty among our people, and those who replaced and scorned our customs, knowledge and skills are responsible for it."*

David: *"What do you suggest to alleviate poverty?"*

Elder Nso: *"The government should certainly look at issues related to material poverty. But poverty in knowledge, skills and spirituality should be addressed at the same time!"*

Cosmovision in northern Ghana

In northern Ghana the traditional cult of 'worship of the ancestors' is central in the worldview of the rural people. There is also the general belief in an Allfather, and the ancestral arrangement traces itself to the founder of the village or community. Gods are symbols that allow for or facilitate communication with ancestors. The people sacrifice to their ancestral spirits for various favours, and the earth spirit is central amongst the spirits worshipped. The land priests perform the necessary rituals and sacrifices, which ensure the prosperity of the land, fertility of the people, their crops and livestock.

Sacrifices and rituals take place during funerals, pacification, intercessions, calamities, festivals associated with productivity and seasonality. Although grains, especially millet and sorghum, are major inputs in sacrifices -especially the use of sorghum for pito brewing - livestock is also important. All consultations of ancestral spirits require an animal: the lowest-order sacrifice is done with a fowl or a guinea fowl; the next in order is a goat, and then a sheep and a cow. In relation to agriculture, people distinguish between crops and animals that are used for rituals, for consumption and for commercial purposes. Commercial crops are frequently introduced from outside and lack a relationship with the ancestors. Rituals are associated with food crops and ritual crops, but to a far less extent to commercial crops. In the worldview of the people the traditional crops were received from the ancestors. The spirits of the ancestors are the owners of humankind and responsible for their well being. A decision to adopt a new crop or a new variety, for example, can therefore not be taken without the advice of the ancestors.

Among the societies of northern Ghana, the family of the original settlers on the land have a special role. The head of this family is the *tendana*, the traditional earth priest and spiritual leader. This person allocates land use rights to the people in the village. Almost invariable a raised piece of ground on the outskirts of the village is chosen by the first settlers as a sacred place for worship, and for sacrifice to the spirit of the earth. With such a specialised function, this area usually also becomes the 'home' for other spirits or Gods that are communally owned. The spiritual world is integrated into nature, because the spirits reside there. Working with natural resources and agriculture, therefore, implies working with traditional leaders and institutions, because they are the ones who can mediate with the spiritual world in nature. While the ritual control of the land is vested in the land priests, the legal control is vested in the chiefs. The chief acts as the custodian of the communal land for the people in the Bongo villages, while the government is like an anonymous entity imposed on them.

Relatively recent introductions to the belief system of the people are the Catholic, Pentecostal, and Muslim faiths. The converts to these faiths, concentrated in the urban and commercial centres, often live in two worlds: though not formally accepted by the churches, they tend to practice their traditions in combination with their new religion. Thus, in this blended belief system, the converts to Christianity and alternative forms of worship, have not eradicated the ancestral cult. Therefore, in northern Ghana, it is common to find Christians blending their forms of worship with traditional ancestral sacrifices, especially in times of need for 'higher order discourses'. Moreover, there is always a lingering commitment to the perceived rewards and punishments associated with the belief in ancestral spirits.

Images of land and the environment. Imagery is very strong in the perceptions of the people of northern Ghana. Despite the external influences of Christianity and Islam, the traditional images described here run through entire communities. Nature is considered the visible part of the spiritual world, and referred to and treated as a collection of smaller Gods. Some parts of nature express themselves in the spiritual world and vice versa. From this perspective has arisen the Earth God, the Rain God, and the God of the Skies (sun, moon, stars and the wind), which give essence to the material aspect of life. A special tree, mountain, river or stone may also be classified as a God. In this perspective, nature as a whole is conceived as a living entity, like an animal, with all parts interrelated and needing each other to function. Nature does not belong to the people, but the people to nature. Therefore, human life is intimately related with nature and constitutes the irreplaceable basis of human life.

Gender differences in cosmovision. In northern Ghana the position of women and men in relation to the spiritual world shows significant differences. Most traditional leaders are male. Occasionally there are women chiefs, women tendana and women soothsayers. The only strong spiritual relationships that women have are when they establish spirit mediums of their own. The ancestral spirits of the men are considered as related to the land of the household, which, in turn, makes their spirit linked to the location. Women have more claims to land belonging to their fathers than to their husbands, except in cases of special re-allocation. In their homes, the husband takes care of the Gods on behalf of the wife. The women explain it in this way: *"My son or my husband sacrifices for me. I provide the animal for the sacrifice, I speak to the ancestral spirit and tell them the purpose of my sacrifice, but the man does the actual sacrifice. I get the answers for my sacrifices, which satisfies my purpose."* The woman, therefore, has a weak link to the spiritual relations both in her husband's home as well as in her father's home.

CECIK

The Centre for Cosmovision and Indigenous Knowledge (CECIK) is an NGO that promotes cosmovision-based endogenous development, providing services to rural communities in northern Ghana. Beyond actions at the community level, CECIK asserts itself in the areas of networking and collaboration, and advocacy for endogenous development. The existing staff is one full time director and three field assistants, two men and one woman, one is a community member and one is from the Ministry of Food and Agriculture. CECIK also collaborates with extension staff of other regional organisations expecially with BAFP (Bongo Agroforestry Project) and MOFA (Small Ruminant Programme).

Methodology used for field activities. It is now accepted that in order to improve traditional farming technologies, the knowledge of both the rural people and of outsiders is important. Relating these two sources of knowledge requires a delicate process of formulating, comparing, merging, dialoguing and negotiating between rural communities and outside experts. Participatory Technology Development (PTD) is one possible methodological instrument for this process, which consists of several phases: getting started, looking for things to try, designing the experiment, execution, sharing the experiences, and sustaining the process. In my experience the phase of 'farmers designing the experiment' has been the most complicated one, as it is relatively easy if the researcher is 'in the driving seat', dictating the pace and direction of the experiments.

　　Since the start of its activities, CECIK has gradually recognised the vital role of the worldview of the people in community initiatives and responses. This is not always easily understood, however. When elders of the indigenous communities in northern Ghana discuss important issues, for example, it always seems as if they are 'talking at cross-purposes'. But, in fact, they are using a creative way of communicating, which is often lost when it is interpreted or translated. The worldview of the rural people of northern Ghana expresses itself in their everyday life and conversations. The link between spirituality and the solutions to their problems, therefore, reinforces the relevance of cosmovision in the farmers' practices. This explains why we need to make cosmovisions a central part of our development interventions.

The general model used by CECIK for field level activities is the Empathic Learning and Action Framework (ELA framework, see box 5d). While the project representatives enrol the so-called beneficiaries in their actions, they also allow themselves to be enrolled in the communities' programmes. The ELA framework is an attempt to establish farmer-driven experimental designs, and is based on more than 20 years of experience in agricultural development. It makes explicit and addresses two different perceptions of reality: that of the rural people and that of outsiders, such as CECIK, who want to work with a rural community. By addressing these two perceptions mutual learning processes can be designed, ultimately leading to an improvement of rural peoples' practices and the quality of the interventions by outsiders.

Examples of field activities

Entering the community in cosmovision perspective. The field work of CECIK in Bongo started early 1998. During the first meeting in Bongo I introduced myself and tried to find out whether I was welcome. A tendana as well as a soothsayer and an elder, consulted their ancestral spirits and the Gods to find out what to do with me. While a libation - a sacrifice for the ancestral spirits - was performed, the tendana asked for the guidance of his ancestors. He also asked if both his ancestors and mine would clear the path and guide our actions. During our second meeting I was told that the response of the Gods and the ancestors had been positive. I was welcome to work with the community, especially on farming matters. Entering the community in this cosmovision perspective was a new experience for me. As a former government extension worker I had learned that you need to ask permission from the village chief when entering a new village. Now I have found out that entering a community implies much more than this. Clearance from the ancestral spirits is sought before people accept you. Only by accepting and respecting these rules can a relationship of confidence be built with a community.

In seeking clearance, another issue that we had to deal with was transparency in our relationships. The elders decided to have a village meeting to discuss a programme of co-operation between us. During this inception workshop I wanted to be very honest about my intentions, my doubts and our commitments. On this occasion the elders had this to share with me: *"It is true that we play games with you, the Karachis* (local term for government workers). *Every farmer is guilty of this. Just imagine the difficulty of paying back the loans. Parting with a substantial amount of the harvest that should sustain you till the next one is not easy, and when we can avoid it we will do so. We are sure you would do the same if you were in our shoes. But let us tell*

Box 5d   Framework for Empathic Learning and Action (ELA)

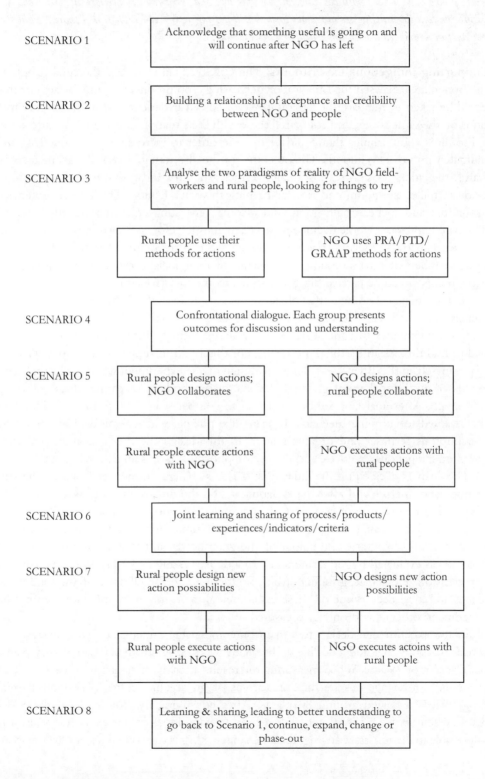

SCENARIO 1 — Acknowledge that something useful is going on and will continue after NGO has left

SCENARIO 2 — Building a relationship of acceptance and credibility between NGO and people

SCENARIO 3 — Analyse the two paradigsms of reality of NGO field-workers and rural people, looking for things to try

Rural people use their methods for actions

NGO uses PRA/PTD/GRAAP methods for actions

SCENARIO 4 — Confrontational dialogue. Each group presents outcomes for discussion and understanding

SCENARIO 5 — Rural people design actions; NGO collaborates

NGO designs actions; rural people collaborate

Rural people execute actions with NGO

NGO executes actions with rural people

SCENARIO 6 — Joint learning and sharing of process/products/experiences/indicators/criteria

SCENARIO 7 — Rural people design new action possiabilities

NGO designs new action possibilities

Rural people execute actions with NGO

NGO executes actoins with rural people

SCENARIO 8 — Learning & sharing, leading to better understanding to go back to Scenario 1, continue, expand, change or phase-out *you this. With our ancestors' way of building our relationship we cannot cheat you. We know of cases where people have cheated with the name of the ancestors and, as a result, have lost all their crops. We assure you that the activities we are about to start will not suffer. We will support and share the plight of one another - provided it is in line with the ancestral rules."*

Supporting indigenous experiments. The CECIK field staff and the rural people in the Bongo area analysed the situation of decreasing crop productivity and the actions that could be taken to mitigate the situation. We discussed experiences from other organisations on the same issues, and compared these with the situation in Bongo. This discussion led to ideas about 'things that could be tried' in order to increase food productivity and ultimately improve livelihoods. The outcome for the different groups reflected their social status: the elders took to rearing small livestock - poultry and goats; the youth chose to cultivate millet, sorghum, and rice, combining this with fishing. The women opted for groundnut and soybean cultivation, and income generating crafts, particularly weaving. The community as a whole decided to start activities to reforest the shrines and groves in the area. The low soil fertility and *striga*, or devil weed, were identified as general problems by all members of the community, irrespective of their social position. It was agreed that experiments would be carried out to try to overcome this problem.

In the striga experiment the objective was to reduce the incidence of striga and increase productivity. The experiments involved 10 farmers. After the possibilities of using organic matter to control striga was analysed with the farmers, I realised that they had to lead the design of this experiment. For this I had to suppress my own inclination to put myself in the driving seat. Thus the design of the experiment was done by the farmers, based on the analogy of giving directions to somebody to reach the village following a footpath. After analysing various methods to combat striga, the farmers decided that they wanted to combine mechanical means like pulling, with chemical means of using phosphorous fertiliser and organic matter. In this design the mechanical aspects were based on indigenous practices, and the use of phosphorus was an external input.

The farmers decided on the indicators to assess changes in the weed's status: the striga population before and after the experiment, and the time required to weed the fields. Their indicators to monitor crop performance included: crop growth rate, structure of the crops (strong or weak, short or long, big or small), time for maturation, reaction to seasonal moisture stress, size and colour of the grain heads, and fullness of the seeds. The harvest was evaluated by the farmers in terms of harvesting time, quantity and quality of harvest, storage qualities, grinding quality, flour colour and smell, taste of the food, local dishes and local beer. Some of these experimental indicators were measured during the experiment; others could only be measured off-farm.

In the experimental design two main outcomes were anticipated: yield increases of cereals by about 25% and a decline in the incidence of striga from 100 plants to 50 plants per test plot of ¼ acre. When measuring the results after the first year we concluded that yields did not change despite the applications of an organic matter/phosphorous mix. Striga weeds averaged around 80 plants. After consulting my colleagues at the SARI research station, we realised that we had been too ambitious in our expectations, as it is impossible to demonstrate any significant change with this experiment after only one year.

Village meeting in Bongo: field staff of CECIK and traditional leaders plan rehabilitation of sacred groves.

Three years on the same piece of land would be necessary. The community had learned, however, that when weeding is combined with the application of organic matter and chemical fertilisation, the weed pressure can be reduced, costs lessened and benefits optimised.

Impatient outsiders might call this result a failure because we were unable to demonstrate more significant positive change. But during the 'learning and sharing workshop', the community had this to say: *"The problems we encountered now should not be counted as failures. Outsiders may call them failures, but in the Gowrie community we call them steps towards success. This is because in the process we have achieved several things. We have become united both in religion and in knowledge. It has facilitated the organisational work in the community. Moreover, more knowledge, both indigenous and external, has been acquired and our community has been recognised by surrounding villages for its work with CECIK. Our ancestors have been satisfied by the procedures followed and the sacrifices we have made to them. We would like to repeat this experience all over again because our ancestors say so."* In the following years, the results were indeed more positive. In fact, after 3 years the incidence of striga was reduced by 80% and the yields of the crops increased by about 25%.

Supporting women's experimentation. At present there is a lot of NGO attention given to women's groups in the region. In the area of formal education women still lag behind, but this is not the case in extension, where several income generating activities for women are being promoted. Yet, CECIK is the only one that includes the spiritual dimension, carrying out various endogenous development activities based on the cosmovision perspective, involving men, women, and youth. Of these three categories, the women are least resource-endowed, but at the same time the most innovative group in finding ways to generate income. Several constraints have been identified as limiting and retarding the opportunities of women in agricultural production. One is the refusal or reluctance of men to release land to women, which is a great setback to women in gaining control of their lives through improved access to economic resources. Moreover, due to their poor economic status, women cannot procure the required inputs, such as farm tools, improved seeds, chemical fertilisers, and hired labour. Socio-cultural constraints include the attitudes related to crops: crops such as maize, sorghum, millet, yam, cassava, and pigeon pea are grown by men and are branded 'male' crops. Though sometimes women venture into the production of these crops, the practice is an exception rather than a rule. Women can cultivate other 'cash' crops, mainly legumes and rice; there are no specific 'female' crops, however. This restriction with so-called male crops denies women the advantages of mixed cropping [Millar, 1993].

Dialogue with women's group
When I went to the community for a pre-season discussion, I had this dialogue with Mrs Apangabasia, leader of the Gowrie-Kunkwa women's group.

David: *"...Do the women have their plots ready for this season?".*

Three women, almost at the same time: *"No!!!"*

David: *"Then I do not need to leave their share of the fertiliser here. I might as well take it back and leave only that for the men".*

Mrs Apangabasia: *"We said NO because we really do not have land. But we shall get a piece. We do not own land but we do have access to land when the need arises. We only need to ensure that our plots are situated within the men's cropped lands so that animals cannot enter and damage our crops".*

David: *"What makes you so sure about getting access to land?"*

Mrs Apangabasia: *"Since the onset of your activities with us, the men are more willing to give us land.*

David: *"Why is this so?"*

Mrs Apangabasia: *"Because we are the better farmers. The men know this but will not accept it".*

David: *"How come you say that you are the better farmers?"*

Mrs Apangabasia: *"Take what happened last year. They gave us the poorest parcels for our groundnut production, land that they considered dead. What did we do? We prepared it, applied the 'petiliza' (local name for fertiliser) that you gave us. We then planted our own groundnuts and bambara beans mixture, and vegetables as border plants. We also planted a strip of the fodder grass you gave us around the plots. The animals owned by the men liked the grass very much. All the village animals, allowed to graze free after the crops were harvested, concentrated in our fields".*

David: *"How does all this make you better farmers than the men?"*

Mrs Apangabasia: *"Don't you see? We did not have organic matter to mix with the 'petiliza', but the planting of our groundnuts and bambara beans with the 'petiliza' enriched the soil so much that the men saw that the performance and yields of our crops were better than theirs. We do not have cattle but the men noticed that we provided fodder to their animals with the grasses we planted. We even sold some of this grass. The vegetables we cooked for the family. The men also observed that we had less striga in our fields than theirs hence, this year, they quickly took back this parcel of land for their cereal production. Are we not better farmers? Within one year we brought a dead piece of land back to life. They will surely want us do it again this year. Am I lying? So who are the better farmers: we the women or the men?"*

Mrs Apangabasia and David Millar.

Farm-family concept

In dealing with issues of gender in agriculture, and the need for rural women to support their families economically, new strategies and approaches had to be designed that took into consideration the different constraints of the women to surmount their basic problem of gaining access to agricultural land. To build and sustain team spirit, a total of 124 rural women were organised and mobilised into three groups. Four training sessions per group were conducted on the improvement of the nutritional status of indigenous foods. The training programme culminated in a community food bazaar.

One activity, which the women themselves organised, was the mixed cropping of legumes and vegetables. CECIK encouraged the groups to take up the challenge of improving the fertility of the land granted to them by the men, by incorporating phosphorous fertiliser and by planting velvet beans (*Mucuna puriens*) as a source of green manure. The three groups were given fertiliser for their one-acre groundnut plots, and groundnut and soya bean seeds. All this - the chemical fertiliser, the leguminous crops (groundnuts, beans and soya beans), the vegetables and the use of mucuna as green manure - supported the women in being better farmers.

To operate effectively we had to ultimately consider men, women and youth as key actors in the development process - 'the farm family concept'. Thus whole families were involved in activities at the community level, which helped to enrich the indigenous knowledge. With both men and women involved, problems related to the transfer of ideas, experiences, skills and information were reduced. This reduced misunderstandings and conflicts between women and their husbands. In almost all cases, the men were willing to co-operate and help their wives to supplement the family income.

The women say that CECIK's approach yielded significant results: land is now more available to women's groups in the project to cultivate the crops they desire, and the mentality and attitude towards women in crop production has changed drastically. Not only do women have access to land, they can also buy their own hoe and cutlass without being reprimanded. An increasing number of women have gone into crop production, even cultivating the supposedly 'male' crops. Many of the women can now go independently to their farms, and sometimes, join their husbands in weeding on the farms. In most cases, the husbands prepare the women's land for them, and in return expect the women to help out on the men's farms when weeding is due.

Working as groups has also helped in breaking the lack of confidence and trust among the women. Raising awareness and addressing gender concerns as a group lead to the re-establishment of traditional solidarity arrangements, which had been largely forgotten. Child nutrition has improved significantly: the combination of soybean with local foods resulted in weight gains of children up to 20%. Women's income has also improved significantly, both from selling crops as by keeping livestock. Two women's groups now have bank accounts that they use to access credit, and one women's group is running a rotational livestock supply system. CECIK realises that its strategy should be to provide even more assistance to women's groups.

Improving natural resources: shrines and groves. In the Boosi Chiefdom in northern Ghana most of the land is barren, depleted of permanent vegetation. Yet various small clusters of bushes, trees and grasses are prominent. Almost invariably these are shrines or groves. To survive the test of time some degree of protection must have regulated these isolated clusters. A shrine is a sacred place or item of worship, sometimes in a natural environment, sometimes within the house. A grove is a forest patch - sometimes a remnant of an original forest- that is perceived sacred by the people. Shrines and groves vary in their physical and biological appearance. They can include a cluster of trees and shrubs, water bodies, a range of rocks, a river with a valley or a few stones gathered in a heap. The location of a shrine or grove is related to a historical site. It may indicate the location of settlement of the first ancestor of the village or a site identified by a soothsayer.

CECIK has conducted a study to look at natural resource management of the shrines and groves. The following questions were addressed: what are the historical changes of shrines and groves in the Gowrie-Kunkwa area? What structures guarantee the survival of shrines and groves and how do the regulatory mechanisms operate? How are the shrines and groves perceived by individuals and by communities? What is their role in bio-cultural diversity maintenance; can they be regenerated and how? A total of 20 shrines and groves were encountered in an area of about four square kilometres. The largest shrine occupied an area of about four acres. It consisted of a chain of rocky mountains. The smallest shrine of half an acre was found in a valley. The average size of the shrines is around two acres.

It is our experience that one can rely on key informant interviews in order to connect with people's spirituality. So we started talking with the chiefs, the tendanas or earth priests, the spirit mediums, elders and opinion leaders in the communities. On a few occasions we started with one person and a group was formed spontaneously. We wanted to deal directly in the local language and were lucky to find a key facilitator from a *tindamba* family, the family of the Earth God. Funerals, markets and festivals were good opportunities to have more in-depth dialogues. We also used participatory observation during the visits to the shrines and groves. We wanted to see what was there and feel the sacredness of these places.

The spirits inhabiting the shrines and groves are important to the people; not the shrines and groves themselves. When sacrifices are performed correctly and by the right people, the spirits will protect the community. In this way the ancestral spirits serve as a vital communication link between the living, the dead and the yet unborn. The physical role of the shrines and groves is to provide rain, fertility and health. They propel livestock development, and ensure peaceful co-existence between mankind, vegetation and other parts of nature like stones, mountains and rivers. Socially, shrines and groves are significant because they provide a common place of worship, where the community meets to perform sacrifices and resolve conflicts.

Traditional rules have to be followed for all shrines and groves. Replanting is not done but natural regeneration is stimulated. The traditional rules are quite strict and offenders face strong punishments. Hunting, fishing and cutting wood is only permitted on special days, and the community is not supposed to harvest the vegetation for private use. Wildlife in the shrine or grove is considered sacred and should not be killed without the consent of the tendana. Trees should not be cut for musical instruments and dead wood should be picked before live wood can be cut.

The tendana explains: *"With the coming of Christianity and modernity, the position of the shrines and groves has been undermined. The traditional rules for the use of shrines and groves are weakening. We have lost some of the trees, but the spirits of the good trees still remain there. Most of the wild animals have also escaped but their spirits are also still in those shrines and groves. Above all, the spirits of our ancestors have remained intact. People that claim to be Christians go in to fish, kill wild animals, pick dry wood or cut trees. Only the elderly keep to the tradition. However, when the young encounter problems in their newly chosen way of life, they run back to us to 'look into things' for them."* One of the elders: *"We lament it that a majority of our youth today has become the victim of these unfortunate ideas. Despite this we foresee the return of our youth to their roots at a more advanced age. They need to be sufficiently informed about important aspects of our culture."*

The communities in the Gowrie Kunkwa area reacted very positively when discussing the idea of working on the shrines and groves, indicating the need to work in partnership with outside organisations. Concrete ideas have been developed, such as planting trees, de-silting water bodies, re-activating the water bodies that have dried up, and re-stocking them with fish. Community members argued that shrines and groves can only be developed when the right process is followed. This includes allowing the people to do it their own way, abiding by the traditional rules. Appeasing the spirits is an important component in the conservation effort, as well as proclaiming the shrine or grove as a restricted area with traditional regulations.

Lessons learned

Over the past years we have learned that working from a cosmovision perspective has many challenges. In the process the following constraints were encountered:
- Limited experience with and understanding of local cultures by the outsiders (in this case CECIK staff) in the initial phase.
- The evolution of new ways of working with no precedence to guide us.
- Dealing the cultural gender inhibitions proved quite difficult.
- The role of youth in cosmovision has been problematic, as they are relatively more responsive to indigenous technical knowledge than to the spiritual aspects of it.
- The communities are still poverty-stricken, which often leads to short term solutions rather than long term developments.
- It is difficult to show quantitative impact when development is dealt with from a cultural perspective.

The project had to go through several growth paths. The initial intention of working with one village and one group had to be abandoned in favour of dealing with 3 sections different cultural identities. Each of these three groups were further divided into 3 men's, 3 women's, and 3 youth groups, as proposed by the communities. This has had implications for staff numbers and slowed down. The CECIK working strategy involves not having full-time staff but taking advantage of existing staff of various development agencies, people based in the communities who are knowledgeable and capable, and paying them an allowance for time input. It is our experience that this arrangement sets the stage for early networking and active involvement of the community in self-development processes. It also takes advantage of certain untapped skills that exist within the communities. With this approach, you also find yourself working into the existing dynamics of the community with minimal interference or destabilisation of the social organisations. The only risk is that such staff may give certain favours to special members of the community.

CECIK has succeeded in establishing the fact that spirituality and cultural performance are an essential part of rural people's worldviews, and critical in ensuring that local and demand-driven development is sustained. In order to work from a cultural perspective, we had to make adjustments. New activities were included as the programme progressed. Such a demand-driven approach has budgetary and logistical implications.The general development strategy, promoting development based on peoples' own indigenous knowledge systems and spirituality, was found effective. Development workers who support rather than ridicule, who do not demand a change of worldview or anger their ancestors, are well accepted by communities. One elder remarked: *"The project respects and values us because they do not look down on our belief and value systems. It is therefore bound to succeed."* This is a very important basis for a development project. As much as possible, the ability to communicate in the local language is our guide for resource persons and field staff. Sensitive issues such as the position of women, elders and spiritual leaders can be touched once the relationship between the outsider and the community has been established in the cultural (and spiritual) context. The implementation of the project activities has had a positive impact on gender and gender relations. Women are now able to speak up during general

Box 5e   Results of endogenous development support by CECIK

Aspects of endogenous development	Field activities implemented	Environmental, socio-economic, and cultural impact
Building on local initiatives to use resources	Start with local leadership Use community based staff for implementation. Start with existing IK and then introduce improvements.	The use of elders, soothsayers, and women leader has helped in community mobilisation. staff has built local capacities. Soil fertility improvement increased about 25% yield of indigenous crops. 3 Groves are being rehabilitated.
Building on local needs	Livestock improvement for men Craft development for women Gardening and fishing for the youth.	60% of the elders reached have doubled their livestock holdings. Women dry season incomes have increased by over 80%. The youth made income gains of about $100.
Improving local knowledge and practices	Striga weed control activities. Livestock improvement. Child feeding/ nutrition improvement.	All 6 plots are about 80% striga free. More livestock available for sacrifices and income. From soyabean combination with local foods child weight gains of up to 20% is visible.
Local control of development options	Working with natural social grouping Separating women and youth groups Responding to different livelihoods Evoking ancestral spirits through sacrifices.	They are more response to environmental issues pertaining to each group. Dialogue and social dynamics have improved and they have been differently challenged. Empowerment through income generation for the women has increased to even 100% of previous incomes.The fear of the unknown has resulted in responsible actions.
Identification of development niches	Legumes in livestock feeding. Conservation of indigenous seed. Introduction of finger millet.	Although some was used for livestock feeding, the sale of this for cash for the women resulted in about 10% of their offseason income. Indigenous seed conservation and propagation of finger millet is identified for Phase II.
Selective use of external resources	Phosphorus in organic matter for striga control. Fish farming and piggery combination. Grinding mill for women.	Reduced the incidence of striga by about 80% and yield of cereals has increased by about 25%. Feeding pigs and using their waste to feed fish has generated incomes form the sale of both to $ 100/yr. Women labour is saved, walking distance of 4km is no more and women make income of $ 200/yr.
Retention of benefits in the local area	Women saving accounts with Bank. Conversion of grain incomes to livestock. Gardening for local vegetables.	Two of 3 women groups have bank accounts that they use to access more credit. One women group is running a rotational livestock supply system based on sale from group farms. Two youth gardens have provided local vegetables to the communities.
Exchange and learning between local cultures	Poster exchange with India. Workshops and meetings Excursions and visits.	A poster was received from India, the community discussed it and are now developing a reply. Staff attended 4 workshops and director 6 meetings. 2 excursions were organised for community members; one in the Upper East the other in the Northern Region.
Networking and strategic partnerships	Conferences attended by Director. Publication of The Horn and other documents.	2 national and 3 international conferences attended to share on cosmovision and indigenous knowledge. Quarterly publication of The Horn, contributions to The Savanna Farmer, and 7 documents printed.
Understanding systems of knowing and learning	The role of the ancestors 'Male' versus 'female' sacrifices. Tutelage as in schools programme.	Annual 'Ndaam Koya' festival Annual competition of schools collecting indigenous knowledge on trees and plants from their parents.
Other aspects	Social recognition as in chieftainship.	The Gowrie Kunkwa community acknowledge the valuable contributions of CECIK by installing the director as a functional Chief.

meetings, and both women and men have expressed the changes related to the tasks and responsibilities as a result of the project. Women have also extended their support to and working relationships with group members beyond project activities. The sharing of benefits accruing from development activities is more profound and far reaching with women than with the other groupings. More gender awareness training and general education (literacy courses) are needed, however.

Working on the basis of the ELA approach has strengthened the farmers' capacity to experiment. The approach has motivated the community to experiment within their own cultural context and, in this way, has moved participation a step forward. The approach has led to considerable confidence of the people in their own capacities to change, learn and develop. It has provided us with new ideas about 'the process of farmer experimentation'. In our quest for endogenous development this process can be adapted and the basic principles can be replicated beyond the Gowrie community.

We believe that it is better to work with groups, especially for the women. It is important, however, to deal with naturally occurring groups rather than those that are 'project-made'. The idea of cultural differences should be reflected in group formation as well. The women's groups are more responsive to their developmental needs, followed by the elders and then the youth. The youth tend to be complacent in their actions and easily run into conflicts. The effect on youth has been considerable, especially in the fishing activity.

Plans for future activities include: continuation of the successful livestock programme for elders, stimulate growing and consuming indigenous foods by women and children, income generation activities for women, crop production with focus on legumes, striga control and soil fertility, youth and fishing, and development of shrines and groves. Conscious efforts in networking,dissemination of information, collaborative workshops and peer reflections. have been made at various levels. A quarterly newsletter 'The Horn' has been published by CECIK and distributed throughout the country. Close collaboration with some local NGOs and Ministries have been established. Possible new linkages include the University for Development Studies, the Ministry of Food and Agriculture, various NGOs, and various World Bank Projects in the area. This will be further extended in the form of in-country linkages, regional networking within the west African sub-region, and international linkages as envisaged within the Compas Consortium of Universities. These platforms will serve as opportunities for policy advocacy on a broader basis.

We can conclude that endogenous development has a considerable perspective, but is a time consuming process. All actors involved have to assess the relevance of both types of knowledge: outside knowledge and indigenous knowledge, and think creatively about new options for combining these is the most favourable way under local circumstances. The methods and approach for endogenous development needs to be developed further, however. Enhancing endogenous development is a continuous and challenging learning process.

5.2 DEVELOPING CENTRES OF EXCELLENCE ON ENDOGENOUS DEVELOPMENT

Cosmas Gonese, Raymond Tivafire and Nelson Mudzingwa, AZTREC, Zimbabwe

AZTREC - the Association of Zimbabwean Traditional Environmental Conservationists - was formed in 1985 by freedom fighters, chiefs and spirit mediums, to focus on environmental conservation and cultural survival. AZTREC's activities are centred on eco-cultural villages, where many income-generating activities are taking place.

Since time immemorial the African worldview is based on the understanding that the living world depends on the tripartite relationship between humans, nature and the spiritual world. Nature is considered to be the habitat of the spirits. In addition to agriculture, people lived from collected fruits, mushrooms, honey and meat from the forests, while traditional medicine was used to cure and prevent diseases. During the Zimbabwean liberation struggle in the 1970s, the chiefs and spirit mediums worked closely with the freedom fighters in training them to interpret signals from the natural world, and in advising them to respect nature. A lot of blood was shed during this period, and, according to our tradition, the people and the natural resources had to go through a cleansing process thereafter. When the war ended in 1980, war veterans, chiefs and spirit mediums took upon themselves the task of facilitating the reburial of war victims, and cleansing the sacred woodlands, wetlands and shrines.

After the liberation struggle. During the liberation struggle the fundamental principles of the new free Zimbabwe were handed down through the spiritual world. Some of these fundamental principles were that: the colonial socio-cultural order was to be replaced by a truly African one; the colonial economic system was to be replaced by a system that reflected African identity which could be complemented by other worldviews; and the land should be equally distributed. As time went by, the new government did not address these pressing issues that the people had been struggling for. In fact, in the early 1980s laws were passed which withdrew the power of the chiefs, and created local councillors, who failed to recognise the responsibilities of chiefs and spirit mediums as the ancient administrators of land and natural resources. This led to a dramatic loss in the quality of woodlands, wetlands and other natural resources, as the traditional rules and regulations, which had protected them thus far, were no longer enforced by the local leaders.

Shona cosmovision

The people of the three communities areas mentioned where AZTREC is working are of the Karanga ethnic tribe of the Shona peoples. According to the Karanga people, the ancestral spirits are the owners of humankind and responsible for its wellbeing. Their cosmovision is based on the three pillars of African philosophy: the human world, the natural world and the spiritual world.

Human world. In the human world every person has a personal spirit. Spirit mediums are a special category of human beings, who are 'possessed' by the ancestral spirits. Thus important ancestors are able to communicate with living beings and guide the people. There are different levels of spiritual authority, ranging from individual to family, sub-clan, clan, tribal, ethnic national, regional and continental levels. Within the human world there are traditional leaders, such as chiefs and sub-chiefs, who represent a particular area. Usually a new chief is appointed by the spirit of the one who founded the clan, who returns as a spirit through one of his descendants. A group of headmen and kraalheads constitute the highest board of chieftainship.

Natural world. Sacred places include shrines, water bodies and particular species within the natural world. In the animal kingdom, lions, baboons, snakes and birds such as the bat- teleur eagle, are considered sacred. In the Karanga cosmovision, the human world heavi- ly depends on special messages from the spiritual world, which are transmitted through these sacred animals. For these animals to perform their functions as intermediaries, a conducive habitat is required, which implies the need for ecological diversity. When diver- sity is degraded, these sacred animals migrate to other places, and can no longer serve the humans in the area. Therefore, people are not permitted to hunt wild animals, fell trees or collect wild fruits for sale in specific places. Violation of these rules and regulations are believed to result in the disappearance of the voice of *Musikavanhu*, or God.

Spiritual world. The spiritual world encompasses both the natural world and human soci- ety, inhabited by the spirits. Musikavanhu is supreme in this hierarchy, the creator of the natural and human world that has existed since the beginning of times. The spiritual world consists of different spirits with various meeting places, responsibilities, tasks and func- tions. There are, for example, spirits specialised in war strategies, technology development, rainmaking and human health. Some of the spirits warn people about diseases and prob- lems, which could affect the entire nation.

AZTREC

During the year 1985 local consultative meetings were held in 7 provinces, where local authorities like traditional chiefs, village heads, and spirit mediums, who were at the same time farmers, met to discuss the degradation of nature, lack of land, and food security. They discussed a new strategy for Zimbabwe, which would take into account indigenous practices and traditional leaders in natural resource and land-use management. They decid- ed to form the Association of Zimbabwean Traditional Environmental Conservationists, AZTREC. This NGO, presently based in Masvingo province in southern Zimbabwe, has about 20 field staff. The majority of the members of the executive committee, as well as the spirit mediums, is female. The three community areas where AZTREC is working in the context of Compas are Zimuto, Mupata and Charumbira, which are characterised by low rainfall (400-600 mm per year) and poor sandy soils. Deforestation, uncontrolled graz- ing, mono-cultures and inappropriate tillage systems have led to widespread soil erosion and destruction of natural resources. Soils and water bodies are polluted with chemical fertilisers and insecticides, and the rivers are no longer reliable sources of drinking water. Altogether, these processes have resulted in low crop yields, loss of biodiversity, desertification and health hazards. The influential spirit medium Mrs Ambuya Nehanda was appointed as the patron of the new organisation. Since 1985 these general meetings of the traditional leaders are held twice a year, to guide and advice the organisation.

Tree nurseries as central element. Because of its obvious importance for the farming families, AZTREC decided to take woodland management as the starting point for activities. This included both sacred and ordinary forests and water resources. In order to start community based natural resource management, the chiefs talked to the kraalheads assemblies *(matare)* in their respective areas. They analysed the status of the local natural resources, and discussed the need to resuscitate traditional rules to protect them. Land for planting new trees, existing degraded woodlands, dried springs and vleis, and sacred natural sites in their area were identified, along with the traditional regulations necessary for managing these sites. Each chief held meetings with the respective communities to discuss these issues. The village heads began to take over responsibility for natural resource management, though officially this task was still in the hands of the government elected councillors. Under the guidance of the traditional leaders and their assemblies, nurseries with indigenous tree species were set up by AZTREC in seven districts.

As had been expected, this process faced considerable government resistance at different levels, for example the Forest Commission officials. It reached a head when, in 1998, AZTREC decided to become a formally registered organisation, and therefore required government approval. At first this request was rejected. But having visited AZTREC's nurseries of indigenous tree species, the Forest Commission officials were impressed, as they had considered it impossible to grow indigenous seedlings in a relatively short period. The seedlings were offered by AZTREC for the National Tree Planting Day organised by the Forest Commission, on condition that the local chiefs would perform the rituals during the planting activities. The ceremonies were conducted, the activity was highly successful, and the survival rate of these seedlings was much higher than that of ordinary seedlings offered by the Forest Department. This was the start of the formal recognition of AZTREC by the Government.

Once AZTREC was officially recognised and donors could be approached for financial support, extension staff was based in the tree nurseries. The villages around the nurseries would bring in seeds according to their requirements for the season ahead. School children would come to collect humus, fill polythene bags, and prune seedlings roots. When it was time to plant the trees, the community would take the seedlings to their homes, or used them in community orchards and woodlots. This work developed over the years and AZTREC manages 12 central tree nurseries at present. Altogether the nurseries provide nearly 50,000 seedlings each year, with 75% indigenous species, and 25% exotic fruit trees, such as mango. Since 1985 a total of 500,000 seedlings have been planted in the woodlots in some forty communities in each of the seven districts. Moreover, AZTREC has gradually taken over all the government-run tree nurseries from the Forest Commission. Many of the woodlots established in the early days have matured, and are now providing fruits, medicine, honey, and construction material, which are used for home consumption and for marketing. The central tree nurseries have evolved into commercial centres, where these products are processed, stored and sold.

From tree nurseries to eco-cultural villages. Ten years later, the idea to diversify the activities was conceived. Thorough consultations amongst the people in the communities, traditional leaders, and local government were carried out, which resulted in the idea of intensifying the activities on the locality of the tree nurseries. The spiritual world, through the national spirit medium, advised that the traditional assemblies should be revived at the level of each ethnic group and clan for providing guidance. This traditional assembly is the gathering of local spirit mediums, chiefs, headmen, kraalheads, elders and youth, both men and women, to discuss current social, economic, environmental and cultural issues. When these traditional assemblies started to meet regularly at the central nurseries, the spirit mediums advised them to construct a sacred hut and assembly hall. The central nurseries were thus transformed into eco-cultural villages.

The patron of AZTREC and national spirit medium, Ambuya Nehanda, lives in Mashonaland West, where the first Chikuti eco-cultural village was established nearly 20 years ago. Here, all chiefs and spirit mediums meet regularly to get advice and refresher courses on indigenous knowledge systems, culture and African cosmovision. The second centre is the Zimuto eco-cultural village, which was established in 1998 on 10 ha of land. The physical layout of this centre consists of sacred areas, including a *dendemaro,* or sacred hut for rituals, and a *dare,* or meeting place and residence for spirit mediums, as well as research and training areas. The latter comprises a showroom, a traditional health clinic and pharmacy, a culture and entertainment area, as well as a tree nursery and fields for organic crop production. Another area is designated for the construction of chalets for tourists. In Charumbira and Mupata the physical infrastructure of the eco-cultural villages is being established.

The transformation of the nurseries into the eco-cultural centres has been, and still is, a process guided by the traditional assembly. Formulation of policies and approval of annual strategic plans for the centres is facilitated by this assembly, which also presides over cultural events, rain-making ceremonies, rituals, and the management of sacred woodlands and mountains in the area. Decisions are taken by consensus, in consultation with the ancestors through spirit mediums. The appropriate rites to appease the spiritual world are performed before, during and after any development initiative. Experience shows that after such rites have been performed, communities tend to own and sustain the initiatives.

Building on committees of natural experts. Natural experts, such as farmer innovators, medical practitioners, hunters, architects, foretellers, conflict managers, rain makers, warriors, tool makers, craftsmen and musicians are found in most communities. These custodians of traditional skills can, given proper support and recognition, accelerate the process of endogenous development by providing demonstrations to other community members. AZTREC, and its collaborating partners, have identified the thematic areas on endogenous development, and organised committees of natural experts accordingly. Thus, the cultural committee in Zimuto is composed of three chiefs, senior spirit mediums, elders as well as knowledgeable men and women, who are responsible for conflict resolution in the area, ritual performances at the centre and co-ordination of the different committees.

The agriculture committee includes men and women who have above average harvests, and possess natural talents related to aspects like water conservation, pest management, grain storage and seed selection. There are also biodiversity experts who possess in-depth knowledge on the characteristics of woodlands, wetlands and sacred groves. The technology committee includes natural experts in sculpture, tool making and garment making, while the natural medicine committee includes natural health experts for humans and animals, as well as health spirit mediums. The entertainment committee includes traditional music and drama experts, while the food committee is responsible for food processing and marketing of the products of surrounding forests and orchards. According to African cosmovision, these different natural experts are linked to supernatural powers, either through dreams or the interpretation of natural signs. Each committee is responsible for documenting the knowledge in its own field of expertise, exchanging the knowledge with other groups, testing selected practices, and imparting the results to local communities, visitors and tourists.

Links with other institutions. AZTREC has been one of the training organisations within PELUM (Participatory Ecological Land Use Management) College Zimbabwe. This mobile training institution is made up of community-based organisations and higher learning institutions, such as the University of Zimbabwe, Africa University and the Forestry College of Zimbabwe. AZTREC facilitates the use of indigenous knowledge systems, culture, cosmovision and community organisation, while Zimuto eco-cultural village hosts the trainees during their visits to the area.

In 2000 AZTREC was appointed by the Government CREATE programme, (Community Based Resettlement Approaches and Technologies), to assist in training 400 resettled farmers in sustainable agriculture and natural resources management. In the Mushandike Conservancy, AZTREC will implement research on biodiversity and wildlife management, traditional medicine and eco-tourism.

Activities in the communities

Woodland and mountains. AZTREC decided to take woodlands and mountain ecosystem management as the starting point for its activities in the communities. This was due to the obvious importance of these natural sites for the farming families. People consider these habitats of the spirits and places where rituals and ceremonies can be performed to appease and communicate with the spiritual world. Some of the tree species in these woodlands and mountains, such as *Brachystegia* and *Ficus spp,* are used to forecast the weather, the types of crops to be grown during each season and the times of sowing.

As has been described earlier in this chapter, the work on woodland improvement started off with discussions between spirit mediums, chiefs and kraalheads on re-establishing the traditional rules and regulations. Together they started to identify the different sacred sites in their area, and held meetings with the communities to discuss these issues.

The village chiefs began to take over responsibility for the natural resources again, and tree nurseries with indigenous tree species were started in several districts. Over the past decades tree planting has been a central element in AZTREC's activities. The villagers would bring in seeds of indigenous trees, and, at the start of the tree planting season, the community would take the seedlings to their homes, or for community orchards and wood lots. In this process the 12 nurseries are providing some 50,000 seedlings a year, of which 75% are indigenous and 25% are exotic.

A total of 400 ha of sacred woodland have been rehabilitated in the areas of Zimuto, Mupata and Charumbira, as well as 29 springs and 5 shrines. Forestry products, such as mushrooms, honey, wild fruits, timber, medicine and meat, are collected for consumption and marketing. Processing and marketing the fruits of the orchards has become a successful activity: in the Zimuto eco-cultural village, fruits are processed for the local market. It is planned that fruit processing will be commercially carried out for local and export markets in the near future. This process is supported by the food processing division of the Bulawayo Polytechnic University.

Another positive aspect of this activity is improved biodiversity and habitats for spiritually important beings, such as snakes, birds, animals and mermaids, which enhance the communication between the human and the spiritual world. The role of indigenous knowledge, culture and cosmovision in natural resource management has been re-valued and recognised in the lives of the people. At a more tangible level, the income per household has improved from the consumption and sale of meat from game and birds, construction material, crafts and natural medicines. On the longer term, we have observed positive effects on the rainfall pattern, the soil structure and the water holding capacity of the soil.

Improving wetlands. Outside the eco-cultural villages, some 30 wetlands with an average size of six hectares have been rehabilitated under the guidance of chiefs and spirit mediums. The Masvingo province is often affected by droughts, leading to a severe shortage of grazing for domestic animals. The wetlands provide an oasis of food and water for both humans and animals, an abundance of grass for thatching, reeds for baskets, while relish in the form of mice, birds and locusts also come from these wetlands. Potters collect the clay soils from the wetlands to make clay pots for sale in the community. As a result of these uses, and due to drought, soil erosion and desertification, the wetlands in the area were severely threatened.

AZTREC conducted a study to understand the situation of the wetlands in the area, and to find entry points for participatory rehabilitation programmes. During the first consultative meeting with the local traditional leaders and spirit mediums, the objectives were agreed upon, and the resource persons were determined. Each wetland turned out to have its own historical development and cultural dimension. Traditionally, the spirit mediums make decisions about the wetlands, and the chiefs, headmen and kraal heads enforce the regulations. These regulations state that certain trees in the wetland cannot be felled, washing is not allowed, soap is prohibited, and only traditional utensils such as earthen pots are allowed for collection of water. During menstruation women are not allowed to enter the wetlands and men must remain celibate when working therein. The study also revealed that the wetlands have great development potential, and that the communities were eager to conserve and manage this resource in a sustainable way. Many wetlands have the capacity to provide water for micro-irrigation activities, while for the people, protecting these wetlands also means protecting the habitat of the spiritual world.

In the areas of Zimuto, Charumbira and Mupata, nine traditional practitioners who could support the rehabilitation of wetlands were identified, and the traditional regulations to protect them were re-established. The experience has been positive, 6 fish ponds, 10 ha banana plantation, 26 market gardens, and 35 bee hives have been established in the 23 rehabilitated wetlands of around 5 ha. each. All are managed by the local communities, and have enhanced the local food security and income situation.

Traditional health practices. The terrible pandemic HIV/AIDS has affected a great number of young and middle-aged people. The natural medicine committee is composed of experts in medicinal plants and other health practices for humans and animals. These experts exchange their knowledge and practices to draw up and maintain a register of medicinal plants and uses. This register now includes some 100 plants for common diseases and 180 plants for a variety of more complicated ailments. Traditional healthcare clinics for humans and animals have been established at the Zimuto and Chikuti eco-cultural villages. Patients receive treatment with plant-based medicine, while payment may be in the form of labour or the gift of a chicken or goat.

To systematically integrate traditional medical practices into the mainstream health delivery system, networking with like minded institutions is encouraged. For example, three members of this committee have received a two-year course on how to process natural medicine into tablets, capsules, oils and perfumes at the department of medicine of the University of Zimbabwe. As a result, herbal medicines are now readily available in the community at affordable prices. Over the past three years collaboration with like-minded traditional medical practitioners within Zimbabwe and other Southern African countries has been established. Traditional medical practitioners from South Africa, Swaziland, Mozambique, Botswana, Malawi and Zambia have visited the cultural village during its inception in 1999, where they observed striking similarities with their own traditional medical expertise.

Organic agriculture. The activities in the eco-cultural centres also include experiments and training in organic agriculture. The concept of organic agriculture is also filtering into the communities. Three communities have committees of agriculture, which include men and women with varied expertise. The local committees are further divided into smaller groups with specific topics like seed varieties and selection, inter-cropping, pest and disease management, grain storage, soil fertility, and animal health and nutrition. A register of the different traditional techniques has been made, as well as a baseline of each area in terms of the history and current status of natural resources, arable plots, vegetable gardens, and the type and status of soil. The process of farmer experimentation included workshops on Participatory Technology Development (PTD) with the communities in each area, where farmer innovators and traditional practitioners presented their experiences. Participants also discussed the role of spirit mediums and other spiritual elements in agricultural activities, and agreed on a framework for experimentation. Thus, for example, various varieties of drought resistant indigenous crops were selected, and are now being tested to evaluate their performance. Documenting this process at field level has been difficult, however, and AZTREC has sought the collaboration of PELUM College Zimbabwe.

Over 40 farmers who combine indigenous knowledge and experiences of organic agriculture have established organic farming plots on their homesteads. They have divided themselves into two groups: one group works with vegetable gardens using organic manure, intercropping and bio-pesticides; the second group focuses on organic dryland crop production. The vegetable gardens have generated considerable income for the families and have led to improvements in their nutritional status. The farmers working on dryland farming have carried out experiments with finger millet, bulrush millet and maize based on organic manure, non-toxic herbicides and different inter-cropping techniques. Traditional ceremonies are held to request the ancestors to protect crops from pests and diseases. It was found that organically produced crops could withstand drought better than chemically produced crops. During the 1999-2000 and 2000-2001 seasons the crops gave a good harvest. On half an acre of each crop, farmer innovators harvested between 2.5 and 3 tonnes, where earlier harvests had been less than 1 tonne. Moreover, 19 farmer innovators have opened seed banks of millets, sorghum, maize and groundnuts, while other agricultural inputs, such as manure and implements, are now more readily available in the communities. Slowly, extension staff from the government is becoming convinced of the value of organic agriculture. Some of them are now being trained by AZTREC.

AZTREC staff participate in a ceremony to celebrate the establishment of organic vegetable gardens.

Technology development. People in Zimbabwe have over the centuries gathered a wealth of knowledge on the extraction of mineral deposits of chrome, gold and copper, and processing them into finished products such as spears, hoes and plates. This reinforces the African belief that the discovery of a new technology does not require formal education, but rather the influence of supernatural forces: an innovative technological genius gets his expertise through dreams. AZTREC, in consultation with traditional authorities of Zimuto, Mupata and Charumbira, has identified at least ten experts in each community who make farming tools and handicrafts, such as weaving, carpentry and pottery, for sale to the local communities, visitors and tourists. The Technical Colleges in Zimbabwe have shown great interest in working with these natural experts, so as to enhance their capacity with elements of modern technology.

Activities at the eco-cultural centres

Learning about indigenous knowledge. Indigenous knowledge, culture and cosmovision are generally known from the memories and stories of the elders. African history that is taught in Zimbabwean schools today does not adequately cover the traditional systems of its indigenous peoples. The rapid disappearance of the local languages is re-enforcing the need to research and document the experiences, knowledge systems, practices, values and norms of local communities. A part of this wealth of information has been documented by AZTREC and the subcommittees of natural experts, and stored in the library established at the Zimuto cultural village. The local primary and secondary schools are benefiting from this information in their environmental and cultural education, while adults and elders in the communities are using it for their experiments. There is a considerable collection of traditional artefacts on display at the cultural village, while the documented knowledge and experiences are also presented through videos and the AZTREC magazine called 'The Three Worlds'.

In-depth research in the three communities was done in close consultation with the chiefs after consultation of the spirit mediums. The spirit mediums advised the chiefs to call for gatherings to identify farmer innovators and traditional practitioners, and traditional ceremonies were held to bless their research. This idea was endorsed both by the communities and the traditional leaders, and was carried out using the methodology of Rapid Appraisal of Agricultural Knowledge Systems (RAAKS). The influence of the different individuals in the different spheres of traditional knowledge was thus determined. In the area of natural resources, for example, it turned out that the chiefs, together with their kraalheads and elders and with guidance of the spirit mediums, have the greatest amount of influence. In agriculture, ordinary farmers and the 'master farmers', who have received special agricultural training in high-external-input farming and intensive support by the government extension service, appear to have less influence than successful organic farmers.

Training and education through traditional experts. The eco-cultural centres promote spiritually endorsed innovations, and provide training to members of the community and school children, organised by the committees of traditional experts. These activities take into account gender and age differences; for example, experts in pottery are usually female, professional farmer innovators are both male and female, while foresters are often youth. There is a wide range of activities organised by the cultural committee, as well as the subcommittees on agriculture, natural medicine, technology, food processing and entertainment. Here, we present the activities of the entertainment committee as an example.

Many communal activities and festivities, including music, songs and folk tales, take place at the Zimuto eco-cultural centre. Ten traditional music experts train several entertainment groups in traditional music and dance, explaining to them the meaning of each type of expression. African communities cannot do without song and dance during events such as funerals, marriages, and worship, as it is an integral part of their way of life. The committee has documented the different categories of songs, each with its own dancing style and musical instruments, such as hunting songs, war songs, revolutionary songs, funeral songs, rainmaking songs, and worship songs. The natural music experts also entertain visitors and train foreigners who want to learn and practice African music. In fact, entertainment has turned out to be an extraordinarily sustainable activity.

Promoting educational tourism. Another more recently developed activity at the eco-cultural centres, is the promotion of tourism. It is on the one hand for the national and international researchers, who come to carry out participatory research on the cultures and livelihoods of the people, and on the other for groups of tourists who want to experience African culture. To encourage the latter, a relationship was established with an organisa-

A village planning workshop is concluded with a traditional festival with youth, elders, chiefs and spirit mediums taking part.

tion in the Netherlands, which sends groups of 18-20 tourists for a stay of one week. They are received and guided by the community and the traditional leaders, and have to abide by the traditional rules set by the spirit mediums. Tourists in turn offer their knowledge in managerial and administrative skills, some of which have been used to improve systems in the cultural village.

Other activities. Communities can also organise special meetings to discuss specific problems at the centres. A community with a problem like an increased incidence of rape can discuss the situation and analyse how it can be improved. This process is guided by a spirit medium.

Lessons learned

Some constraints. The experiences with enhancing endogenous development have certainly not been without contradictions and constraints in the politically and socially unstable situation of present day Zimbabwe. We will mention the most striking aspects here.
- Cultural erosion has been serious, and the persisting conventional practices often overshadow the value of indigenous practices.
- Indigenous knowledge systems, culture and cosmovision have never been documented for use in education from primary to tertiary level.
- The top-down style of working with the communities, which is still dominant with a part of the government extension staff, is in contradiction to the AZTREC approach which assumes that communities are in control of their experimentation and innovations.
- There is no government policy to support the integration of indigenous knowledge systems, culture and cosmovision into mainstream development.
- The relationship between traditional spiritual values and practices and the formal church and religion leads to some tensions.
- The market for traditional products is still limited, while the quality of the local products does not always meet the requirements of the market. Although the ceremonies are well attended, it is possible that some people come for the food, drinks and entertainment, not identifying themselves with the beliefs and values contained in the ceremonies.
- Language differences between ethnic groups, and between rural people and academia, is a major obstacle for more people to benefit from the documented indigenous knowledge.

Towards endogenous development. AZTREC is a community-owned organisation totally engaged in development initiatives. Its philosophy and development agenda is above party-politics. The focus is to promote the welfare of every Zimbabwean notwithstanding tribe or political affiliation. This is demonstrated by 17 years of lobbying and advocating for reinstitution of chiefs, spirit mediums and natural experts. The majority of the people in Zimuto, Charumbira and Mupata have made a turn from exogenous to endogenous solutions for their problems. In this process, however, it is imperative to make a good choice of solutions from outside and fuse them with the traditional way of solving problems. There is an increasing feeling among this population that, unless people go back to their roots, there cannot be true sustainable development, because: *"What is borrowed shall never be yours"*.

The five main thematic areas on endogenous development, culture and entertainment, natural resources, organic agriculture, traditional health, and technology and food processing, will continue to be the major focus for AZTREC's future activities. Indigenous languages and policy formulation will also be given attention. The aim is to further empower the different kinds of natural experts through capacity building programmes at individual level, while on-farm demonstrations and the eco-cultural villages will showcase the outcome of their practices. The results will be documented, and will allow for scientific analysis of the findings on each of the thematic areas.

Schools of higher learning are increasingly supportive of this development path, spearheaded by traditional leaders. AZTREC is presently collaborating with Bulawayo Polytechnic University in establishing an innovative training university on endogenous development, the future International Centre on Endogenous Development (ICED). This university will enrol students from the south African region who will be trained in the different thematic areas of endogenous development. The Ministry of Higher Education, through the Bulawayo Polytechnic University, will collaborate with ICED in research, curriculum development, documentation and practical assignments of students. The Government of Zimbabwe has allocated 40 hectares of land to AZTREC on which the ICED will be established. The establishment will be done through the guidance of the traditional national assembly of spirit mediums who will work closely with natural experts.

This International Centre for Endogenous Development will build on the experiences built up over the past 17 years in the communities and eco-cultural villages. The positive effect on the income and culture of the people involved, can thus be spread to other regions and countries throughout South Africa.

6. KNOWLEDGE AND BELIEF SYSTEMS IN LATIN AMERICA

Freddy Delgado (Agruco, Bolivia) and Felipe Gomez (Oxlajuj Ajpop, Guatemala)

The majority of the people in Latin America are so called Mestizos, a mix of Spanish and indigenous origins. The cultures of these populations reflect a combination of their historic roots. Although the European influence often dominates, the indigenous culture plays an important role. Especially in the more isolated and marginalized areas the traditional cosmovisions, knowledge and technologies are still very relevant and influence the community organisations, the notion of time, the relationship of people with Mother Earth, the animals and crops. Traditional leaders perform important functions in land use practices, mutual aid and rituals. This chapter focuses on the knowledge and belief systems of the indigenous groups in the Andes and in Central America where Compas is implementing various activities.

The peopling of the Americas began approximately 30,000 years ago when climatic changes permitted migration from Siberia across the Bering Straits. It took another 8,000 years for these small wandering human bands to reach the southern edge of the continent, Patagonia, and to spread throughout Central and South America. Those who undertook this 'Great Journey' through the New World survived by environmental adaptation, which enabled them to fan across two continents. Somehow they managed to compensate for infant mortality by high levels of reproduction. Those who adapted to the Amazon Basin continued in a hunter-gatherer mode, learning the skills needed to survive in a tropical rain forest. Agriculture arose simultaneously in the Andean highlands and in Central Mexico some 5,000 years ago, first as a supplement to hunting and gathering, and later on as a response to growing populations. Gatherers observed the plants yielded by different seeds, and then began to cultivate on a trial and error basis. Teosinte, a high protein precursor of corn, was first cultivated in Mexico, while potato was an early, ecologically adapted crop in the colder Andes. The list of cultivated edible plants soon expanded to include manioc, maize, squash, peppers, pineapple, and other American originals, especially several varieties of beans.

Native Americans

Native agricultural technologies evolved slowly to include the use of digging sticks, irrigation channels, terracing and ridging, intercropping and seedbeds. Food processing and storage technologies were also innovated and widely diffused. As towns and cities grew, especially in the Andes and Central America, hunting declined in favour of limited domestication of chicken, turkey, pond fish and other animals. However, animal protein was hard to come by in all the predominantly agricultural societies. Transport was an obstacle for all the American peoples, though alpacas and llamas were semi-domesticated and used for limited local transport in the Andean region.

Being confined to small home markets, these pre-colonial societies invested their agricultural surpluses in exquisite crafts. The royal courts that developed around ceremonial centres stimulated artisans to turn out specialised products of high quality, apart from items they made for daily use. Ceramics and basketwork were closely associated with agriculture, but with time became important forms of ceremonial art. The different peoples throughout the Americas constructed magnificent and long lasting buildings in environ-

ments varying from the lowland jungles to highland mountains. While we can still marvel at these sites, such as the ruins of Machu Picchu built by the Incas in highland Peru, and of Tikal built by the Mayas in the tropical lowland of northern Guatemala, it is much more difficult to penetrate the intellectual world of their builders.

The Mayas, prior to their collapse in AD 800-900, had a sophisticated writing system, such as the Maya codices. These documents were systematically destroyed by the colonisers, however, as were many of their ideas about astronomy and mathematics. The Aztecs in Mexico excelled in urban planning, irrigation and public health, but showed little interest in writing. The Andean civilisations never developed a system of writing identified as such. Therefore, the main

Guatemalan Mayas honour Mother Earth at the temple pyramid of Huehuetenango.

written sources of knowledge of these cultures at the time of the conquest originate from the Spanish colonial chroniclers. These are replete with names of sacred places in the form of mountains and rocks, lakes and springs, and other kinds of natural and man-made objects with a ritual significance.

Pre-Columbian agriculture. Malnutrition was relatively unknown in pre-Columbian times. In the Amazon and other tropical forests, the descendants of the original settlers built societies, characterised by low population densities and high mobility, combined with a rotational system of resource use for hunting, gathering, fishing, and gardening. For millennia this system ensured ecologically and socially sustainable livelihoods. In the valleys and highlands the productive systems included different kinds of terracing and ridging, irrigation canals, intercropping and seedbeds, as well as slash-and-burn (or shifting) cultivation. Wetland cultivation was developed to an art form by the pre-Columbian peoples throughout the Americas. The most elaborate systems involved the construction of artificial island platforms and adjacent channels or ditches within the wetlands. Moreover, the Spanish conquerors reported managed forests and extensive orchard-gardens.

These strategies included complementarity of different ecological zones, communal land use, and a complicated system of labour exchange based on solidarity and reciprocity. As a result, traditional agriculture was small-scale, but highly productive. Pre-Columbian Andean biotechnology, for example, has produced around 40% of all the plants consumed by humans today, and has developed around 3,500 varieties of potatoes and 50 varieties of maize [Earls et al., 1990]. These agricultural achievements help to explain the consistently large populations found in settlement studies of, for example, the Maya, and the large number of city-states that emerged in this classical period.

After the conquest

The European conquerors came from an age of iron and steel with wooden ships, navigation, steel swords, guns, explosives, and literacy. They brought horses, cattle, pigs; also diseases such as smallpox, measles, diphtheria, trachoma, whooping cough, chicken pox, bubonic plague, typhoid fever, scarlet fever, amoebic dysentery, and influenza [Segal, 1997]. The local elite was destroyed and their power replaced with that of the Spanish conquerors based on a State-Church structure that controlled the means of production. The colonial times that followed witnessed the exploitation of the lands, the resources, and the people of the conquered regions. Local tribes were exhausted in the search for cheap labour, and slave labour became part of the model. Food habits were modified, as wheat, rice, coffee, banana and sugar cane were introduced and produced for export. Famine, little known in the pre-Columbian times, became a major concern in the Americas.

The conquerors settled permanently in these areas, and mixed with certain parts of the indigenous populations, thus forming the dominant *ladino* or *mestizo* populations. Independence from the colonial powers in the nineteenth century saw power transferred to the dominant ladino populations, while for the native indigenous populations throughout the three Americas the situation changed only marginally.

After colonisation Catholicism became the dominant religion. Seen as a rebellious return to pagan beliefs, the religious animistic expressions of the indigenous populations were destroyed. Christianity was preached as the only true religion. Europeans tried to educate Maya children, for example, in the ideas and language of the conqueror and through the mass destruction of Maya art and images, the repression of rituals, the burning of books, and the methodical eradication of literacy in the old writing system. Where once Maya communities had been in intensive communication and interaction with one another over long distances, they were now fragmented and kept in deliberate isolation. Today there is not a single Maya society, linguistically and culturally; what remains is a mosaic of different Maya ethnic groups.

Post-colonial agriculture. From the time of the conquest to the present, agriculture in this region has been dichotomised between small-scale subsistence farming and large-scale mono-crop operations producing for the market. Some native agricultural methods have continued, but other techniques perfectly adapted to local conditions, such as terracing and raised fields, have largely disappeared. Early colonial institutions and legislation were designed to exploit native labour and mineral resources, and to produce surplus food to support the European economies as well as the colonial administration. Large landholdings were taken away from the native populations and granted to Spanish and Portuguese immigrants, who transformed it into plantation enterprises for lucrative trade with the home country. The system called *hacienda*, with its labour secured through debt peonage, stood at the basis of these plantations. This resulted in the persistent dichotomy between large, extensively cultivated holdings (*latifundios*) and small, intensively cultivated properties (*minifundios*). This system has survived in many Latin American countries until today, and stands at the root of the major economic and social problems.

The small-scale farming enterprises are based on minimisation of risk and adaptations to local ecological conditions, as well as on heterogeneity and diversity within the production system. In spite of their suitability to local conditions, and often exceptional productivity, pressure of the larger society has led to the erosion or abandonment of these techniques. Yet, there are efforts to re-introduce ancient agricultural techniques, like the 'ridged fields' in the Titicaca basin of Bolivia.

Indigenous worldviews

Combining Indigenous and Christian beliefs. A significant number of pre-colonial beliefs from the deep past of the Maya and other indigenous groups have survived to date. A process of synthesis between the traditional beliefs and Catholicism has taken place, which is expressed in various ways by different indigenous groups throughout Latin America. Van den Berg [1989] explains how the Aymara people have become followers of the Catholic Church, without loosing their Aymara religious identity. Whilst the Catholic mass is celebrated and attended by community members, the church and the churchyard is also used for ancient rituals. Hatse et al. [2001] describe how for the Q'eqchi' people, one of the Maya indigenous groups in Guatemala, has transformed the ancient Maya traditional cross figure to the Catholic cross in the course of colonisation. For these people, the cross represents God, as well as the sacred hill and valley. The Q'eqchi' bring food and ritual offerings to the cross, asking for rain or sun, for the blessing or healing of animals, and the health of their families.

Another example is the incorporation of a selection of Christian festivities into the Aymara ritual calendar, according to the agricultural production cycle, as well as astrological and climatological considerations. Pre-harvesting rituals are combined with the catholic carnival festivities, which are celebrated widely all over the Andes and other parts of South America. Other expressions of religious synthesis in the rural indigenous communities of Latin America include the celebration of the catholic *Todos Santos*, or All Saints' Day, the 2nd of November, which coincides precisely with the celebration of *Difuntos*, or Spirits of the Dead, in the indigenous world. Reciprocity between the living and the dead is celebrated at the funeral sites: meals, music and prayers are shared between the living and their ancestral family members.

The way both religious expressions are integrated into daily life is described by Rigoberta Menchu, the Maya woman and Nobelprizewinner of 1992. She explains: *"My mother prayed to Nature. Whenever a problem arose in the community she would go out at night to pray. She greeted the rising sun every morning. My mother's religion was the Maya faith. My father was a catholic. He was a sacristian and had to place candles and flowers in front of the saints. Reverently he would burn aromatic incense. Never the balance between my father's and mother's faith has been broken. We, their children, learned two ways of intense prayer and believe from them. The Creator knows how to deal with that"* [Wijsen and Nissen, 2002].

Community organisation. Rural indigenous communities in the Andes today have a mixed form of traditional organisation: in the form of *Ayllu* - or indigenous organisation for communal and individual land use - combined with colonial traditions in the form of rural villages, and in the case of Bolivia a syndical organisation. The rural communities have multiple functions, such as to administer communal resources, to solve differences between families, as well as to form the basis for expressions of spirituality. The social organisation is based on *reciprocity*, or mutual help, which lies at the heart of the Andean indigenous culture and is expressed in agriculture as well as all other aspects of life. There are many different systems of reciprocity, such as *ayni* ('today for me, tomorrow for you'), *minka* (payment in agricultural products) and *faenas* (working together on a communal project) [Bilbao, 1994].

Cosmic harmony. The traditional Aymara and Quechua worldview is based on the perception of the 'totality of the universe', which includes three major spheres: *Pachanka-macha* or the human sphere of life, *Pachamama* or the natural-material sphere of life, and *Pachakamak* or the extra-human, spiritual sphere of life. Human society includes communities, families and individuals, and the relations between them; the natural sphere includes all material aspects of nature. The extra-human sphere includes all super natural beings like God and Angels, personified natural beings, such as the Sun, Mother Earth or *Pachamama*, as well as the spirits of the agricultural products, the saints and ancestors. There is a hierarchy in the importance of these spiritual forces. From this confluence emanates a fourth sphere, *Pachankiri* - or daily life. It is in this sphere that all the shared practices such as the necessary techniques and technologies for the continuity of life, and the social, material and spiritual reproduction take place, be it for agriculture, animal husbandry, forestry, art or other activities [Rist et al., 1999].

Harmony in the cosmos is considered optimal, not only when there is harmony within each of these three components of the universe, but also between them. Both the indigenous groups of Maya and Andean origin believe that, when man respects his natural environment and adapts himself to it, nature will maintain its equilibrium and supply man with what he needs. When man attends to and respects the different spiritual forces, through correct conduct as well as rituals and sacrifice, these forces will remain quiet and will offer him protection, support and abundance. For example, when something happens in the human world, such as a provoked or spontaneous abortion, this is related to a (natural) disaster, both for the family involved as for the community it belongs to. Abortions are often related to hailstorms, which seriously affect the crops in these regions. In the same way, bad crop results are often perceived to be a result of faltering human conduct.

In this way the equilibrium of the spiritual forces has its effect on the equilibrium of the natural environment, which can then support man in his quest for survival. Thus, the circle is closed: 'all is related to all'. This cosmos equilibrium is not stable, however, as each of the three spheres is contrary to the other and tries to dominate. Thus, in Aymara cosmovision, the fundamental equilibrium between the different spheres is recognised on the one hand, whilst on the other hand the constant tensions that threaten this equilibrium, within the spheres as well as between them, is encountered.

In this tension, another common concept in American indigenous cosmovision can be identified: the concept of duality, or antagonistic forces. In the natural world these include light-darkness, male-female, cold-heat, and drought-humidity; in the human world they include wealth-poverty, and community- individualism; while in the spiritual world they imply protective-dangerous spiritual forces. These antagonistic forces are not perceived as an obstacle to life; they are rather referred to as basic elements in life, as long as they remain in equilibrium and do not exceed their limits. Therefore, the equilibrium in the cosmos is perceived as the encounter between opposite forces that are, at the same time, necessary and complementary.

Spiral notion of time. Up to the present day, the essential elements of the Andean and Maya cosmovision are widespread. In the Andes, the spiral notion of time leads to the understanding of life in terms of *jakakha*, or karma, and *kutimithaya*, or re-incarnation. Time is seen not as a linear process with a beginning and an end, but as a spiral process. This implies that the future is a repetition and expansion of cycles and rhythms. A Maya priest, José Serech explains: "*For us time has no end. Time links us with who we were, with our ancestors, and with who will come, with our children and grandchildren. We are but a part of a chain, and part of a whole. But as an essential part of this whole we have a special responsibility. We cannot simply live our lives, we have to guarantee continuity. And all we do as human beings has its effects in this life and in this world. After we die there is a completely different life, in another world*" [de Walsche, 1992].

Within this concept of time, the concept 'development' is also perceived as a spiral movement, as 'the unrolling or expansion of the past, where only the context of every specific moment changes, as well as the movement from the centre to the periphery'. The moment obstacles arise, the movement returns to the origin, to the sources of knowledge and survival strategies that have been proven in the past. But it is only a phase of development. Once the solutions for the obstacles are found and integrated, development continues, but with renewed potential.

Religious origin of indigenous crops. Amongst all natural forces, it is the earth that receives most attention in Aymara cosmovision. The earth is perceived as sacred, and is expressed in the concept of Pachamama, or Mother Earth, in the Andes. But within the concept of Pachamama, the *chacra* - or agricultural plot - in the Andes, and the *milpa* in

Central America, is what the campesino has the most intimate relationship with. This is expressed in numerous beliefs and rituals [van den Berg, 1989].

These indigenous beliefs in which agriculture and culture form a central unity, provides the basis of life in the uncertain climatic environment.

The potato has its origins in the Andes similar to maize in Central America. The mythical origins of these and other Andean indigenous crops include their creation out of the different parts of a divine body: *"Ashkoy fell on the ground and from the various parts of his body wild plants and crops emerged. From his eyes potatoes and ollucos emerged, from his teeth maize, from his fingers other tubers, such as ocas and mashuas"* [Salas, 1996].

In Central America, Mayas consider themselves 'the people of maize'. Not only because tortillas, or maize cakes, constitute a major part of the daily diet, but also because maize is the ultimate source and inspiration of the myths, rituals and customs that guide their every day life. The ancient and sacred Maya book, the Popol Vuj, contains the story of the creation of man. It explains how God, after two failed attempts to create man from clay and wood, finally succeeded in moulding the bodies of the first Maya people with maize-dough, four men and four women. Today, maize is seen both as the mythical origin of the Maya people, as well as the holy and necessary food. Maize production, therefore, is filled with ritual activities and beliefs. Rituals start the evening before sowing, when all the participants accompany the seeds that will be sown with incense, candles and prayers. The rituals are observed until the final phase of the harvest, when in a procession the 'spirits of the lost maize seeds' are taken home. It is believed that losing one single seed may reduce the strength during the next production cycle. According to Maya cosmovision, producing maize is not just another activity, but an exercise for a dignified life, a process that keeps one on the right track of good thoughts and behaviour,

Within the Andean concept of Pachamama (Mother Earth), the agricultural plot is considered sacred.

reminds one of his origin and destination, and binds one to the generations before him as well as to the coming generations. He who grows maize helps to maintain creation: *"he who sows is being born, and he who dies will be placed in the earth like a maize seed, waiting for new seasons"*. The Maya farmers are, therefore, convinced that for a good harvest, you not only need knowledge and experience, but also 'the heart of a good person'. But today, the Maya are threatened, as many of them own little or no land at all to produce maize, while almost 600 local varieties of maize are under threat due to the influence of multinationals and their genetically modified varieties [Garcia et al., 2000].

Traditional spiritual leaders. For indigenous peoples the mysterious world of spirits, myth and religion occasionally breaks into the natural world, for instance in dreams and rituals. Since the spiritual world is more difficult to understand than the natural and human world, the interpreters of that world, medicine men, shamans and priests, are more important than experts in the everyday world. In native America the range of spiritual experts was much wider than that of technology experts [Hultkrantz, 1997]. Plants with psychoactive or hallucinogenic properties have been considered sacred. They allow medicine men, or even ordinary individuals, to communicate with the ancestors and the spiritual forces of the mysterious world, who are able to inflict sickness, suffering, death, or calamities on people and whole tribal groups.

Maya local spiritual practitioners, or shamans, as a social institution have survived the last two and a half millennia. Modern village shamans cure individuals of their illness, assuage afflictions of the household, and help neighbours find peace with the spirits of the maize fields. But their work is not exclusively confined to the personal or local realm. Besides the local divinities, shamans are also responsible for community propitiation of the broadly acknowledged Gods, such as the Chakob, or raingods, Yum Kaax, the spirit of the ruins and the forests, and Halal Dios, God Almighty, who is the sun.

Traditional healers are often specialised in a particular area of health. Spiritual matters, emotional affairs, the use of herbs, bone setting, massage or birth attendance are some of these areas. There are also specialists in 'fear' and 'greed'. Most traditional healers combine medical/herbal, psychological and spiritual activities in some way. They do not understand disease by focusing on specific organs, nor do they have knowledge of microbiology. Disease is considered to be a result of a disturbed balance between elements, such as diet, climate, infection, constitution, emotion, behaviour and energies. Many of these factors can make a patient either 'hot' or 'cold', and remedies are also divided into these categories. Most healers belong to the same social group as their patients, and combine their activities with another occupation, such as housewife, carpenter or farmer [Garcia, 2000].

Living astronomy. Over 3,500 years have passed since the Andean societies built observatories to register the passing of seasons, to measure eclipses, to observe planet rotations, moon and sun phases and the rising or setting of the stars. The careful and elaborate design of those structures show the importance attached to astrology and its relevance for the socio-territorial organisation of the agricultural cycle. The most important spiritual moments, today marked by Christian feasts, are also vital dates for astronomical observations. Many of them are used to predict the climatic characteristics of the coming rainy season. Another important element in the organisation of social and productive activities is the inter-relation with the phases of the moon. Many activities such as sowing, cutting of trees or animal castration, for example, are limited to periods with certain moon phases. The interest of the Andean farmers goes beyond an abstract scientific interest in the movement of the stars and planets. They try to synchronise their social and productive life with the rhythms of the cosmos, and this leads to what could be called a 'living astronomy'.

Gender aspects in cosmovision. In the Andes, as in many other indigenous societies, the woman is associated with fertility and reproduction. The feminine and the seeds, *muhu* in Quechua language, constitute a symbolic unity. The female character has a divine dimension, when it is included in the concepts that refer to earth - or Pachamama - which in this case refers to the world, the space where humanity and the family lives [Salas, 1996]. Moreover, in the process of religious synthesis between indigenous and Catholic beliefs, the female Pachamama has become associated with the Virgin Mary.

Daily rituals. Agricultural rituals are related to the activities and time of year, take place at various levels, and include social conduct based on the concept of reciprocity. At family level simple rituals are performed on a daily basis, such as *ch'alla*, which includes a small offering by sprinkling drops of an alcoholic drink on top of agricultural products or the Pachamama, in order to show gratitude and fulfil her needs. Through these and other small rituals - sometimes in the home, other times on the agricultural field or specific natural sites - the farmer appeases the natural forces and attracts good luck and abundance. Many rituals are combined with a sacrifice of an animal, which is later on consumed by all present [van den Berg, 1989].

Endogenous development

Today indigenous peoples in Latin America manoeuvre between their faith in ancient knowledge and their aspirations to become 'modern people'. Therefore, endogenous development will have to take both aspects into account. We can build on the natural endogenous process of synthesis of cultures, which has enabled cultural survival over the centuries in the Americas. This synthesis can be interpreted by some as a weakness, but in fact is a strength and opportunity. As was expressed during a conference on Culture and Maya spirituality in Guatemala, February 2000 [Garcia et al., 2000]: *"The major force of the Maya culture has been to incorporate, to direct elements that came from afar which, over time, have become part and parcel of this culture. Like the güipiles (*Maya traditional colourful clothing*) are the very part of the Maya culture today, the colours, the wool and the designs have come from another world. The great strength of the cultures is not to isolate themselves from the rest of the world, but to incorporate, to translate and to adapt what has come from other parts. The question today is: how do we combine the two worlds, our Maya culture and modernisation, and how can we incorporate things from the modern world within the lines of our own culture and spirituality?"*

Several organisations in Latin America are trying to enhance practices and methodologies aimed towards endogenous development. An example is Educe in Mexico, an NGO that works with Maya health practices. These traditional practices are usually fragmented, often combined with elements of western medicine. They are used with many limitations, under ideological pressure and with severe scarcity of resources. They depend on an oral culture and lack a homogeneous theory. Garcia [2001] describes how this NGO in Mexico re-enforced traditional Maya medicine by systematising the knowledge and experience of 40 traditional healers, comparing these with other medical traditions, such as Chinese health systems. Striking similarities were encountered, both in concepts as well as practices, such as acupuncture, massage and the use of certain herbs and spiritual healing techniques. This was used to reinforce the local traditional health system, as well as to disseminate the experiences among traditional healers elsewhere in Central America.

Moreover, Educe sought to bridge the concepts between traditional Maya medicine and western medicine, in order to enhance the formal education programmes aimed at diminishing the incidence of diseases, such as cholera. The traditional Maya concept of 'wind' resulted similar to the concept that diseases can be transmitted if, in western terms, they are 'infectious'. Adapting to this indigenous concept of 'wind' in these educational programmes has greatly enhanced their effectiveness in preventing cholera in the rural communities.

Agruco, in Cochabamba, Bolivia, is one of the Compas organisations that has stimulated indigenous markets, in which different concepts of purchase and sale are included. This market system is the centre of exchange of agricultural products between communities in the highlands, who bring many varieties of potatoes and other local tubers, and communities from the valleys, who bring the local varieties of maize. Enhancing these traditional markets are a way to re-activate the production of Andean crops and to support the indigenous forms of solidarity, which may well be viable alternatives to the economic crisis that Bolivian rural population is facing today [Delgado and Ponce, 2001].

In the next chapters, the field experiences of endogenous development within the Compas network in Latin America are presented in more detail.

6.1 ENDOGENOUS DEVELOPMENT AND UNIVERSITY EDUCATION

Freddy Delgado and Dora Ponce, AGRUCO, Bolivia

AGRUCO is a university centre dedicated to higher education, scientific research and social interaction with farmer communities, in the field of agro-ecology and sustainable development. It is part of the State University San Simon (UMSS) in Cochabamba, Bolivia. This university-based Centre for Agro-Ecology has two roles: it carries out field-based activities and it teaches university courses in crops, animal husbandry and forestry, based on agro-ecological principles and the culture of the Andean farmers. Participatory research and the involvement in small development projects in the Bolivian highlands permit constant feedback of experiences in endogenous development into the contents of teaching.

The province of Cochabamba includes a large number of natural eco-systems, which vary from highlands and valleys to tropical lowlands. The communities that AGRUCO is working with in the context of the Compas programme are in the highlands, some 25 km from the city of Cochabamba. Together they have a total of 2,500 inhabitants of Quechua indigenous background. The communities are located in the Jatun Mayu watershed, at elevations varying from 2,800 to 4,300 meters above sea level. The ecological variety in the area permits a diverse and complementary production system, in accordance with Andean cosmovision and the risk-avoiding strategies related to the climatic uncertainties. The main crops are tubers and grains, especially potatoes and oats in the highlands, and corn, wheat, barley, legumes and vegetables in the valleys. The produce is mainly for people's own consumption, and to a lesser degree for exchange and sale. Animal husbandry is diversified, with llamas in the highlands, and sheep, cows and goats in the lowlands.

University education in Bolivia, as in other Latin American countries, has numerous effects on young people. The fact that the students originate from the Andean culture, often direct descendants of the Quechua or Aymara indigenous peoples, does not imply that they identify with the local culture after they have graduated. On the contrary, the acceptance of the materialistic vision of life, learning about modern agricultural production within the curriculum, and the lack of linkages between higher education and the concepts of the rural people, often leads students away from their cultural background instead of bringing them closer to the potentials of endogenous development. That is why the State University San Simon has created AGRUCO: to enable students to receive an education that is supportive of endogenous development. The link between the university department and the rural communities of the Jatun Mayu watershed is essential in this process.

Cosmovision and farmers' organisation

Because the inhabitants of the Andean communities have been and still are predominantly farmers, their religion has evolved from agricultural experiences. This emphasises the relationship of society and nature in a certain *Pacha* (space-time) and results in a ritual calendar that is in fact an agricultural calendar. This calendar permits them to synchronise the productive practices with the rhythms and cycles of the cosmos. The European and Christian colonisation could not change this: the communities chose to accept the Catholic feasts that coincided or were very close in time to their own festivities. Thus, below the layer of Catholicism, most ritualistic activities maintain their original meaning to a large extent.

In the Andean worldview, the human, natural and spiritual worlds are inseparable: they are in constant dynamic interaction with each other. The notion that people have to relate both to the natural and to the spiritual world implies, therefore, that they not only develop knowledge and skills to survive materially, but that they also have to carry out their own spiritual activities in order to be in tune with the spiritual world. In this worldview, a good crop, quantitatively and qualitatively, does not only depend on the appropriate technologies, but also on the accompanying rituals. The moment that farmers begin to create adequate physical conditions for plant growing, like ploughing for example, they ask *Pachamama*, or Mother Earth, through a ritual, to contribute to this by creating optimal spiritual conditions.

Organisation of farmer communities. The organisation of the Bolivian rural communities is twofold: it combines a syndicate and a traditional organisation. Both forms of communal organisation respond to the same cosmovision. The agrarian syndicates were founded in 1952 in the context of the Agrarian Reform, and are organised in one confederation, which is divided into departmental and provincial confederations and local farmers' subcentres, such as the 'Subcentral 8 of August' in the Jatun Mayu river basin, where AGRUCO works. The role of this organisational structure is to represent the communities to the outside world, such as during their negotiations with the state, NGOs and other entities.

The traditional organisation is reflected in two institutions: the *Alcalde de indios*, or mayor, and the *Juez de Aguas*, or water manager. The alcalde is the traditional religious authority responsible for ensuring cohesion within the community. He has to be involved in all community discussions, including the planning of agricultural activities, and all actions need to be legitimised by him. Moreover, he has to resolve conflicts, is part of the juridical administration and also presides over the ceremonies and rituals of the community. His symbol is the *vara*, a kind of stick. In Jatun Mayu a new alcalde is elected each year on the 3rd of August, during a ceremony in which all villagers participate. The water manager also has a significant responsibility. This person has the difficult role of ensuring the equitable distribution of irrigation water in the community.

Principle of reciprocity. The rural indigenous communities are linked by the principle of reciprocity that permits the reproduction and continuity of the families. There are various forms of reciprocity, and several of them are related to agricultural production. The most frequent form is called *a partir*: one farming family owns a plot of land and another family does the work; the profits are shared between both families. *Ayni* is a work-exchange arrangement practiced at family level. These systems of reciprocity are well adjusted to the heterogeneity of the climate, topography and biodiversity of the Andean ecosystems, as the variety of climatic conditions poses significant risk to agriculture. The Andean logic also includes the concept of *El Don,* which refers to moral reciprocity, not only between people, but also with nature and the spiritual world.

Today, the continued functioning of the syndicate structure, the traditional communal organisations, and the system of reciprocity shows that, in spite of the effects of globalisation and westernisation, the Quechua and Aymara communities are still organised in accordance with their own worldview. It is quite remarkable that in the course of history, in spite of many fierce efforts to dissolve their structure, these indigenous groups have been able to withstand total cultural erosion and destruction. It is, however, necessary to avoid romanticising these cultures and to open up the Andean cosmovision through intercultural dialogue, to improve the quality of human life and the sustainability of nature.

Bolivian woman performs a thanksgiving ritual to emphasise the reciprocity between humans, Pachamama and animals.

AGRUCO

Changing approach over time. AGRUCO's main goal is to support sustainable rural development through a revaluation of local knowledge, culture and agro-ecology. Over the past years we have gained experiences in supporting the process of endogenous development without interfering too much with social structures, values and the specific contexts that make each community unique, and are finding ways of including this experience into the university curriculum. Chronologically, this process can be divided into three phases. Between 1985-1989, during the 'agro-biology phase', our programme worked with rural communities, taking organic agriculture as practised in Switzerland as its starting point. We concentrated on interrelated systems, like those between soils, plants and mixed cropping, for example. Over time, however, we came to understand that the agro-ecosystem is the result of the co-evolution of nature and human society, rather than only a nat-

Farmers and fieldworkers review the results of experiments with traditional Andean crops, Agruco, Bolivia.

ural process.

Therefore, between 1989 and 1995, we implemented an 'agro-ecology' approach, working in an interdisciplinary way in research and extension. Education and technical assistance was provided to the communities in an attempt to overcome the gap between research and its application in the field. Our methodology involved participatory research, revaluing local knowledge and local decision making models. This implied the search for a reciprocal relation between researchers and community members. The task resulted to be easier than we had thought, because the agro-ecological principles are congruent with the essence of traditional Andean agriculture. Over time we found, however, that in the process of handing over more research responsibilities to the farmers' communities, we had unintentionally continued with the conventional 'transfer of technology' model.

While entering the third phase of supporting 'sustainable rural development' in 1996, we concluded on the need to get a deeper understanding of the concepts of life of the communities we were working with, in order to develop a context for our actions. We developed a methodology based on the material, social and spiritual life of the rural people. Participatory research and intercultural communication between farmers and scientists became central in our actions. For the first time we became aware that experience and sensitivity are required when entering indigenous communities, and that we had made some critical mistakes in this respect. For example, we would try to meet with the leader of a community at a time of community fasting or during spiritual withdrawal, without taking this into consideration. We learned the necessity of understanding the indigenous concepts of life, and found that respecting, sharing and becoming part of the ritual in a deeply spiritual way are important principles in the process of educating professionals, who intend to work in sustainable rural development. In this approach, from 1996 onwards, AGRUCO has been involved in Compas.

Combining higher education with support to rural communities. Some fundamental conditions and actions enabled AGRUCO to evolve from an university organisation with a conventional development programme, into an organisation that initiates and practices an intercultural dialogue between the scientific and local knowledge systems. Three questions were important in this process of change. Firstly, how can we establish an institutional framework that permits harmonious and permanent interaction between the university and the rural communities? Secondly, what are the main attitudes necessary to enhance the exchange between the community and the university? And finally, how can we encourage technical staff to overcome the limitations of conventional and specialised education, that prioritises the use of quantitative methods?

In order to establish the institutional basis for the intercultural dialogue we had to take two basic realities into account. On the one hand, it was the university of which we are part of, and its academic programme based on scientific knowledge and values. And on the other, it was the native communities, with an entirely different system of knowledge, objectives and concepts of life. This meant that AGRUCO had to find an institutional configuration that allowed a horizontal and reciprocal interaction with the communities. Since we wanted to ensure that our work interacted with all parts of the communal

University students exchange their views and findings with the community.

process of learning and action, we could not organise ourselves as in a conventional university: into departments for education, investigation and extension. Instead, we had to structure AGRUCO into three other units. First we created a unit called 'support to communities'. This provided the basis for the activities of the other two units, namely 'participatory research' and 'education', which imply activities both at communal and university level.

This combination of education, research and support to the communities now permits the integration of local experiences into the educational process at the university. When we describe a farmer's technology, or when a student produces a thesis in and with the community, we simultaneously contribute to participatory research, support of the communities and reciprocal education. During courses located within the communities for students, university teachers and professionals, the local people are able to transmit their knowledge and capabilities, their needs, pre-occupations and aspirations to them.

The support given to the local communities is focused on strengthening their organisation, and the elaboration and management of projects as prioritised by the community members, which are called Integrated Community Programmes for Self management and Sustainable Development, or PICADS.

Self-education of university professionals. Having overcome the artificial separation of research, extension and education, we realised that the methodological instruments we used still needed to be revised. One aspect of utmost importance was the process of re-education of the professionals involved. For example, we had to learn to behave as an interdisciplinary team rather than as a multidisciplinary one. In AGRUCO we maintain a permanent and obligatory process of self-education for the whole staff, which starts with a phase of de-schooling and an analysis of the experiences of conventional agricultural extension.

Our experience shows that it is possible to overcome the problems of extension by openly analysing the contradictions and the failures, and by making serious efforts to achieve dialogue on an equal basis. In this process the issues raised by the professionals included: how can we understand the reactions and decisions of the community? How can we learn with them about their reality and their strategies? What is extension? Who decides what? What is it we all want and what can we offer? We concluded that we should move from extension to 'guiding the dynamics of community knowledge'.

Another important factor has been the re-encounter as university professionals with our own cultural identity, as we all have our origins in Andean rural communities. This experience of re-encounter with our own roots is actually the methodological basis of the work with our pre- and post graduate students.

University training programme. In the graduate programme, the training starts with the life of the farming communities, and goes on to co-operating with the families in their search for alternatives to strengthen endogenous development. This co-operation is carried out both in the field and in workshops, with themes identified by the communities, which may vary from agro-ecology to policy and organisational issues. The basis of this work is the process of permanent reflection and dialogue between local knowledge and scientific knowledge. In this way, the research projects of the students start, when possible, with the problems expressed by the farming communities; they then engage in looking for solutions and alternative ways of solving them.

In AGRUCO, the investigations and projects related to the re-valuation of local knowledge and agro-ecology fall into 3 major domains: plant diversity (including wild plants, forestry, and soil conservation), animal diversity (including wild fauna) and cultural and socio-economic diversity (including community strategies, social organisation and alternative community economy). Each domain has diverse projects and sub-projects, and takes general concepts such as sustainability, gender and empowerment into account. The postgraduate programme is based on the same concepts, and offers actualisation courses, as well as a masters in 'Agro-ecology, Culture and Sustainable Development in Latin America'.

Case studies, theories and experiences from other parts of the world also contribute to this educational process. The works of Rist [1992] and Apfel Marglin together with PRATEC, as well as the exchange of experiences through magazines, such as Compas Magazine, have stimulated this process.

Examples of field activities

Supporting endogenous development in Jatun Mayu. In 1998 we started working with the four villages of the Jatun Mayu watershed near Cochabamba. Together they form the subcentre '8th of August' founded in July 1991 in the Jatun Mayu river basin of the Municipality of Sipe Sipe, province Quillacollo. The general aim with the communities is to support farmers' organisations, so they in turn can identify and define their own strategies for endogenous development. More specific objectives include: strengthening the farmer organisations within the new social, economic, political and legal context; supporting and innovating farming practices and technologies related to health, food and biodiversity; supporting local initiatives that strengthen cultural identity; supporting communities in the elaboration, management, execution, administration and evaluation of sustainable development projects.

In the initial process of revitalising the community, we consider three major steps: orientation, consolidation and transfer. During 'orientation', the main emphasis is on understanding the natural, social and spiritual world and their interrelations by means of a 'participatory community diagnosis'. The outcomes and plans for action are then fine-tuned in the context of the whole watershed. During 'consolidation', we support and participate in indigenous research activities, especially in the field of irrigation or production. During 'transfer', AGRUCO provides follow-up support and training in project management to ensure sustainable rural development.

Apart from the monthly meetings of the communities, seminars on political and socio-economic themes of interest to the communities are organised once or twice per year. Through resolutions the farmers express their positions on various issues, like the need to improve education and health in their communities, or their discontent with certain laws. In some cases this has resulted in concrete action directed to national authorities. For example, when the farmer leaders signed an agreement against the development of genet-

The field work of AGRUCO strengthens community organisation and activities such as soil erosion control.

ically modified food and crops in Bolivia, they wrote a letter to the Secretary for Sustainable Development soliciting him not to permit experiments with genetically manipulated potatoes in Bolivia. As a result of these and other actions, the tests were temporarily suspended. The people of the communities have recognised the importance of these seminars and congresses, as enabling them to analyse fundamental aspects of community life. Moreover, this has revitalised the community organisation, the role of traditional leaders, and their relations with local authorities.

The farmers in Jatun Mayu have expressed keen interest in learning how to develop projects for their communities and how to improve their relationships with the municipalities, who, due to the Popular Participation Act, now control government funds for local activities. Permanent reflection between the communities and the AGRUCO project team has resulted in a strategic vision for the development of the river basin, which is now gaining importance in the annual plans of operation of the Sipe Sipe municipality. Community members submit their problems and requests to the appropriate authorities, such as the municipality, and express their points of view about solutions in The Integrated Community Programmes for Selfmanagement and Sustainable Development (PICADS).

These PICADS are also the basis of the interaction between the communities and the municipalities, which - according to the 'Law for Popular Participation' established in 1992 - handle government funds for local development activities. This law enables communities to receive financial support from the state through the local municipalities, which means that successful experiences can be replicated by building them into the operational plans of the PICADs.

Documenting indigenous practices. Over the years AGRUCO has established a large number of documents based on Quechua and Aymara local knowledge and practices in the form of IK-information sheets. These documents are authored by farmers with an innovative practice or knowledge, and are used in community meetings for diffusion. The IK information sheets have proven useful tools in energising the discussions and reflections on the importance of local knowledge, and the way it is adjusted to fit the needs of each local context. Moreover, it has stimulated self-esteem and motivation of the farmers to continue experimenting with these practices. Based on these and other experiences a series of calendars have been designed and distributed, which show the inter-relation between agrarian production and the celebration of rituals and fairs.

Within the university context, a large number of publications have been brought out throughout the years, organised as different series. Several small booklets resulting from small research projects of students about specific alternative technologies in the fields of agriculture and livestock comprise the 'technical series'. The 'reflection series' includes reflections about a specific theme based on concrete experiences in the communities, while the 'memorising series' systematically documents the methodologies used in the work with the communities, research and educational activities. Finally, books are published within the 'series Kumakapi': these result from thesis research of the students following different courses. These documents form the basis of the educational activities, both in the university and in the field work, and have also resulted in a series of publications in national and international magazines.

Strengthening and revitalising indigenous practices. Within the Jatun Mayu area we are presently conducting three investigations: 'Farming strategies to gain access to potato (*Solanum spp.*) seeds for conservation of biodiversity under conditions of climatic risk'; 'Influence of social relations of reciprocity and kinship on farming production systems for a sustainable agriculture' and 'Conservation of biodiversity of cultivar seeds by a cultural value system centered around the role of the Andean woman, in the case of potato (*Solanum spp.*)'. These documentation activities, and the dialogue necessary for them, have strengthened, on the one side, the eroding local knowledge, and, on the other side, the education of graduate and postgraduate students.

Dialogues and reflection with the communities have led to ideas about specific ways towards endogenous development. For example, it was decided to establish a common seed bank in the community of Chorojo, which is now being managed autonomously. This seed bank is supplying and safeguarding the main varieties of local tubers and grains. This positive experience has been spread to other communities for reflection and analysis with a view to replicating it. In another community, Capellani, a water tank was constructed and soil improvement activities were carried out to enhance horticulture. Members of these communities also visited other parts of the country for exchanging experiences related to community organisation, organic agriculture, horticulture and local management of natural resources.

Strengthening local fairs. A fundamental element in the educational process has been the support of the fairs and festivities of the farming communities. These festivities are of strategic importance, especially in times of crisis when cash flows are restricted. Documenting and supporting these events, therefore, is of didactic significance for all involved farmers, technicians, students, as well as development scientists. It provides the chance to learn more about the depth of the ethical principle of reciprocity in the Andean cultures.

Seventh Friday Fair. AGRUCO has devoted much attention to the Seventh Friday Fair, carried out on the 7th Friday after Easter, in the town of Sipe Sipe. The exchanges that take place during this fair are guided by the traditional concepts of *cambiacuy, trueque,* and *purchase sale*: each system complements the other in terms of objective, time and importance. The cambiacuy is the most important form of exchange, based on affinity rather than on interest in gain; the produce is handed over as a gift to satisfy and please the receiving family. It has a strong spiritual and emotional dimension, strengthens the ties between families and signals new friendships. Trueque, or barter, is the other form of exchange at the fair, through which farmers can exchange ceramics, woven baskets, or agricultural products, without the involvement of cash. Purchase sales enable the farmers to buy household items, like sugar, rice cooking oil, radio batteries, and enables transport and buying *chicha,* or local corn beer.

During these exchanges, community and family news is shared, which strengthens feelings of solidarity. This fair shows how two sets of economic logic complement each other: the indigenous logic of 'reciprocity' and the modern logic of the market economy. The fair is very important for farmers in the region because it contributes to food security through non-monetary and monetary exchange, and strengthens social relationships between relatives, friends and compadres, or godfathers, from different communities in the valleys and highlands. Moreover, it is an occasion when religious feelings are expressed. According to elderly farmers in villages near Sipe Sipe, it may date back to the times before the Incas. The Seventh Friday Fair, like other indigenous fairs and festivities in Bolivia, has been losing ground over the last decades due to the influence of religious sects and increased consumption of agroindustrial foods, such as sugar, rice and noodles. These factors have also led to reduced production of Andean crops.

The project to strengthen the Seventh Friday Fair is a result of joining the farming families in several rural communities in the highlands of Sipe Sipe. Over a period of 10 years AGRUCO has supported the production of Andean crops, and small agro-ecological projects have been carried out to increase biodiversity and improve food security. Organising of farmer workshops to reflect on the objectives of the fair, and its importance in times of crisis, has been another activity, as well as publishing on this subject in local papers and radio. The results of these activities have been positive. We have had a good response not just from the communities where this experience was born, but also from other communities and from people in the city of Cochabamba.

This year, the process of strengthening the fairs has been broadened with the active participation of the municipality of Sipe-Sipe. This project not only stimulates fairs and festivities, but also aims at increasing access to Andean foods, strengthening indigenous cultural identity, and educating the urban and rural population about Andean cultural practices. But, most importantly, the support given to these socio-cultural indigenous activities point out new ways of reactivating the production of Andean crops and supporting indigenous forms of solidarity. These may well be viable alternatives to the crisis that the Bolivian rural population is facing today.

Supporting local health traditions. After more than a decade of working with local agroecological knowledge, AGRUCO concluded that it would not be possible to support sustainable agricultural production without taking the communities' concepts of health and disease into account. In the Andes agriculture, food, health, and cosmovision are parts of a diversified whole: there can be no health without culture, food and biodiversity. AGRUCO's experiences with local knowledge have allowed us to get a better understanding of the way these concepts of health and disease fit into the daily lives of the people. Health is based on the principle of 'being united with everyone to live well and better'. This implies being in harmony with the family, the community, the *Pachamama,* or Mother Earth, and all supernatural beings. Consequently, a disease cannot be cured by simply applying a medicinal plant. The medical treatment needs to be combined with a ritual that re-creates adequate spiritual conditions for a healthy life.

The indigenous inhabitants of the Andes identify three types of supernatural diseases. First there are 'diseases due to supernatural punishment'. These diseases are caused by the accumulation of 'sins' for not obeying the norms of the community. The second category of supernatural disease includes those caused by 'unbalanced' people. This especially refers to negative practices in love life, such as envy or desire for revenge. These diseases are 'sicknesses put upon someone', 'sicknesses due to hurt' or 'diseases sent by humans'. The third type of supernatural disease is known as 'spirit loss'. Its usual symptoms are headaches, stomach aches, and rashes and itching all over the body. The villagers attribute this illness to emotions of fear, for example due to stepping on an anthill or the sudden appearance of a snake. The one who treats the 'loss of spirit' is the traditional healer, or *coca khawador,* 'he who foretells the future and cures with coca leaves'.

AGRUCO has worked on participatory research to collect the medicinal plants and the knowledge related to them in the communities of the Jatun Mayu basin. More than half the wild plants in the Chorojo community have a local medical use. A total of 112 species with medicinal properties have been found. This has been analysed in community meetings, and documented in small booklets that are distributed to other communities and regions.

International networking

Latin-American Compas Network. AGRUCO hosted the First International Compas Workshop in Capellani in 1996, and since 1999 assumed responsibility to co-ordinate the Compas network in Latin America. Within this context, a Latin-American Workshop on Indigenous Cosmovision and Biodiversity in Latin America was organised in the community Chorojo in February 2001. Besides AGRUCO, Compas and the Department for Rural Development of the Faculty of Agronomy of UMSS, experts in the subject matter from various indigenous organisations in Peru, Chile, Ecuador, Guatemala, Nicaragua, Colombia and Bolivia were present at this event. The central themes of the workshop were 'indigenous cosmovision' and 'local knowledge and biodiversity', which are essential components of development programmes for the revitalisation of culture, natural resources and indigenous knowledge.

Presently, the Latin American Compas Network is divided into units along the lines of ethnicity: Quechua and Aymara indigenous groups (with organisations from Bolivia, Peru, and Colombia), Mapuche indigenous groups (with organisations from Chile), and Maya indigenous groups (with organisations from Guatemala). In the future, the network may also include Amazonian indigenous groups.

Other networks. AGRUCO also has a co-ordinating role in other international networks, such as MAELA (Latin American Agro-Ecological Movement), which includes over a 100 organisations involved in organic agriculture in Latin America and the Caribbean, GRAIN (Genetic Resource Action International), and LEISA (Information Centre for Low External Input and Sustainable Agriculture), and participates in the Platform against Genetic Modification.

Towards endogenous development

There is an urgent need for a new relationship between the scientific knowledge system and the hundreds of native knowledge systems all over the world and recognition that, after all, we are all immersed in the same adventure. Or as the native people would say: *"we are all fish in the same sea, we are all birds of the same sky"*. Fifteen years of permanent work have made AGRUCO a pioneer in the field of agro-ecology and in revitalisation of indigenous knowledge and Andean culture within the university context. This has permitted AGRUCO to develop into a centre of excellence, recognised by the academic world and by other Latin American institutions.

One of the questions that keeps coming up is: 'In view of the existing difference between conventional rationalism and the native concept of life, what are the options for the Andean population to develop and yet maintain their identity?' It is obvious that one of the ways to express cultural identity is through using the native language. Over the years we have learned that as outsiders we should be very careful with the interpretation of local concepts. We refer not only to the literal, but also to the conceptual and the symbolic dimension of these languages. This is an aspect that we have had to take into account throughout our activities.

Concept of poverty and well-being. It is also essential to study the meaning of concepts, such as 'poverty' and 'development', according to the worldview of the rural people. For the people in communities of Jatun Mayu, 'development' means *Allin Qausay*, or 'living well', which implies not only material well-being, but also living in community, having good relations within the community, and with the natural and spiritual world. It is only when a person can comply with the demands of the social, natural and spiritual surroundings, can he or she reach this stage of 'living well'. In this sense, anyone in the community who does not have enough food to eat, or cannot totally support his family in a material sense, is not considered poor, but rather as 'lazy'. The concept 'poverty' is related to a person who, while he or she has reached considerable material well-being, is not able to share this with the community, nature and spiritual beings, who have facilitated this success to start with. Poverty is thus related to a person who has lost the spirit of reciprocity. Such a person is not seen as being apt for community leadership nor for working towards 'development'.

These indigenous concepts of poverty and development are not in line with the concepts used in official and conventional development programmes. In fact, many laws relating to the management of natural resources go directly against the internal norms and functions of the indigenous communities in the area that are for preserving the same natural resources. This lack of understanding, and perceived differences in interests between the official organisations and farmers, has led to many confrontations, such as road blockages and other forms of protest. These are often seen as the only way to make the government listen to the farmers. Dialogue is still a far cry.

Intercultural dialogue in universities. Yet there is hope. We have learned that the Andean communities have plenty of potential in moving towards endogenous development. The indigenous concepts and community organisation structure, in spite of numerous conflicts and difficulties, form an important basis for endogenous development, as they imply cultural values geared towards community well-being. Another potential is the continuous experimentation and innovative capacity of the community members, to include and adapt external practices and strategies into their lives without loosing their cultural identity. Moreover, the recent laws for decentralisation give local communities the possibility to negotiate their interest in the municipalities, and obtain funds for local projects.

The support of qualified technicians, who have received an education that includes the indigenous cosmovision, is essential in this process. We are convinced that a university education, which is based on enhancing the synthesis between western-based scientific knowledge and traditional Andean knowledge, is required to educate fieldworkers who would gain the capacity to truly support endogenous development.

6.2 COSMOVISION AS A BASIS FOR DEVELOPMENT

Felipe Gomez and Oscar Pacay Caal
Oxlajuj Ajpop and ADICI-Wakliiqo, Guatemala

Compas started its activities in Central America in 2000. During a workshop in Guatemala different indigenous groups discussed their situation and made plans to co-ordinate activities for endogenous development. In this chapter we present some elements of the Maya cosmovision and the experiences of two Compas partners in building development on the culture, traditional leadership and local resources of the people.

Nowadays, the greatest prevalence of Maya culture is in Guatemala, where the Maya makes up around 60% of the population. In the other central American countries the prevalence of indigenous peoples is much less, making up 14.7% in Belize, 7% in El Salvador, 1.8 % in Nicaragua, and 1.3% in Honduras [Stavenhagen, 2002]. The other part of the population is generally referred to as *mestizos,* a mix of Spanish, black and indigenous origins. The Maya in Guatemala consist of 22 ethnic groups, of which the Quiché's form the majority.

Maya cosmovision

Maya society in Central America has changed profoundly over the past 3,000 years, especially since the arrival of Columbus and those who followed him. The Spanish conquerors and their descendants worked hard to destroy all vestiges of the indigenous government and belief system. Under this pressure, the cultural reality of the Maya changed and adapted - but endured. The Maya adapted Spanish Catholicism to their own worldview. Perhaps the most capturing example of the Maya's capacity to transform their model of the cosmos without destroying its basic structure, is the adaptation of the Cross of Christ, the main symbol of European domination on this continent [Freidel et al., 1993].

The *Popul Vuj*, the 'Book of Council of the Quiché Maya of highland Guatemala', is a touchstone and the closest to a Maya bible surviving to the present. This book describes how the Mayas consider themselves 'the people of the maize'. Not only because tortillas, or maize cakes, constitute a major part of the daily diet, but also because maize is the ultimate source and inspiration of the myths, rituals and customs that guide their every day life. The Popul Vuj describes the story of the creation of man: God, after two failed attempts to create man from clay and wood, finally succeeded in moulding the bodies of the first Maya people, four men and four women, out of maize dough. Today, maize lives both as the mythical origin of the Maya people, as well as the holy and necessary food. Maize production, therefore, is filled with rituals and beliefs. Growing of maize is not just another activity, but is an exercise for a dignified life - a process that brings one on the right track, good thoughts and behaviour. Maya farmers are therefore convinced that for a good harvest, you not only need knowledge and experience, but also 'the heart of a good person'. And it is for achieving this state of being that performing rituals is considered imperative.

Effects of modernisation. Today the Maya in Guatemala are threatened, as many of them own very little or no land at all to grow maize and other food crops, and limited or no access to credits. Moreover, around 600 local varieties of maize are also threatened by genetically modified varieties being promoted by multinational companies. Government policies keep the price of the locally produced maize varieties low, while hybrid maize is imported from other countries [Garcia et al., 2000]. Large landholdings, as well as the main economic activities such as mining, construction and industry, are in the hands of a privileged few. This has caused a lot of social unrest and political protest, which, especially in the rural areas, was repressed fiercely by military governments during the 1980s. Complete communities were destroyed; people were killed or became refugees in Mexico. It is only over the past decade that these displaced people have been able to return to their original lands and start building up their lives anew. The difficult process of reconciliation has been made somewhat easier by the re-burial of family members who were killed or disappeared during the unrest.

The influence of the modern world has left its traces in Maya thinking and agricultural practices. Most farmers in close proxinity to roads use chemical fertilisers, whilst many of them have lost the custom of crop rotation. Dependency on chemical inputs is increasing, not only in the fields, but also in the minds of the people. Today many Maya people are absorbed by products from the modern world, and do not carry out the old practices based on traditional values related to the earth, the crops, the harvest and its distribution. Individualism is replacing collectivism, and the spirit of exchange and co-operation within the communities is faltering. The loss of land and diversity, and the deterioration of spiritual practices, social organisation and productive systems, is affecting the Maya's capacity for taking collective steps towards community improvement.

The agricultual policies of the state are focused primarily on the main export crops, such as coffee, broccoli, cardamom, tomato and asparagus. Many NGOs focus on organic agriculture and support processes of change, though often in a paternalistic way. As a result, people in the communities have developed an attitude of 'waiting to see what comes' and often abandon the newly acquired practices when external support is withdrawn. At the same time there are also many positive experiences such as communities with fertile lands, producing a diversity of products and handicrafts, with small enterprises based on local organisational structures. It is important that we build on and improve our own organisational capacity, in order to find ways forward. The process of endogenous development calls us to build on our own Maya knowledge and experience, paying attention to the relationship between man, nature and the spiritual world.

ADICI-WAKLIIQO

The name ADICI - or Association of Integrated Development of Indigenous Communities - is complemented by the term *Wakliiqo*, which means 'let us come up'. This NGO works with 25 Q'eqchi' communities in the mountainous zone of Alta Verapaz with the aim of strengthening community organisation based on their own cultural identity. ADICI focuses on land rights, agro-ecology, health, gender, community organisation, culture and spirituality. One of the main activities is to enhance the production of threatened traditional crops and plants, which provide food, medicine and timber.

The Compas programme. The Q'eqchi' is the largest population group in the forested areas of north-eastern Guatemala. Traditionally, they live in small, often isolated rural communities, where a strong sense of community and mutual help is still common. Q'eqchi' farming is an intensive diversified subsistence activity, characterised by great respect for the earth and the *Tzuultaq'a,* or the sacred hill-valley. But, as a result of the civil war and influence of modern forms of production, the character of their agricultural systems and social relations are changing.

From January 2001 to June 2002 the Compas activities of 'enhancing spirituality in traditional Q'eqchi' agriculture' have complemented the other activities implemented by ADICI in these communities. While documenting aspects of spirituality in traditional Q'eqchi' agriculture - especially maize - and analysing the outcome with traditional healers and spiritual leaders from different communities, the importance of the Q'eqchi' cross has become clear. For the Q'eqchi' the cross is a way of visualising the sacred hill-valley. The cross is not only the symbol of the Christian religion; in the Q'eqchi' cosmovision it also symbolises the 'first tree', the origin of all creation, and is the symbol of fertility. In the words of Mr Manuel Paau, a Q'eqchi' spiritual leader and staff member of ADICI: *"The holy cross shows me the way. It is the place where our Lord Jesus Christ died, and it also shows us the heart of the sacred green tree. Its colour is green, the sign that it is alive. The cross shows us the love we must have for the sacred forest."*

No large crosses have been built in the Q'eqchi' region for at least two generations. The chapels and crosses, symbols of indigenous social unity and identity, had been the targets of repression during the 1980s. Therefore, the traditional crosses have become scarce, while the elders have forgotten some of the prayers and secrets necessary to build them. In analysing the importance of the cross for the Q'eqchi' it was decided to revive the tradition of construction of these crosses.

Reviving the Q'eqchi' Cross. Initially, and with the support of the local church, 'the Council of 13 elders' - the regional indigenous organisation of traditional leaders - was revived. Then a series of meetings were held with this group of elders and young people from different communities. The objective was to motivate the people and to bring together available knowledge regarding the construction of the traditional cross.

Then, over a period of several weeks, in a mountain forest at an hour's walking distance from one of the communities, 39 crosses were built from one mahogany tree. These crosses were to be placed on chapels, sacred sites and in the houses of the elders who participated in the construction. Except for the help from a foreign painter, the elders did all the work themselves, while the entire construction process included various ritualistic practices. On the 2nd and 3rd of May 2000, the 'Day of the Holy Cross', the crosses were brought down from the mountain, and received by the community as well as interested people from other communities in the region. On the second night of the festivities, a catholic cleric read the bible and food was shared.

The revival of this traditional practice implied considerable progress for the communities. This was seen in the positive relationship between young people and elders, between women and men, between different communities, as well as between traditional religion and Catholicism. The progress was also reflected in the revival of the role of the elders, both men and women, together with the many secrets involved in building the crosses, as well as traditional ecological views. Many spiritual practices related to the cross are

The women of the communities went to greet the Q'eqchi' Cross with incense and candles.

an expression of the respect of the people towards the forest and the sacred hill-valley, and highlight the importance of the forest as a source of rain, soil and fertility. This vision on natural resources can be built upon by projects aiming at managing the environment sustainably [Hatse et al., 2001].

Exchange between Q'eqchi' and Lacandones. During the meetings in the Q'eqchi' communities, the desire to visit the Palenque ruins and exchange ideas with the indigenous communities of the Lacandones, in Chiapas, Mexico, was mentioned several times. The Lacandones live in isolated communities in the forest, and still maintain their language, long hair and intimate relationship with nature. The Q'eqchi' felt that an exchange could stimulate both groups, who despite different historical backgrounds share common concepts. After 8 months of preparation, a group of 6 Q'eqchi' men and 2 women visited the communities of Lacandones in June 2000. The visit was returned in April 2001. The experience was quite revealing and interesting, though complicated due to the necessity of 2 translations: from Q'eqchi' to Spanish and from Spanish to Maya-Lacandón.

The exchange visits touched on many aspects such as ceremonies, rituals, practices and experiences. The women shared practices related to food preparation, animal husbandry, and handicrafts of dried seeds. They also visited the maize fields in the middle of the forest, and found out that the Lacandones, too, are loosing part of their social and spiritual traditions related to food production. Then the ruins of Palenque were visited by both groups, who held ceremonies for the ancestors. Later on the Q'eqchi' group analysed the outcome of the visit, indicating that the spirituality preserved by the Lacandones and the Q'eqchi's offers important opportunities of fortifying both cultures.

Oxlajuj Ajpop

Oxlajuj Ajpop - National Conference of Ministers of Maya spirituality in Guatemala - was started in 1991 by seven organisations of Maya priests from different ethnic groups throughout Guatemala. The name Oxlajuj Ajpop means 'the thirteen spiritual leaders'. Some 1,100 spiritual leaders, coming from 12 departments with 9 different languages, are participating. These leaders include traditional healers, mid-wives, musicians, and others with a central role in indigenous communities. Their objective is to promote endogenous development in the communities, based on their own cultural identity. They wish to revive the philosophical, spiritual and moral values of the Maya in the process of enhancing economic development.

One of the organisations within Oxlajuj Ajpop is the Centre of Investigation and Diffusion of Maya Sciences 'Oxlajuj Baqtun'. This academic entity aims at systematising Maya knowledge in order to revitalise and diffuse positive practices. These include aspects of traditional medicine, agriculture, handicrafts, astronomy and the use of the Maya calendar, which are diffused through radio and during meetings. Oxlajuj Baqtun is responsible for the Compas project in four communities in the department of Santa Cruz del Quiché.

Activities. At community level, several activities are being implemented throughout the country by the spiritual leaders within Oxlajuj Ajpop. These include enhancing community organisation, stimulating traditional health services and the use of medicinal plants, maintaining a dialogue with members of Catholic and Evangelical churches, stimulating forms of organic agriculture, and enhancing bi-lingual education in schools. At regional and national level, the exchange between communities is being enhanced, while Maya ethical values towards development and peace are being promoted. Oxlajuj Ajpop participates in several national dialogues. Moreover, Oxlajuj Ajpop is involved in the research of the traditional Maya judicial system, the Commision of identifying Sacred Sites, while it also participates in the proces of curriculum transformation started by the government.

Meso-American exchange. Oxlajuj Ajpop, together with ADICI and the Compas co-ordination team in Latin America, organised a workshop on the 'Exchange of ancestral knowledge and practices to enhance indigenous cultures'. In August 2001 this workshop was held in the community of Panajxit, in Santa Cruz del Quiché. During this event, representatives of different indigenous groups from Guatemala, Honduras and Nicaragua, discussed their situation and made plans to co-ordinate activities. Several rituals and exchanges were celebrated during the workshop, the highlight of which was the pilgrimage to the mountaintop of Tojil y Qumikaj, the sacred mountain in this region.

Several days were spent on intense discussion on ways to enhance indigenous cultures. One of the main issues was about how leaders can stimulate the process of passing on the values and experiences to the younger generations. Apart from NGOs, also representatives of the ministry of education, the police, military and local authorities participated in the workshop. In the highly politicised environment of Guatemala, with its history of violent political confrontation between indigenous groups and the military during the past decades, this was considered a major step forward in the direction of endogenous development of the Maya communities.

7. KNOWLEDGE AND BELIEF SYSTEMS IN EUROPE

Bertus Haverkort

The early European peoples, such as the Celts and Germanics, expressed reverence to nature and worshipped different Gods. The fate of mankind was considered the result of the forces of Gods, giants and nature. From the 3rd century onwards, the Roman Empire became the stronghold of Christianity. The combination of indigenous and Greek-Christian worldviews allowed the emergence of a culture where thrift, planning the future and hard work were held in high esteem. These values, combined with missionary zeal, led to colonisation of large parts of the globe in the 16th and 17th century. The industrial revolution and the Enlightenment resulted in important economic and technological developments. After the colonial period, market protectionism and economic expansion kept Europe, and increasingly its former colony USA, in the driving seat of international power. Problems related to the environment, social stability and inequalities between the regions of the world have led to a renewed interest in diversity and sustainability.

Historical overview

The earliest hominids in Europe arrived from Africa some 700,000 years ago. The fluctuating climate and sea levels influenced human survival in the region, which depended on hunting and gathering. Migration in order to make use of the natural resources was common, and fluctuated over the seasons and years. The main tools were hand axes, made of stone and wood, while fire and clothing were necessary to live in this temperate climate. Some 120,000 years ago the Neanderthals lived in caves, and were the first type of humans known to bury their dead and to display a variety of ritual behaviour and social organisation.

Between 35,000 and 12,000 years ago, a period of technological change took place, as the pressure- flaking technique enabled people to produce more finely shaped tools, spear throwers, bows, fish nets, hooks and spears. Hunters were no longer forced to follow their herds all the time, but could live on stored meat, plants and smaller animals such as rabbits, fish and birds. The population increased and specialisation of roles emerged. This led to increased competition and group identification, or ethnicity, each with its rites and symbols. Rituals were practised for hunting, fertility and initiation of the young. Artistic expressions played a role in these rituals: mural paintings, sculptures, and engravings on animal bone, antler and stone have been found from this period.

Original inhabitants. After the most recent ice age came to an end some 10,000 years ago, temperatures rose, allowing people to inhabit the northern part of Europe as well. 3,000 years later agriculture was well established in northern Europe. The hierarchical, metal-using societies of the Copper and Bronze ages introduced the plough. People of the Celtic and Germanic cultures built places of worship, had their own creation myths, systems for maintaining law and order, and artistic expressions. Natural Gods, giants and natural forces had to be worshipped and respected, and a variety of rituals were held in sacred places.

These early European societies had some matriarchal characteristics: women were respected as spiritual leaders and held important positions. Clairvoyant women, quite influential in these indigenous religions, could look into the past and future, reveal the myths of origins, and predict the future. The oak was considered a sacred tree, and often provided an appropriate place of worship in celebrating and respecting natural forces. The peoples built stone circles and ritual monuments with astronomic functions, such as Stonehenge on the British islands, while on the continent remnants of graves with enormous boulders and menhirs can still be seen today.

As the original occupants of Europe did not have an elaborate system of writing, the main sources of information on their belief system still available today are observations of Roman occupants, and the Edda, a book on Germanic wisdom, myths and saga written in the 13th century AD.

Classical civilisations - the Greeks and Romans. Inspired by both the Mesopotamian and Egyptian cultures, the first European urban-based civilisation emerged in Crete, around 4,000 years ago. This was the start of the Greek culture, which had its climax between 2,500 and 2,000 years ago. Later on its centre shifted to Rome. The Greek developed an elaborate cosmovision, with a pantheon of Gods, semi-Gods, and giants. Religious ceremonies were held and impressive temples and sculptures were constructed to honour the Gods and invoke their blessings.

This period also produced a class of people who were to think and teach about basic questions: the philosophers from this period, Socrates, Plato and Aristotle, are considered the three pillars of western philosophy. Socrates developed a system of reasoning and thinking aimed at finding the truth. He put great emphasis on ethical values, such as modesty, justice, courage, and truthfulness, and pointed at the immense potential of mankind once prepared to know itself. Plato developed ideas about the ideal state, which should be ruled by enlightened philosophers. Women and men were to be equal, with equal education and prospects. Marriages were to be arranged by the state, and children were to be removed from their parents in order to minimise personal and possessive emotions, and to foster public spirit. He put forward the notion of 'divine perfection': objects we can observe in the world are merely appearances of the perfect idea or form. Trees in the material world are merely copies of God's perfect tree. Aristotle made the distinction between 'form' and 'matter'. The form of something is its essence. Matter without form is just potentiality, but by acquiring form, its actuality increases. Humans, by increasing form to matter, by building bridges and making sculptures, make this matter more divine. Aristotle is also considered the founder of 'logic', the system of propositions and deductive arguments, which has had great influence on western scientific thinking

The Greek city-states had strong and centralised governments. Military technologies and organisations were developed, which allowed the Greek, and later on the Romans, to conquer the original inhabitants and occupy major parts of the Mediterranean, Asia and western Europe. The Greek empire lost its dominant position around 1,700 years ago, and Christianity became the dominant religion. Under the influence of the Roman emperor Constantine, state and church became strongly interrelated in the 4th century AD, and western Europe was christianised from the 7th century AD onwards. The Holy Roman Empire and the Church of Rome formed an interdependent system of spiritual and political authority, which controlled the continent politically and substituted the traditional religions of the original inhabitants with Christianity.

Christianity and colonisation. Christians believe that the whole creation is an act of one God, who continues to take care of all aspects of its existence. People have one life in which their destiny after death is determined: either eternal bliss in heaven, or the eternity of torment in hell. Christ provided for the redemption of humankind by his death. Humans are permitted to explore and exploit nature, but not destroy it: people are to act as good stewards of natural resources. At the same time values like thrift, planning the future, and working hard to reach specific goals in life, became part of Christian societies. The new religion and church were male dominated, and women were not allowed to fulfil roles in rituals and priesthood any more.

The Church of Rome led the Christian missionaries within Europe. They were faced with widespread indigenous belief systems of the original inhabitants, in which worshipping of different Gods, the sun, moon and other elements in nature were common. In order to destroy these ancient religions, specific laws were established by the new Christian authorities. For example, clairvoyant women of the traditional belief systems were considered to be witches, and prosecuted by the Inquisition, a church based court of justice.

In a general sense, it is interesting to note the similarities between the strategies used during the early colonisation process of Europe, and the strategies used later on in colonising other parts of the world (see also chapter 2). These strategies included the following elements: the original culture and religion were declared to be barbaric and inferior, based on a superstitious belief system. Introduction of the new religion was presented as a liberalisation and as a general benefit for the people. Sacred places of worship of the original religion were destroyed and, where possible, replaced by churches on the same location and using the same materials. Traditional practices not wholly in contradiction with the new religion, were given a new label, and were thus gradually taken over by the new religious system. Alliances were made with the ruling political leaders, and the legal systems were changed to take on board the new morality and values. Indigenous traditional leaders were declared demonic, witches were prosecuted and killed, and non-believers in the new religion were convicted.

In this way the Inquisition could condemn and punish -even to death- those who did not comply with the laws of the new church. Through education, welfare and technological innovations the new religion was able to gain popularity, and to create an elite educated in the new system. These new leaders had the tendency of rejecting the old religion even more vigorously than the missionaries before them, as their new position and status in society depended on this. Policies that reinforced the dominant trend were adopted. But, the new religion and value system could not easily wipe out all traditions, and in spite of the threat of persecution and ridicule, the traditional leaders often continued to perform their roles as religious leaders, unnoticed by the new rulers. Europe was, initially, no exception in this process, which we still can observe in dominated traditional societies in other parts of the world today. But, after 700 years of domination by Christianity and subsequent social, economic and political developments, most of the indigenous original European belief systems have been reduced to a vague memory, though a range of European values, popular beliefs, festivals and costumes can still be traced back to the Germanic and Celtic cultures.

In the course of its history, Christianity has strongly influenced the policies of the emerging nation states and has played an important role in the colonisation process in other parts of the world. Christianity has spread itself far beyond Europe: Latin and North America and Africa were strongly impacted by missionary activities. Meanwhile, Christianity has also gone through a number of reformations and changes. At present Christianity has a wide range of denominations, and its influence on the European society is no longer as prominent as in the past. In western cultures, the church and the state are separate identities. Christian values, however, as well as the linear time concept, the attitude towards nature, and emphasis on the material world, still have a major impact on European cultures today.

Enlightenment and the industrial revolution. European rulers of the middle ages were appointed, sanctioned and ordained by the Church. In the 18th century, a number of scientists decided to work without the limitations imposed on them by the religious dogmas. Francis Bacon, Isaac Newton and Descartes, considered the founders of modern science, formulated a new scientific paradigm: they shifted from the concept of a world controlled by God to the concept of a material world, which functions like a machine. This mechanical picture of nature, or Cartesian worldview, became the dominant paradigm of western science, and guided all scientific observation and formulation of theories. This new paradigm was called Enlightenment, as it implies an optimistic view on the potential of the human being, based on its rationality. In this perspective, humans were to use science to dominate and control nature (see also page 17, chapter 2).

In the 18th century, the new machinery developed for textile and metal processing through technological innovation could no longer be installed in small-scale home industries due to its size. As a result, factories gradually replaced home industries. Coal, iron and steam engines were used in the railway system and on steamships, which, combined with the construction of roads and railroads, allowed for more efficient transport of people and goods over large distances. This so-called industrial revolution led to high productivity of labour and capital, and to considerable economic growth. Its success is ascribed to factors such as: technological innovations, availability of capital to invest in equipment, availability of labour and raw material from colonised countries, as well as free and expanding markets. The growth of towns led to increased demand for food and increased agricultural productivity. At the same time, employment opportunities moved from the rural areas to the towns, and a poverty-stricken labour proletariat emerged, who over time started a class struggle.

The industrial revolution started in England, but spread to the USA, continental Europe and Japan. It did not get a foothold in tropical countries, as the necessary investments in infrastructure did not take place there. Instead, tropical produce was transported to the industrialised countries for processing. From the 16th century onwards, Spain, Portugal, England, France, Belgium, the Netherlands, Italy, Denmark and Germany expanded their colonial activities. The New World of the Americas, Africa, and major parts of Asia came under colonial control. Slave trade resulted in major changes in populations, as well as de-humanisation of a part of human society. In 1914, European countries controlled 84% of the land surface of the world [Schultz et al., 2001].

This expansion was made possible by scientific advances, such as navigational devices and cartographic techniques. The 'newly discovered areas' were studied scientifically: botanists and geologists and ethnologists took stock, made inventories and studied the natural and human resources and potentials for its use. According to Adas (1997), the science carried overseas by European colonisers, was considered value neutral, objective in its procedure, privileging abstraction and reason, empirically grounded, somehow transcending time and space, and therefore universally valid. These assumptions about western science gave its practitioners and advocates confidence that the spread of western science, and the instruments and procedures associated with it, was beneficial and somehow inevitable for the local populations. In this process indigenous ways of learning and knowing were consciously pushed to the periphery.

Post-modernity. The scientific paradigm that emerged during the Enlightenment is considered to be modern. The impact of the technologies developed by this approach has been tremendous, and has enabled food security and wealth in various parts of the world. At the same time the disadvantages and limitations of this materialistic-mechanistic approach is now clearly visible, and the sustainability of present day food production systems, and economies in general, call for a new approach.

In the early 20th century, Einstein formulated his laws of thermodynamics and the theory of relativity, thereby laying the foundation of new physics and post-modernity. Development in quantum mechanics, pioneered by Niels Bohr and Werner Heisenberg, further modified the hitherto conventional concepts of time and space, matter, gravity and cause-effect relationships. They concluded that subatomic particles have a dual nature: depending on how we look at them they sometimes appear as particles, or matter, and sometimes as waves, or energy. Bohr considered the particle and the wave as complementary descriptions of the same reality. Heisenberg postulated the 'uncertainty principle', which is based on the concept that, at subatomic level matter does not exist with certainty at a definite place, but shows a 'tendency to exist'. In contrast to the former mechanistic Cartesian worldview, this post-modern worldview can be characterised as organic, holistic and ecological. The universe is no longer seen as a machine, made up of a multitude of objects that can be controlled, but as one indivisible, dynamic whole, whose parts are interrelated.

In the 1980s the General Systems Theory emerged, in which an organic, living system is not considered as a machine-like organ, that can be managed and controlled separately once its dynamics are known, but as a combination of living, interacting and self-organising elements. Competition, symbiosis, self-renewal and innovative creativity are important processes in a living system. Chaos can be a necessary step in the evolution of a system towards a new order of higher complexity and quality [Prigogini, 1984]. The notion of Gaia [Lovelock, 1979] assumes that earth behaves like a living organism, and her properties and processes cannot be understood and predicted from the mere sum of its parts. In this notion, the reductionist description of organisms can be useful and necessary, but is considered dangerous when taken as the complete explanation of its characteristics. Reductionism and holism, analysis and synthesis are seen as complementary approaches, which, if used in a proper balance, help us to gain a deeper understanding of life [Capra, 1983].

Capra also pointed at the relationship between this Systems view and Taoism and other elements of eastern mysticism. The dualism, observed at sub-atomic level coincides with the Yin Yang duality within Taoism. Ruppert Sheldrake (1990) has elaborated the theory of morphogenetic fields and resonance. Other authors, like Ken Wilber (1996), are elaborating holistic theories to link science and spirituality. The boundaries of post-modern science are difficult to indicate. New paradigms are sometimes difficult to defend, prove or explain within the conventional paradigm; some may be speculative and many meet with resistance. Yet, post-modern science presents an interesting panorama of a diversity of approaches, perspectives and theories.

Agricultural policies

Though the colonial system came to an end by the middle of the 20th century, the economic relationship between the new tropical countries and the formal colonisers maintained a character of dependency. With the exception of a number of countries in South Asia, the newly independent states continued to be suppliers of raw materials, while international enterprises did little to invest in the South. Export subsidies and import levies for food prevented access of tropical countries to the northern markets, and thus contributed to a stagnating agricultural development in the South. This combined with the policy of international debts has worsened the situation over the past decades. Development cooperation, now the responsibility of the governments of rich countries in the world, has not been effective in alleviating poverty, or in building local capacity for economic growth, in major parts of Africa, Latin America and Asia. Local capacities are hampered by corruption, undemocratic processes and unevenly distributed resources.

After the Second World War, Europe, USA and Japan adopted agricultural policies, which included the combination of market protection, technology development, human resource development, credit and improvement of physical and institutional infrastructure. Governments invested heavily in the development of knowledge and technologies in the process of rationalising agriculture. The triangle of research, education and extension was the major tool for strengthening the internal dynamics of the agricultural system. The Land Grant universities in the USA played a major role in research, training and agricultural extension. A number of agricultural universities and research centres were established in Europe, and rural extension was carried out by government agencies. Technologies for plant and animal breeding, soil management and fertilisation, mechanisation, irrigation, pest management, energy management, storage and processing were developed, and became even more sophisticated with the high-tech computer and genetic modification technologies.

The investment in agricultural technology development was far more intensive in the western than in the tropical countries. Evanson (1986) compared the expenditure in agri-

Investments in agricultural technology resulted in a dramatic increase in productivity and farm scale.

cultural research and extension across the globe, and concluded that in the 1980s, only 6% of the total expenditure on agricultural research and extension were spent in Latin America and Africa. In these regions the expenditure on extension exceed the expenditure on research: the number of researchers per extension worker in Europe is around 1:1, in Asia 1:3, in Africa 1:10, and in Latin America 1:4. At the same time, the research focus in the tropics has long been a replication of the type of research being carried out in the North, with a focus on Green Revolution technologies, such as mono-cropping, fertilisers, herbicides, pesticides, irrigation and machinery.

The price policies of the northern countries were initially intended to reach self-sufficiency in food. The combination of import duties and export subsidies stabilised off-farm prices, and provided an acceptable income to the farmers. In the process, the domestic prices for products like grain, sugar, dairy products, and meat were between 1.5 and 2.4 times higher than the border prices! In contrast, the policy chosen in many developing countries kept the consumers prices as low as possible and provided subsidies for agricultural inputs as well as for food imports. These policies over-stimulated agricultural production in Europe and the USA, while agriculture in tropical countries was seriously hampered.

Other investments in the North included infrastructure, water management and land consolidation. This further increased soil productivity and allowed market access for remote areas. Rural institutions and farmers organisations successfully lobbied for the interest of farmers, to provide credit, insurance, processing industries, input delivery and other services. These government policies led to a dramatic increase in productivity and farm scale. Yields of 9 metric tons of grain or 60 tons of potatoes per hectare and 10,000 litres of milk per cow per year were within reach, and the productivity per unit of farm labour increased dramatically.

Crisis in European agriculture. Yet today, in the same northern countries, agricultural development can no longer be considered an undisputed success story: The export subsidies are no longer affordable, the reduction of agro-biodiversity is dramatic, and nature is hardly present in the landscape. The use of agro-chemicals has been a major contributor to the pollution of the soils, air and water, while the energy efficiency of agriculture is negative. Animal welfare is threatened by intensive animal production systems, which in turn are threatened by swine plague, foot and mouth disease and BSE. Over the past decades farmers have been confronted with a range of laws and regulations, first to increase the scale of farming, later to reduce environmental impacts. This has resulted in enormous bureaucracies, low farm incomes, and large numbers of farmers being pushed out of business.

Currently, there are several efforts to redirect European agriculture, though this is not without controversy. The mainstream innovation policies aim at further developing technologies for large-scale production, but with fewer disadvantages for the environment and animal welfare. In this option, genetic engineering and trade liberalisation are to lead to new technologies and economic opportunities. An increasing number of initiatives, however, advocate rural renewal, which builds on ecological and cultural diversity, and stimulates multipurpose farming. In this perspective, farming enterprises include nature management, processing of local produce, and rural tourism.

From agricultural modernisation towards rural development

The scientific approach used for the rationalisation of agriculture mentioned above, has also been labelled 'the Cartesian theatre' [van der Ploeg, 1999]. In this approach the scientific (physics, biology, chemistry) and economic laws are used to control and influence the production process towards increased productivity and farm income. Once the processes involved are understood, and the technologies to control them are developed, the 'ideal farm model' and agricultural production system is determined. Extension services, subsidies, rules and regulations are then used to get the farmers to where the policy makers want them to be. These generic policy measures apply to all farmers, and are not adapted to sub-regions or cultural values held by the farmers.

Van der Ploeg found empirical evidence, however, that despite the consistent influence of the instruments of agricultural developments on the farming communities in the Netherlands, differences can be observed between regions and localities. The same is true for Europe. The value added by the Frisian dairy system, for example, is lower than that of the Italian region around Parma. In the latter, the farmers have not adopted the development process identified as the ideal farm type, but have built on their own traditions of ecological farming and on-farm processing. They have been able to market their Parmesan cheese as a well known, region specific, and high quality product.

Van der Ploeg also found that, despite the application of generic policy measures over several decades, farmers in Europe still have a wide diversity of farm styles. Depending on their personal preferences and regional cultures, farmers have opted for intensification and rationalisation, or have attached more value to production systems based on local diversity. This includes the combination of farming with tourism or on-farm processing, animal welfare, and nature conservation, and has resulted in a diversity of farm styles. This diversity is now considered a major potential for developments within the European agricultural systems, as well as for enhancing diversity in the landscape and ecosystem. (see also box 9a on page 249)

This discussion about universality versus diversity has become a central theme in the search for new agricultural developments in Europe. As we have seen, the application of the universal paradigm in the North has brought progress as well as problems. A major challenge

Dairy farmer in Italy. Despite the modernisation in Europe, family farms are still prevailing in a wide diversity of farm styles.

now is to find the best relationship between science and technologies. Schakel [Van der Ploeg et al., 1990] has no doubt that soil chemistry, theoretical crop ecology, biochemistry and genetics can contribute to the improvement of local production systems. This depends, however, on the possibility of translating these insights into specific technologies that can contribute to sustainable livelihoods in the different corners of the globe. The cases presented in the next two chapters, illustrate that a diversity of cultures and farm styles exists in Europe, and interesting innovative processes are taking place.

7.1 BIODYNAMIC FARMING AND FARMERS' REALITIES

Joke de Jonge, Coen ter Berg and Jos Pelgröm, BD-Union, the Netherlands

Biodynamic farmers are organic farmers who add earth-cosmos relations and spiritual dimensions to their farming activities. The participation of the Dutch Biodynamic Union in Compas focussed on clarifying and documenting the biodynamic cosmovision among farmers, and experimenting with new methods to enhance the vitality, or life forces, on their farms. Central to many biodynamic farmers is the question: How can I develop my spiritual connection to the farm?

The Biodynamic Union is a small organisation with some 2,600 members, including 200 farmers, as well as processors, traders and consumers involved in biodynamic farming in Dutch society. The Netherlands is one of the most densely populated countries in the world, which leads to a permanent pressure on the scarcely available lands. Most farmers work with high input technology, including the use of chemical fertilisers, herbicides and pesticides, though this is decreasing due to environmental regulations. Only a small group works in a more sustainable way. In December 2001, there were 1,510 organic farms (1.64%), working on 1.54% of the total farming area. Biodynamic farmers are organic farmers, thus working without chemical inputs, who go one step further: they include attention to earth-cosmos relations, as well as spiritual beings in their farming activities. In 1999 organic farming in the Netherlands had a market share of € 234 million [Melitta, 2000]. The Dutch Ministry of Agriculture is supporting organic farming through subsidies and fiscal regulations to reach the aim of having 10% of the area under organic farming by 2010.

The origin of biodynamic farming. Biodynamic agriculture developed out of eight lectures on agriculture presented by Rudolf Steiner (1861-1925), an Austrian scientist and philosopher. In 1924 these lectures were published in a book called 'An Agricultural Course - spiritual foundations for the renewal of agriculture'. The lectures were given in response to farmer observations that the health and quality of their soils, crops and livestock had deteriorated after the introduction of chemical fertilisers, around 1900. According to Steiner, the basic principle of biodynamic farming is to conceive the farm as an organism in itself, a self-contained entity. Emphasis is placed on mixed farming: linking crops and livestock, recycling nutrients, improving health and well-being of soils, crops and animals, and the farmer him or herself being part of this whole. Many organic practices such as green manuring, crop rotation, companion planting, cover crops are applied.

Today, the norms in biodynamic farming are more strict than in organic farming: 60% of the manure, 100% of straw for the manure-straw mixture, 80% of the fodder, and 100% of the concentrates should be of organic origin; cows should maintain their horns, chickens their beaks and pigs their tails. In addition, biodynamic faming has elaborate non-obligatory guidelines related to composting, nature development, and the balance between the physical realities and cosmic forces. Farmers work with these forces to enrich their farm, its products, and its inhabitants with life energy or etheric forces. In fact, the regeneration of etheric forces that work through the soil to the plant, is the central aim in bio-dynamic farming. These forces are enhanced in various ways:

- *By using biodynamic preparations,* which are compositions of specific minerals (like silica), cow manure, weeds and weed parts, prepared in animal organs such as intestine, bladder, skull or horns. When crops are harvested, it is not only the substances that are removed, but also the life forces and vitality gained in that year. The preparations are given to the soil, compost and/or crops, to enhance vitality and make them more alert to cosmic forces.
- *By working according to the sowing calendar,* which recognises the influence of celestial forces on plant growth.
- *By acknowledging the existence of spiritual, so-called elemental beings,* which are related to the four elements earth, water, air and fire. Via these elements the spiritual beings are connected to the corresponding parts of the plants: roots, stem and leaves, flowers and fruits. Some farmers are aware of the presence of these beings as a kind of feeling or mood in different parts of the farm and during specific times of the day.

Steiner founded Anthroposophy, or Wisdom of the Human Being: an elaborate cosmovision in which human evolution is seen as a long process, originating from divine sources and guided by hierarchies of spiritual beings, to a time in which each human being has the freedom to make individual choices to a spiritual way of life and destiny. In this process, the development of advanced cognitive capacities allows the individual to experience the spiritual forces and beings in humans, nature and the cosmos. Steiner often proclaimed his worldview *"a spiritual science for western people, and not a mixture of western and eastern esoteric wisdom. It is the scientific investigation of the spiritual world, that looks beyond the one-sided approach-*

In contrast to conventional farmers, most biodynamic dairy farmers allow their animals to maintain the horns so as to respect the integrity of cows and enable them to perform their own behaviour.

es of mere science or the usual mysticism". According to Lorand [2001] the essence of Anthroposophy is: "A reunion of science, art and religion, not just a renewal or transformation of science. Central in anthroposophy is the understanding of Christ Event: Christ as a great cosmic being, who through his life, teaching, death and resurrection has affected all of humanity, the entire earth, and the whole universe".

Biodynamic Union

When the Biodynamic Union joined Compas in 1997, a preliminary research showed that many farmers found it difficult to explain the biodynamic cosmovision in words. While there are some biodynamic farmers who doubt the effect of preparations, others are becoming increasingly sensitive to the spiritual aspects of their farm and to nature. However, this seems to be strictly individual and difficult to put into words. The activities within Compas started with the stimulation of farmer-to-farmer approaches, such as the 'coaching project'. Selected farmers were trained to individually coach fellow farmers during farm visits. One of the aims was to improve the farmers' skills to develop more feeling and understanding of the cosmovision aspect of biodynamic agriculture. The coach was expected to withhold his or her own knowledge and judgments, and to stimulate the farmers' creativity. In the end, the assessments of the coached farmers and of the coaches themselves came together. 'Coaching' proved to be a successful concept: many farmers joined and later on they continued as study-groups.

Another activity was to write articles in the Biodynamic Magazine with the experiences of Compas partner organisations in Africa, Asia and Latin America. This helped Dutch farmers to realise that there were similarities and differences of their practices with other cultures. Dutch farmers were surprised to note that in India, Bolivia and Sri Lanka traditional farmers also work with moon phases and other planetary constellations to determine the correct time of sowing. At the same time, in many southern cultures, farmers can rely on spiritual teachers, while in the Netherlands, they have to find their way alone or together with other farmers. Attempts to actively link up with Green Foundation in India on the subject of participatory plant breeding were not sustained, though there was mutual inspiration and reflection.

In the year 2000, a next project activity was to clarify and document the biodynamic cosmovision through interviews and reporting. The need to describe the fundamentals of Dutch biodynamic farming, was one of the outcomes of the coaching project. It states that Dutch biodynamic farmers share a common cosmovision, which unites them and enables them to communicate amongst themselves about the essence of agriculture, including the spiritual dimension. The Agricultural Course of Steiner as well as anthroposophy are the main sources of inspiration, though many farmers are not able to spend a lot of time to deepen its essence. The fierce economic pressures make it hard to develop the physical as well as the spiritual side of their farm.

Experimentation. In 1999, some farmers started to explore 'eco-therapy' as a means to better their skills to sense life forces, and to 'communicate' with their soils, crops and animals. This was continued in 2000. In this approach learning to 'measure' life forces and to apply 'energy treatments' were central objectives, and farmers became more skilled in receiving subtle information on the growth pattern and development of their crops, soils or animals, through intuition and a pendulum according to six parameters. This information assisted them to decide on the necessary healing practice. According to 'eco-therapy' every living organism has a radiation, which is similar to the 'aura' of human beings. The size of the aura is a measure of the health and vitality of an organism. With the current changes in ecology across the globe, air, soils and water now contain new chemical substances, leading to decreased vitality and blockages in life forces. Healing nature implies diagnosing the energy levels, and then removing these blockages to renew the life forces. This is expected to diminish the need for more physical control measures, such as organic pest control.

In the year 2001, 14 farmers joined to explore the common fungus disease *phytophtora* in potatoes, and find ways of enhancing the life energy of the potato and the field, thereby expecting to delay the infestation of phytophtora. The locations for learning were the different farms of the participants. According to Coen ter Berg, who joined the course as a participant, observer and reporter, the effects of the course were positive for most of the farmers, as it enhanced their relation with their potatoes and farm as a whole. The infestation of phytophtora was not delayed, however.

Discussion

Participation in Compas proved to be a difficult task for the Biodynamic Union. Though Compas provided an inspiring platform for exchange about cosmovision and agriculture, the difficulty of intercultural dialogue remained. The context and the problems of biodynamic farmers in the Netherlands are fundamentally different from farmers in the South. Dutch farmers were uncertain if healing practices from southern cultures could enrich their own farming, and attempts to sustain bi-lateral links failed. A search for other spiritually inspired agricultural movements in Europe yielded no concrete partnerships. Compas did contribute to a process of further clarification of the spiritual dimension of biodynamic agriculture, however, including the new ways such as 'eco-therapy', which has resulted in a lively discussion in the Dutch biodynamic farming movement.

Through numerous meetings and workshops the farmers try to develop local knowledge based on locally felt needs, such as enhancing the vitality of food and the soil, the spiritual development of farmers, and safeguarding the integrity of animals and plants. Development niches for Dutch biodynamic agriculture include direct marketing, as well as social goals, such as employment for socially derailed persons or mentally handicapped people. The Biodynamic union is actively looking for new ways to interpret and innovate the traditional anthroposophical concepts. On farm coaching, and experimentation on the basis of the biodynamic cosmovision, are valuable but difficult challenges for enhancing endogenous development in a highly modernised country.

7.2 ENVIRONMENTAL CO-OPERATIVES RECONNECT FARMING, ECOLOGY AND SOCIETY

Jan Douwe van der Ploeg and Henk Renting, Wageningen University, the Netherlands

Regional diversity, diversified farming styles and endogenous development are hot issues in the current political debate on European agriculture. This article presents a historical overview of development experiences and elaborates on the emergence of environmental co-operatives in Dutch farming. They are unique 'field laboratories' for innovations toward sustainable rural development. The achievements in terms of environmental gains and social cohesion are coupled with cost reduction for the farmers and the state.

During the four last decades a seemingly unstoppable process has swept through the European countryside. Farming and nature areas have been thoroughly reshuffled and modernisation has managed to penetrate even the remotest corners of the continent. Local specificity appears to have lost its relevance, whilst entrepreneurship, the European market, and adherence to latest technologies emerge as guiding principles. The European Common Agricultural Policy is strongly supporting the use of new genetic technologies for enhancing productivity. But, the negative aspects related to this modernisation process can no longer be obscured.

Diversity in European agriculture. Although empirical evidence indicates that the effect of modernisation in Europe has been one of globalisation, its real scope and impact has been dependent upon responses developed at the grass roots level. As much as the modernisation model, characterised by intensification, larger scale, specialisation and integration into agribusiness chains, was internalised by some regions and some farmers, it was also deconstructed and reshaped by others. Some groups have consciously taken distance from what appears to be the dominant blueprint. In fact, the impressive heterogeneity of current European agriculture shows that agricultural development is a many-sided and highly variable interaction between the local and the global, and that diversity continues to be one of the main features of European agriculture. Diversity is also becoming a keyword in the debates taking place on common agricultural policy. Any European policy on rural development must, therefore, be based on the recognition of this diversity, which can be viewed either as a problematic remnant of the past, or as a major opportunity for the future.

The diversity of Europe's agriculture can be attributed to differences in factors such as climate, soil, distance from centres of consumption, as well as historically created land-use patterns. But above all, agriculture is a social construct: the way agriculture is organised depends heavily on the individuals and organisations involved in it. They decide on the strategies used and the ways practices are linked to markets and technological developments. And it is these decisions within a complex process that makes agricultural practice what it is: a highly diversified whole.

The effects of modernisation. The renewed interest in endogenous development can be explained, theoretically, by the effects of agricultural modernisation. Since the mid-1950s modernisation of European agriculture is increasingly a process originating from, and driven by, institutions outside of the agricultural sector. This view has been consolidated by a concept of development that implied, essentially, a rupture with the existing discourse on the practices in the countryside. Agriculture was considered to be a stagnant sector, and 'getting agriculture moving' and 'transforming traditional agriculture' were amongst the main slogans in the 1960s. Those farmers able and willing to participate in the modernisation process were classified as 'modern' and innovative. Their activities were oriented towards urban dynamics, and fitted in well with mainstream economics, in which agricultural development was considered a process of adapting farming practices to global markets and modern technology.

Modernisation was, and still is, shaped by external interventions aimed at introducing new organisational models, new linkages between farming, markets and market-agencies, new technologies and knowledge, and new forms of socialisation and training. This has resulted in a redefinition of the role and identity of farmers and their families. Meanwhile, the implementation of this integrated policy on agriculture has reinforced the break away from existing practices, relationships and role definitions.

Secondly, certain conditions, times and regions proved more favourable for modernisation projects than others. Thus, modernisation increased inequalities, and has resulted not only in growth, but also in marginalised rural areas. Consequently, the simple repetition of the model based on so-called 'growth poles' and 'centre economies' became, within the less favoured areas, an increasingly less convincing policy option.

Thirdly, it must be stressed that the practice of modernisation, based on introducing exogenous elements into the farming sector, has caused dependency to be internalised into the structure of development. This emphasis on exogenous development has produced a bias in our approach to nature, and to mechanisms of agricultural development. Although considerable knowledge exists on how to design and implement projects for exogenous development, there is a sad lack of knowledge in how to conceptualise and analyse endogenous development patterns, their impact and potential. This is expressed by the widely shared belief that endogenous development has little to offer when it comes to resolving current problems. This ignorance, which has its historical roots, manifests itself today as one of the main problems in rural and agrarian development throughout the world.

Internal and external elements. Diversity in agriculture is a multidimensional phenomenon. One of the criteria we can use to analyse this diversity is the level of autonomy in relation to markets and technology supply. Of course development patterns can neither be defined as being exclusively based on local resources, nor as only on external elements; they contain a specific balance between 'internal' and 'external' elements. The balance in endogenous development is one in which the local resources figure both as the starting point for farming and as the yardstick for measuring the utility of external elements. External elements will only be internalised if they can strengthen the vitality of local farming styles. This entails a process of careful 'deconstruction' and 'recomposition' of the external technology, to guarantee the maximum fit with local conditions, perspectives and interests.

It could be argued that more often than not endogenous development is blocked, not only by global factors, but also by factors in the locality itself. As such, it could be stated that there is no general scheme for endogenous development. It is only the careful and detailed exploration of farming styles, and other local elements embedded in the particular frameworks of interaction with external factors, that can render insights into the prospects for endogenous development.

Re-embedding Dutch farming in its locality

In Dutch farming, the shift to exogenous development due to modernisation is much greater than in many other parts of Europe. Over the past decades, farming has been practically disconnected from its local social and natural environment, leading to environmental pollution, animal welfare problems, as well as social disintegration. Currently, Dutch rural society is deeply divided about the best way forward for the rural areas, with distrust between farmers, the state and other actors. Many 'traditional' farming systems, which were foreseen to disappear under the modernisation paradigm, are now moving to the forefront of the policy agenda and have been revalued for their positive impact on natural resources, or as providers of quality regional food. Pluri-activity, once conceived as an indication of under-developed agriculture, is now increasingly recognised as a phenomenon with important potentials for sustainable livelihood strategies [Kinsella et al., 2000]. A range of new rural development activities has emerged, including organic farming, tourism and marketing local produce, which are being adopted by farm households as a

On-farm cheesemaking in the Netherlands. Forty percent of Dutch farming families get additional income from 'rural development' activities, such as nature management, agritourism and on-farm processing of regional food products.

means of strengthening their business. Many of these new and revitalised 'old' practices correspond to a fundamentally distinct development rationale in contrast to the modernisation approach. They form the contours of a new rural development paradigm, which goes beyond modernisation [van der Ploeg & Renting, 2000; van der Ploeg, 2000].

Environmental co-operatives. The emergence of environmental co-operatives in Dutch farming can be understood against this background. These co-operatives are innovative associations of farmers at local or regional level, which promote activities related to sustainable agriculture and rural development in their locality. In most cases, the activities involve nature and landscape management, as well as the reduction of environmental pollution on the members' farms. They also include water management, tourism, production of quality regional foods and organic farming. These co-operatives emerged in the early 1990s in response to the crisis of high-tech agriculture, concerns over the deteriorating public image of farming and, most of all, the increasing number of environmental regulations of the government.

The number of farms involved in environmental co-operatives is difficult to assess, as there is no official registration. A study undertaken in 1999 [Polman & Slangen, 1999], showed that 81 co-operatives had around 6,600 member farms, with about 134,000 hectares of land. This implies 6% of all Dutch farms and 7% of the total agricultural land. The co-operatives generally attract relatively large, full-time farms. The average size of a co-operative is about 70 members with 1,600 ha of land. Regions with an environmental co-operative count nearly 50% of the farmers in its membership.

The factors that triggered the formation of the environmental co-operatives were often of a highly localised nature. A clear example is the Vel&Vanla co-operative, a combination of the 'Vereniging Eastermar's Lansdouwe' (VEL) and 'Vereniging Agrarisch Natuur en Landschapsbeheer Achtkarspelen' (VANLA), in the province Fryslân in the northern part of the Netherlands. This co-operative represents an interesting field laboratory for innovation towards sustainable rural development. In the case of Vel&Vanla, it was the state regulations on soil pollution, which threatened to block any further prospects for farm development in the area. In other situations it was the obligation to apply manure through injection techniques, which resulted in local discontent.

Crucial elements for innovation. The following elements have been observed as crucial in the process of innovation towards sustainable development:

New institutional relations between the state and agriculture. The environmental co-operatives question the overload of state regulations that apply at farm level in the Netherlands. They generally accept and endorse policy objectives set by state agencies, but claim substantial reforms, and more flexibility in implementation.

Rebuilding networks of trust at the local level. At local level, the environmental co-operatives have actively re-created networks and coalitions between the farming population and other rural interest groups, such as nature conservation agencies and entrepreneurial organisations engaged in tourism and leisure. They advocate integrated development of land use and economic activities in their region. By going beyond distrust and conflicts, doors have been opened for a range of new coalitions at the local level.

The re-embedding of farming. At farm level, a wide range of possibilities exists to realign farming with ecology and wider society, although the exact lines along which to proceed may vary substantially. The environmental co-operatives are an attempt to restore the wholeness, context and specificity of farming, by reinforcing the craftsmanship of farmers and their capacity to produce tailor-made innovations. Examples are nature management plans, nutrient balances, ecological norms, codes of conduct, and farm certification schemes. Common to all these innovations is that they shift the control of farming and rural development back to the locality-specific coordination mechanisms. This renewed embedding, however, requires adequate institutional back-up.

Social, economic and environmental impact. The achievements of the more developed environmental co-operatives give an indication of their potential. The members of the Vel&Vanla co-operative have reduced the level of environmental pollution of their farming operations through reduced use of external inputs and a more efficient use of internal farm resources. Nitrogen surpluses on member farms have reduced from 346 kg N/ha in 1995-96, to 269 kg N/ha in 1998-1999. The regional average during the same period was 371 and 306 kg N/ha respectively. In fact, the N-loss level in the season of 1999-2000 was already in line with the national policy goals set for 2003.

The farmers of the Vel&Vanla co-operative also implement a range of activities that contribute to nature management. At present, 270 ha of land belonging to member farms is under special meadow birds and botanic protection, 240 kilometres of hedgerows and 220 ponds are actively managed, with a positive impact on local natural resources. In general terms, the co-operatives have had their impact on socio-economic performance of the member farms, as local leaders point at the 'renewed spirit' among farmers, leading to positive effects on the local economy. More farmers would have given up farming if not for the co-operatives.

The co-operatives also facilitate members to take up new activities to diversify farm revenues. This is most obvious with respect to payments for nature and landscape management. On the Vel&Vanla member farms, payments for conservation activities contribute on average to € 5,500 of revenues, though the disparities between farmers are large. In the case of organic farms, the farmers receive € 18,000 extra, while agri-tourism activities add on an annual

A Vel&Vanla farmer (left) explains the biodiversity value of hedgerows to tourists who camp on his farm. Agritourism adds to the family income and is one of the 'ways out' of the limitations of agricultural modernisation.

average of € 8,000 [Roep, 2000]. The activities with the local tourist agency have substantially improved the reputation of the area as a tourist destination, creating new opportunities for the farms in the area, directly and indirectly.

The practices of environmental co-operatives have also resulted in important cost reductions. A part of these are reductions in transaction costs [Saccomandi, 1998], as farmers spend less time on bureaucratic regulations, sometimes avoid unnecessary investments, and manage their farms more efficiently. These benefits at farm level are frequently combined with similar cost reductions for state agencies and third parties. Additionally, there is a sharp reduction in state control costs. Monitoring is now conducted to a large extent by the co-operatives themselves, while external state control is reduced to one visit in several years. Other important cost reductions result from reduced environmental pollution. Vel&Vanla has recognised the virtues of low-external-input and sustainable agriculture, or LEISA, [van der Ploeg, 2000] when reducing nutrient losses. The co-operative has started study groups and on-farm research on these subjects. This would have been impossible without this organisational structure, as exemptions from standard state regulations required contacts with research institutes. As a result of these innovations, the associated cost reductions amount to about € 315 per ha, which implies an annual benefit of € 4,000 for an average farm of 30 ha.

Concluding remarks

While public opinion and the Dutch parliament support further development of environmental co-operatives, doubts about this trend have been voiced at local government level, especially within the Ministry of Agriculture, Nature Management and Fisheries. Being used to standard policy regulations that are applied uniformly, the legal experts of this ministry have started to question whether further development of localised regulatory frameworks could be adequately administered, and the results sufficiently monitored. Although the co-operatives were given room for a policy experiment in 1995, and despite positive results, the state bureaucracy has managed to block off any option for the environmental co-operatives to by-pass the standard regulations.

While the co-operatives will receive no official policy status, and while further exemptions from standard regulations are out of the question, they continue their activities at local level. In many cases support of national state agencies is not needed for this. The future of environmental co-operatives depends, however, on their capacity to mobilise other actors, including government agencies, and to establish alliances at local and regional levels. The rise of these co-operatives is in line with general trends in other European countries. With international policy favouring more decentralised, participatory and integrated approaches, these co-operatives can probably show the way to a more diverse European agriculture.

Local market in Valle Alto, Bolivia. A key strategy for endogenous development to reach its potential is regional economic management, in which producers, consumers and traders are ensuring the retention of most benefits within the region.

8. RESULTS AND CONCLUSIONS

This book describes the historic processes that formed the basis of the cultural diversity in our world today. Chapter 3 highlights the basic elements underlying endogenous development within the Compas network. The chapters that follow contain case studies from various continents, as examples of how endogenous development have been enhanced under specific local circumstances. This chapter analyses these experiences and their results, in the light of each of the components of endogenous development, and presents the major opportunities and constraints encountered in this effort.

The work of the Compas partner organisations in enhancing endogenous development is taking place in an environment that is continuously changing. The ongoing process of globalisation has led to the growing influence of international markets and privatisation. The economic situation of the developing nations has been influenced by these processes, often with negative effects for the poorer regions and people. According to the World Development Report 2000-2001, almost half of the world's 6 billion people have to live on less than 1 dollar a day. Alongside this are the growing concerns regarding the climate, biodiversity and natural resources in many parts of the world. According to the UN Convention to Combat Desertification, over 250 million people are directly affected by desertification, while one billion people are at risk. And they are amongst the world's most marginalized citizens. Biodiversity and ecosystems are more threatened today than ever before in recorded history. This loss of species has profound implications on the economic and social possibilities for human survival and, again, affects poorer families the most.

Notable, however, is the growing international concern about food security, environmental changes, and poverty. Improved communication has resulted in an increased interest for biodiversity and indigenous peoples. The number of initiatives that address sustainability, indigenous knowledge and endogenous development are therefore increasing. At international level, for example, the UN Conferences on Environment and Development (UNCED), in Rio de Janeiro in 1992 and in Johannesburg in 2002, have emphasised the importance of sustainability as well as the diversity of cultures and biological systems. Moreover, the recognition of the importance of indigenous knowledge and practices by the scientific, donor and development institutions is growing. During the past decade many indigenous techniques on subjects like soil and water conservation, natural pesticides, intercropping, agroforestry, food preservation, as well as traditional human and animal health practices have been studied and documented. Presently, development agencies such as the World Bank, UNDP, UNESCO and FAO have programmes focusing on indigenous knowledge, while United Nations conventions such as UNCBD (Convention on Biodiversity) and UNCCD (Convention on Combating Desertification) acknowledge its importance.

Results of Compas in enhancing endogenous development

The central aim of the organisations that constitute the Compas international network is to support local people in appreciating, testing and improving their own knowledge and practices. Compas emphasises the local ownership of knowledge, and supports the capacity of local people to learn and experiment so as to improve their livelihoods. In the five years that Compas has been operational, 27 partner organisations in 14 countries have become actively involved in a wide range of field activities. A variety of innovative methodologies, for learning from and with local people, for co-operation with traditional leaders and organisations in the area, for testing and improving indigenous practices, as well as for networking and training, have been designed, applied and tested. The experiences gained have been exchanged amongst Compas partners and with wider audiences during several workshops, while also published in local, regional and international publications.

General effects of field work. The actual outcome of efforts at field level varies according to the economic, cultural and ecological situation of the rural population. The field activities implemented differed considerably among the partner organisations, and positive effects have been reported in a range of aspects. Improvements in terms of income, biodiversity, local natural resources, the position of traditional leaders and healers, the interest of youth in culture and traditions, food and nutritional status, human and animal health, the position of women, increased local organisation and cultural identity, and an improved agricultural curriculum are a few.

In this process, all partner organisations together with the rural populations have improved their understanding of the strong and the weak points of local knowledge and practices. They have found ways to carry out experiments in establishing and enhancing the effectiveness of local practices, which have resulted in conclusions that explain the rationality, effectiveness or limitations of these practices. In many cases modifications of traditional practices have been reported, sometimes by a synthesis with elements of modern knowledge. The relation between the NGOs and the communities has undergone substantial change. Rather than being a development agency with an 'outsider' perspective, the partners have developed into catalysts for development that originates from within the community. Experience shows, however, that changing the relations between the NGOs and the community in this direction requires constant learning and reflection, as paternalistic support patterns are often ingrained in both field workers and community members.

Over the past five years, national and international exchange and training workshops were organised in the Netherlands, Ghana, Zimbabwe, Uganda, India, Sri Lanka, Bolivia, Peru, and Indonesia. Compas partners took part in several national and international meetings and conferences, and contributed to the international debate on bio-cultural diversity. An international co-ordination unit has provided support to the network by organising an inception workshop followed by regional meetings, and by stimulating exchange of challenging views, and publications. Regional co-ordination units have been established in Asia, Latin America and Africa and various regional initiatives have been undertaken.

The Compas Magazine publishes the ideas, views and experiences of the Compas partner organisations and other like-minded individuals and organisations. This 6-monthly magazine contains articles based on practical experiences, presents case studies on different themes, and results of research. The magazine appears both in English and Spanish, and is currently distributed to over 7,000 organisations in 125 countries. The Compas web site (www.compas-network.org) contains all publications and basic information, both on the programme and the partner organisations that constitute the Compas network.

In general terms, the way endogenous development has been supported by the Compas partner organisations is very diverse. And this is exactly the idea. The options for endogenous development should be diverse, depending on the ecological, economic and cultural situation, as well as the skills, values and insights of both the rural community and the development agency.

Some lessons learned at field level

Local initiatives to use resources. All Compas field activities for endogenous develop-ment are based on a variety of local resources. Apart from biophysical (soil, water, climate) and biological (plants, animals biodiversity) resources, these also include local knowledge, values and norms, culture, social organisations and leadership. The experiences of rural people, and the wide range of insights and practices that have enabled them to survive under difficult circumstances, are often underestimated by outsiders. Traditional social organisations, though often eroding, continue to play a subtle but important role in daily activities and decision making. Local economies have mechanisms for saving, investment, income generation and marketing with often undervalued potential. The willingness of field workers implementing Compas activities to accept and respect the peoples' world-views has contributed to a new look at the development process. The cultural and social resources, once taken seriously, enhance the capacity to use all locally available resources.

Initially, the main areas of activity of the Compas partner organisations were agricul-ture, health and natural resources, but this was gradually widened to include many other activities. All field work is based on local resources with clear examples such as enhancing the use of local varieties of indigenous seeds (Green Foundation in India) and animal breeds (KPP in India), indigenous pest control practices (ECOS in Nepal, ECO in Sri Lanka), local management of natural resources (CECIK in Ghana, AZTREC in Zimbabwe, IDEA in India), and local herbs for human and animal medicines (FRLHT and IDEA in India).

As a result of the ongoing dialogue with the communities, almost all partner organisa-tions have expanded their range of activities to include the wider expressions of local cul-ture. Experiences in this respect include supporting music, dance and theatre (IDEA in India and AZTREC in Zimbabwe), supporting indigenous practices related to marketing and trade (AGRUCO in Bolivia), stimulating eco-tourism (AZTREC in Zimbabwe), enhancing the role and organisation of local spiritual leaders (ADICI in Guatemala), and stimulating festivals and rituals (Green Foundation in India). The rural people and the field staff have together re-assessed local resources and sought ways to use, combine and expand them in order to improve local livelihoods.

Box 8a   Enhancing bio-cultural diversity: experiences of Compas partners

Compas partner	Cultural dimension of local practice	Biodiversity issue	Entry point for development	Results
KPP India	Mangos are used in rituals, the leaves protect the house	Varieties of tender mango are declining	Rural competition for revival of tender mango varieties and related traditions	Over 2,000 tender mango plantings distributed to farmers; home made pickle production increased; farmers employ safer harvesting practices
TIRD-p Indonesia	Adat house is place for worship and teaching	Different plants are used in pest control rituals	Revival of adat house and traditional pest control in crops	Pest control rituals combined with biopesticides; ceremonial centre has experimental site in 3 villages
AGRUCO Bolivia	Potatoes have souls; Mother Earth is sacred	Many varieties related to altitude microclimate and traditions	Trace and stimulate traditional potato varieties, enhance local marketing systems	Traditional Andean tuber varieties preserved and revived in production system
IDEA India	Tribals have totemic relations with plants and animals	Plants, trees and animals are protected	Changing hunting ritual into conservation ceremony	Species with totemicsignificance are being protected by tribal people
AZTREC Zimbabwe	Spirits have their habitats in nature	Ecologically diverse wetlands and woodlands are needed	Rehabilitation of sacred wetlands and woodlands	10,000 ha of sacred wetlands and woodlands rehabilitated since 1985
GREEN India	Sacred seeds and ceremonial germination tests	Bio-genetic seed diversity of traditional crops maintained by women	Conservation and dissemination of traditional food crops	52 finger millet varieties, 37 dryland paddy varieties and 32 wetland paddy varieties conserved; 7 other traditional food crops revived Breeders rights protected with register
CECIK Ghana	Sacred groves are habitat of ancestral spirits	Sacred groves contain original vegetation with many endangered species	Traditional leaders are eager to restore and protect sacred groves for religious reasons	Sacred groves are restored and biodiversity enhanced by natural regeneration and planting exotic species
FRLHT India	Local healers use prayers and offerings when collecting medicinal plants	Variety of medicinal plants to be used in primary health care	Kitchen Herbal Gardens to promote positive local health practices and its medicinal plants	Over 40,000 KHG established, now spreading autonomously. Decreasing household medical expenditure
VEL&VANLA the Netherlands	Landscape is an expression of cultural identity	Trees and birds are protected. Local production system enhances agro-biodiversity	Agro-based tourism Nature management by farmers	Trees, insects and birds preserved. Landscape enriched Environmental pollution reduced
ECO Sri Lanka	'Evil eye' can damage crops	Herbs in rice bunds can enhance biodiversity and reduce pests	Demonstrations cannot be used as evil eye would prevent the effects Testing of no-weeding promoted during village festivals	Biodiversity in paddy fields increased (wild plants, insects, birds) Traditional varieties revived

Thematic focus: Enhancing bio-cultural diversity. Each Compas partner has a different thematic focus, depending on the priorities of the rural people and the expertise of its staff. Issues related to biodiversity are an outspoken activity of many partners, and the results gained in this field have been striking (see box 8a). Today, it is a well-known fact that the world's biodiversity is degrading fast. It is estimated that since 1600 AD about 500 animal species and more than 600 plant species have become extinct as a result of human interference. Many more are on the edge of extinction as their habitats are disturbed, isolated or disappear. All over the world modern agriculture has replaced numerous species and varieties of crops, plants and trees with monocultures that are vulnerable to pests and diseases. This erosion of natural diversity goes hand in hand with diminishing cultural diversity. More than half of the 6,000 languages currently spoken is unlikely to survive the next century.

The cases presented in this book show that many traditional cultures have deep-rooted beliefs that the spiritual world resides in nature, where humans can communicate with the supernatural forces. Not only houses of people, but also the lands, waters, forests, mountains, plants and animals are often perceived to be inhabited by spirits. Examples are the holy mountains in Bolivia, rocks and wetlands in Zimbabwe, sacred trees like the Baobab in Africa, the Ficus religiosa in Nepal, India and Sri Lanka, and the oak in the ancient cultures of Europe. These sacred natural sites also have an important social function as meeting places and sites of common worship. Traditional worldviews are often reflected in regulations and taboos in the management of natural resources, for example, by limiting woodcutting, hunting and collecting fruits. Box 8a presents some examples of the efforts which have been undertaken to preserve biodiversity based on the cultural dimension of traditional knowledge. This required a location and culture-specific diagnosis and intervention strategy. The Compas partner organisations have concluded that the combined attention for culture and biodiversity holds important keys for sustainable development.

Analysis of results at field level.

On the basis of the ten activities for supporting endogenous development, mentioned in chapter 3, we will now analyse the results of the fieldwork implemented by the Compas partner organisations over the past 5 years.

1. Building on local needs. All project activities implemented by the Compas partners were based on the priorities set during the dialogue with the rural communities and their local leaders. This resulted in a host of activities, as presented in the case studies in this book. In this process, however, it became clear that understanding and addressing the real needs is a serious challenge. Initially, identifying the local needs was perceived as a relatively simple process, which implied the involvement of local leaders in all stages of planning and implementation. Over time we learned, however, that it requires a more specific methodology to understand and address the intricacies of the intra-communal differences in power, wealth and knowledge, and the resulting differences in expressed needs. Class, caste and gender differences play a role here and are often difficult to tackle.

Community member and fieldworker identify strong and weak points of IK and decide to experiment with improvements CECIK, Ghana

Dealing with these controversies is, of course, a delicate process. Compas partner organisations have encountered these limitations, and included them into their dialogue. This means that the field staff has, at times, enhanced the discussion about moral dilemmas related to local values. Examples are the transformation of hunting into environmental protection ceremonies in the tribal communities (IDEA in India), and the influence exerted by Green Foundation in India to abolish a certain form of buffalo sacrifice in specific rituals. Several partners, for example IDEA, KPP and Green Foundation, have started activities in weed management, nutrition and agro-biodiversity, with a special focus on women. In Ghana, CECIK has developed a special programme to facilitate the access to land for women. In Zimbabwe the most important spirit mediums are women, which is reflected in the staffing of and field programme of AZTREC.

Building up the relationship between the rural people and the NGOs turned out to be an essential and delicate aspect. In many cases it required time and special efforts to show that the field staff indeed wanted to relate to the rural people within their cultural context as part of a mutual learning process, instead of prospecting their knowledge for personal motives. Participation in festivals and rituals and showing interest in learning from the traditional leaders were important ways of building up a relationship of trust. CECIK in Ghana presents a clear example where building up a relationship of confidence involved consultations of the ancestral spirits of both the community and the field workers.

2. Improving local knowledge and practices. The partner organisations found that, though often not expressed openly and increasingly affected by the globalisation process, indigenous knowledge, values and practices are still widespread amongst the rural communities. They concluded that the best way to support the local people was to understand, test and improve their practices within the local context, the in situ development of local knowledge. This process implies an ongoing and respectful dialogue between the staff of the NGOs and members of the rural communities, which challenges traditions as well as modern practices. Care needs to be taken not to romanticise indigenous practices, nor to be too sceptical or prejudiced. The case studies in this book present a wide array of methodologies for this process of in situ development.

An interesting way of validating indigenous practices is cross-checking them with different knowledge systems. FRLHT in India has spearheaded a process in which selected local practices are compared with western bio-medicine as well as other codified medical systems, such as Ayurveda, Siddha and Unani. Priorities for further testing and experimenting were determined during workshops in the communities. Another methodology is followed by CIKS in India. They study ancient classical texts on agricultural practices, called *Vkrshayurveda*, and then carry out experiments on their experimental farm as well as in farmers' fields, to study the potential of these practices for enhancing farming practices. They have come to the conclusion that linking the farmers' practices with the knowledge available in the ancient texts can strengthen and revitalise present day agriculture.

Improving indigenous chicken breeds, supported by IDEA, India.

KPP in India is carrying out on-farm experiments to test and revitalise ancient practices related to local food and cattle. The Compas Network in Sri Lanka is developing a methodology to measure the effect of indigenous knowledge, by relating the degree of 'indigenousness' of the farmers to the outcome of their agricultural practices. AGRUCO in Bolivia is systematically documenting traditional Andean farming practices, which has resulted in a tremendous data base. Local farmers have access to this information, while traditional farming practices have become part of the university agricultural curriculum. Students, fieldworkers and community members carry out joint experiments with traditional Andean crop varieties and animal husbandry practices, and support community organisational structures.

3. Local control of development options. Several methodologies have been developed to enhance local control. Compas partners have supported the communities and local leaders to take control of the development process. This implies their active participation in the diagnosis of the situation, as well as the planning, implementation and evaluation of activities. AGRUCO, for example, supported local communities in formulating community development plans, and presented these plans to the local municipality where increased funds had become available due to the government's decentralisation policies.

Presentation of the People's Biodiversity Register, supported by FRLHT in India.

The protection of intellectual property rights is another point of critical importance in working with indigenous knowledge and practices. Compas partner organisations have developed different ways of safeguarding these rights. For example, Green Foundation in India works with 'Village Biodiversity Registers' in its efforts to protect local crop varieties, while FRLHT in the same country has promoted 'People's Biodiversity Registers' to protect knowledge related to medicinal plants. Indigenous knowledge once published, as is the case with these registers, it cannot be patented by a (foreign) company. The code of conduct agreed upon by the Compas partners (chapter 3), aims at overcoming problems with local control and intellectual property rights in the communities they work with.

4. Identification of development niches. In the process of identifying local needs and potentialities, unexplored development niches were encountered often. Marketing of region-specific quality products such as local mango varieties (KPP in India), seed varieties and products from traditional crops (Green Foundation in India), forest produce (Aztrec in Zimbabwe), local chicken breeds (IDEA in India and CECIK in Ghana), traditional weaving (TIRD in Timor), local cattle breeds (KPP in India) and local cheese and grain products in the Netherlands are some examples. AGRUCO has built up experiences in stimulating traditional marketing systems that are based on indigenous forms of solidarity and exchange.

Traditional areas also have a comparative advantage in relation to international tourism, one of the fastest growing income-generating activities in poor countries. Some Compas partner organisations have already developed some expertise in this direction like Aztrec in Zimbabwe and IDEA in India that have included traditional music and dance in the programmes for eco-cultural tourism. It is a major challenge, however, to develop this eco-cultural tourism into an activity that strengthens rather than weakens cultural identity.

All these cases demonstrate positive effects in terms of nutritional status, ecological improvements and learning processes, as well as considerable enthusiasm of the rural people. Effects in terms of direct monetary income have not been shown in all cases, partly because some rural communities hardly function as cash economies, and partly because it takes time to establish and consolidate income-generating activities. Often, the process of linking local economies with regional or national markets requires interventions at the levels above that of the community.

5. Selective use of external resources. The use of external resources could be done selectively once the locally available resources were well identified and their limitations were understood and accepted. The chemical drugs necessary to complement traditional medicines for ethnoveterinary practices and human health systems were identified by IDEA. FRLHT made use of the pharmacological data on local herbs as produced by bio-medical science. CECIK has incorporated exotic tree species to complement slow-growing local species. The farmers also experimented with a combination of organic fertilisation methods and chemical fertilisers, to reduce the incidence of the 'devil weed', called *striga,* in northern Ghana. TIRD made use of laboratory research to determine active ingredients for bio-pesticides. Of course, the cars, computers and other equipment used in the offices and fieldwork are based on global science. In all cases the complementarity between local knowledge and external knowledge was considered important. This did not lead to substitution of local knowledge by external knowledge, but to a synergy between all available re-sources.

Combination of traditional health practices with outside innovations: a traditional healer interprets X-ray, FRLHT, India.

6. Retention of benefits in the local area. Several Compas partner organisations are experimenting with techniques to improve local storage and processing of products, and to enhance the marketing of these products in retaining their 'added value' in the local area. Often these processes include rituals and communal festivities. The activities in this respect were experiments and training in storage, processing and marketing, as well as investments in infrastructure. Examples are the preparation of mango chutney and organic vegetables (KPP in India), and local marketing of traditional seeds in Green Foundation. AZTREC (Zimbabwe) has reported a decrease in youth migration from the Zimuto area to the cities due to the increased income generating activities in the eco-cultural villages such as processing and marketing of vegetables and fruits, eco-tourism and organic agriculture.

Van der Ploeg [2002] has presented economic data explaining the economic advantages of endogenous development for European farmers. In the process of diversifying agriculture, the income of the Dutch farmers participating in the experiments has risen as a result of cost reduction, use of new market niches and saving of time. Moreover, the solutions developed by the farmers such as increased uptake of roughage by dairy cattle, has had a positive impact on the environment.

Local marketing of regional products in the Netherlands.

7. Exchange and learning between cultures. The Compas partners have organised various exchange activities at local level. Exchange between different villages and population groups was stimulated through seed fairs, demonstrations or school competitions. Often these activities were combined with expressions of local culture, such as dance, music, theatre, or rituals. This exchange was supported by the dissemination of newsletters and other publications in local languages.

Exchange also took place with other organisations in the region and at national and international level. Newsletters, books, websites, calendars and CD-roms in the dominant language, such as English and Spanish, were the main forms of exchange at this level. Various Compas workshops and exchange visits have been organised to share and assess the experiences in enhancing endogenous development. An example of an international exchange between rural indigenous groups were the visits of Q'eqchi' Maya people from Guatemala and the Lacandones in Mexico in December 2000 and April 2001. A poster designed by the tribal people in the North Eastern Ghats was sent by IDEA to the other Compas partners.

These forms of exchange have led to an increased cultural awareness and self-esteem, as people recognise the similarities in the fundamental concepts underlying the different indigenous practices. A specific example of the study of these similarities is the comparison between Chinese and Maya local health systems [Garcia, 2000]. The findings of this study have influenced the work with local health practices of several Compas partner organisations. Similar experiences in agriculture and natural resource management have shown the importance of comparing and exchanging information on the cultural dimensions of endogenous development.

8. Training and capacity building. The Compas partner organisations are engaged in an ongoing dialogue on endogenous development with rural people. To be able to do this, each field worker needs to develop a new set of skills to collaborate with rural people in a truly participatory way. This does not only imply the participation of field workers in activities, such as rituals, sacrifices and festivals of the communities they are working with; it also implies taking the local concepts as the main starting point of the development process. Such an approach requires an attitude of respect, creative thinking as well as communication skills, which is not part of the training in conventional schools and universities. A kind of de-schooling and re-training was necessary, therefore, for all involved in the fieldwork. This turned out to be a truly eventful learning path.

Most of the training activities of the Compas partners have taken place on-the-job. Training materials and training capacities for endogenous development were scarce, and needed to be developed. IDEA has developed a 'dormitory training', with training of staff, community leaders and farmers at their training centre. CECIK describes the learning path of establishing a relationship with the community in a culturally accepted way in Ghana. AGRUCO in Bolivia has quite a specific way of addressing the necessary change in attitude and communication skills of field workers. Their field experiences are included into the curriculum for university students, while rural communities express their ideas and criteria for research activities. The objective is to gear schooling of field workers to a form that creates a high degree of cultural sensitivity. Plans for a similar education and action-research programme exist in Sri Lanka, Zimbabwe and Ghana.

This re-education process of field staff has also had unexpected side effects. Trained field workers with increased capacities to work with rural communities in a participatory

Woman farmer in Iscos, Peru, offers coca leaves during the Santiago ritual for livestock health and production. Her husband explains the meaning of the ritual to a staff member of a NGO supporting them.

manner have been lured away by better paid jobs in other organisations. This has sometimes caused a lack of continuity in the programmes of the partner organisations.

9. Networking and strategic partnership. Individual NGOs in different countries joined hands to start the Compas programme. In most cases these NGOs had on-going and established programmes and local networks in the domain of organic agriculture, indigenous knowledge, or local health. The Compas programme enabled them to work towards endogenous development in a more systematic way. All Compas partner organisations have established or widened their local and national networks; most of them have organised local, regional or international exchange and policy workshops. A number of partners have newsletters in the local language, many have national or regional publications. FRLHT in India, for example, is publishing the magazine 'Amruth', and has organised an international conference on traditional health practices. The linkages with like-minded organisations are growing due to increased awareness on the importance of in situ conservation and development of indigenous knowledge and practices.

In order to address global issues related to endogenous development, a number of initiatives for setting up regional networks are underway. In Africa, a special programme for enhancing endogenous development has been launched. This has resulted in the establishment of regional networks for endogenous development under the name ENEDA

Compas member IDEA (Gowtham Shankar, left) shares the tribal cosmovision in the form of a poster with participants of the conference on biocultural diversity in Yunnan, China.

(Enhancing Endogenous Development in Africa, see box 8b). In Asia, networking between partners so far has been during regional workshops and conferences, as well as exchange visits. The Asian network also produces a newsletter called 'Clarion'.

In Latin America, Compas partners participated in a workshop on indigenous land use systems in Guatemala, and organised a workshop on Cosmovision and Biodiversity, in Bolivia, in February 2001. Presently the Latin America Compas Network is divided into units according to ethnic background: Quechua and Aymara indigenous groups (with organisations from Bolivia, Peru, and Colombia), Mapuche indigenous groups (with organisations from Chile), and Maya indigenous groups (with organisations from Guatemala). Based on the experiences of Bolivia, the Latin American partners will establish programmes for self management and sustainable development. In Europe, the networking activities involve the Ceres network on endogenous development, which has contacts in several western European countries.

Box 8b   Enhancing endogenous development in Africa - ENEDA

In Zimbabwe, a regional network of traditional leaders engaged in environmental conservation was launched in 1997, under the name of ASATREC, the Association of Southern African Traditional Environmental Conservationists. AZTREC, the Compas partner in Zimbabwe, was appointed as the regional focal point of ASATREC. This regional network will implement the ENEDA proposal - Enhancing Endogenous Development in Africa - in Swaziland, Western Zambia, Botswana and South Africa, as a follow-up of ENIAKA and in close co-operation with Compas.

With financial support of CTA (Centre Technique Agricole) a special project for enhancing indigenous agricultural knowledge in Africa was launched in 1999. This programme undertook the following activities: taking stock of the existing literature on indigenous knowledge in Ghana and Zimbabwe, and making an inventory of the traditional practices actually being carried out in these two countries by consulting local and national experts. Then national workshops to assess the situation and to formulate proposals for national activities to enhance indigenous agricultural knowledge were organised in each of these countries.

In December 2000, a Pan-African workshop was held in Masvingo, Zimbabwe, to present the outcome of these country studies and to formulate proposals for enhancing indigenous agricultural knowledge across Africa. Representatives from 14 countries took part and a number of regional co-ordination units were set up, namely West Africa, East Africa and Southern Africa. Since then, two national workshops have been held in East Africa (Uganda and Tanzania) to take stock of the existing situation and to formulate proposals for action. In Southern Africa a number of workshops have been held and an elaborate proposal has been formulated for country-wide programmes and regional support in the domains of methodologies, training, policy dialogue and research. In West Africa the initiatives were hampered by the language divide between Anglophone and Francophone countries. An initiative has been started to organise a country-wide workshop in Ghana with possible expansion to other west African countries.

Regional co-ordinators appointed to each of the regions are taking the lead in networking activities. At the time of presenting this book, the momentum of networking has reached a critical point. With some additional effort, the movement of endogenous development can link up with other movements and spread to many other countries.

10. Understanding the systems of knowing and learning. During the initial years of the Compas programme, partners put most of their effort into understanding the local culture, and implementing joint experiments with local practices. A direct difficulty encountered here was finding the appropriate methodology to base the experimentation on the concepts of the different knowledge systems. Ancient systems of knowledge place their trust in direct *experiential knowing*: knowledge derived through direct experience. This differs from the foundations of western knowledge systems that are based on verified theories and propositions, also called *propositional knowing*. Questions frequently discussed were: how can traditional practices be validated - do we need methodologies derived from western science or can this be done within the own theories and scientific concepts? And,

if so, how can this be done?

Some partners have subsequently made deliberate attempts to understand the epistemology of these knowledge systems, which is the study of their nature, origin and scope. This implies the more theoretical aspects of this knowledge, as well as their dynamics. For example in India, IDEA has studied the knowledge concepts of the tribal people, CIKS has studied the basic concepts of the ancient Vrksayurvedic texts, while FRLHT has made comparative studies of the concepts within the different medical traditions. Balasubramanian of CIKS argues that despite the dominant position of western science, it can not be concluded that it is unique and universally applicable. Specific research methods derived from the scientific concepts of other traditions deviate considerably from those used in western science.

CIKS (India) builds its work on Vrksayurveda texts which are documented on palm leaves.

Similarly, de Zoysa in Sri Lanka has elaborated on the Buddhist concepts of unity and interdependence of nature, the limits of resources, and compassion for life. Modern science bases its observations on the five sensory inputs (smell, hearing, eyesight, touch and taste), and makes no distinction between the mind and consciousness. According to the Buddhist viewpoint, experiential as well as propositional knowledge has to be ultimately experienced by the one who knows, and meditation is used as a methodology to accomplish this. The question of subjectivity is dealt with in Buddhism by developing *sila*, which implies the correct ethical attitude and behaviour in the experiencing individual.

In the context of the ENEDA programme, the dynamics of the African knowledge and value systems have been studied. As explained in chapter 5 of this book, there are many differences between African and western concepts on matter, nature, religion, time, art, agriculture, nature conservation, local governance, community leadership and decision making. Similarly, AGRUCO in Bolivia has studied the knowledge concepts of the Quechua and Aymara indigenous groups in the Andes. The Latin American knowledge concepts (chapter 6) include the spiral notion of time, the importance of festivals and rituals, sacred aspects of nature, importance attached to biodiversity, hot-cold polarity, living astronomy and astrology, and mutual relations between humans, other living organisms and mother earth. Also here, morality of the people is considered an important factor in explaining the cause and effects of processes related to farming, health and community welfare.

It was concluded that the capacity to set up experiments, as well as theory building about traditional knowledge required further strengthening amongst the Compas partners. The epistemological interpretation of the different Asian, African and Latin American knowledge systems, their ways of learning and experimenting, and their relationship with the western knowledge system needs more attention. It is proposed that in the coming years the partners will get increased support from a group of selected universities (the University Consortium for Endogenous Development), to develop ways to compare the concepts and theories behind indigenous knowledge systems.

Opportunities and constraints for endogenous development

These experiences show that the economic and environmental changes have increased public awareness and attention for cultural diversity and local economies. The output of the work of the Compas partners indicates that enhancing endogenous development can be feasible and effective. The basic components of endogenous development have been used effectively by most of the partners as a basis for the field methods. The steady growth of the Compas programme in regional networks has enhanced the institutional capacity of the network as a whole. Biodiversity is a promising theme, while gender and power issues require more specific attention in the future. The cases show that there is a great variability of development options if one takes the worldviews, values, practices, knowledge concepts and ecological and political contexts seriously. However, not all is positive and easy. Here, we elaborate on a number of opportunities and constraints.

Opportunities. A consistent observation of the organisations working with Compas is that there is much indigenous knowledge, cosmovision and traditional leadership still alive in many cultures, although often under threat. The cases presented in this book show that numerous groups are working to revitalise indigenous knowledge and cosmovision. They are not romanticising cultural expressions, but are trying to understand and challenge them by means of experiments and innovations. We observe that at field level there is enthusiasm among farmers, spiritual leaders, NGOs and some policy bodies to experiment with ancient knowledge in the modern context. The initial results are promising, but more time is needed to consolidate them and come to more definite conclusions.

Among NGOs, we see an increasing interest in culture and cosmovision. This implies that innovative methodologies, strategies and policy frameworks to enhance endogenous development are emerging. Due to new communication technologies, indigenous people find it easier to get more support and public awareness for their quests, also on issues related to cultural diversity and biodiversity. Strategic alliances with like-minded organisations can lead to a deeper understanding of the dynamics of living systems, and the development of rules and regulations that protect cultural and biological diversity. Moreover, some major donors, including the World Bank, IDRC in Canada and DGIS in the Netherlands have made funds available to support indigenous knowledge systems. The Compas international network, regional co-ordination, local networks, as well as the recently initiated University Consortium, embody an important institutional capacity that can further enhance endogenous development.

Constraints. The constraints encountered in the Compas activities over the past years have been at two levels: at the level of field work, and at the level of the wider environment for enhancing endogenous development.

Constraints at field level

Constraints have been encountered within the traditional cultures themselves, such as ineffective concepts and technologies, restrictions on women, or abuse of power related to secret knowledge. Based on previous experiences, rural people have found it difficult to build a new relationship of trust with the staff of support organisations or to share the intimacy of their culture and spiritual knowledge. Local experts and leaders have not always been willing to share their knowledge and power. Field staff of support organisations, on the other hand, has sometimes lacked the right attitude or skills to be able to respectfully dialogue about culture and cosmovision. In certain instances, outside agents tended to romanticise or preserve cultures, for example for eco-tourism purposes. Also donors have found it difficult to reserve finances for the purpose of enhancing endogenous development and cultural diversity.

It takes more time than the five years of the Compas programme to make a gender specific analysis of a cosmovision, however, and to develop appropriate methodologies. We can not assume that by working with local leaders, women are logically represented. The majority of the field workers are men and their gender sensitivity can often be improved. It was learned that special training is required to bridge the existing gender and social gaps. The way in which the cosmovisions of women differs or coincides with those of men has not been explored in depth. The gender perceptions within the traditional cosmovisions, with existing limitations in rights or social positions, can be made more explicit. The attention for gender aspects can be improved and strategies need to be developed for gender-specific endogenous development.

Field workers are often of a higher social background than the marginalised groups they are working with. In some cases methodologies were found to overcome this limitation. In the case of IDEA and CIKS, local youth function as project staff, while Green Foundation, CECIK, KPP, and AZTREC work in close co-operation with community based animators. This has helped in overcoming the social differences, but it has also sometimes posed new difficulties of continuity and availability of staff.

The capacity within the Compas partner organisations for understanding the concepts, as well as the methodologies for testing and improving indigenous knowledge and practices, was often limited. This was in part due to the conventional educational system, in which most of the fieldworkers have been trained. Moreover, skill development in the Compas programme was essentially an informal activity based on the experiences and needs of the field activities. More systematic support to the experiments and the understanding of the knowledge systems, as well as training, will be necessary to enhance the capacity of field staff, not only of partners but also other NGOs in the localities.

Constraints in wider environment

Thinking along the lines of diversity as a guiding principle in development, of a diversity of cultures and sciences, and of a co-evolution of cultures, is not yet accepted by many. An important constraint is the notion that all development should come from a western-induced modernisation process. This may even be stronger in the minds of professionals in southern countries than those in the North. For endogenous development to be main-streamed, some important changes in international and national power relations, vested interests and politics are required. The international trade relations between the western and southern countries, for example, hamper economic development in large parts of the South. Recent negotiations in the World Trade Organisation have not yet led to more equi-table access to international markets. Also, the status ascribed to western consumption patterns, science and technology does not favour endogenous development. The threat of patenting knowledge and the pirating of bio-resources is also very real and is taking place.

Challenges for Compas

The experiences of the Compas partners can be characterised as action research for in situ development of local knowledge systems. This action research has effectively developed new methods for building relationships with rural people, for learning from and with them, for conducting local experiments based on local values, knowledge, concepts and leadership, for improving the experimental practices and skills, self development and training, networking and intercultural dialogue.

The results are a variety of innovative and practical ways of enhancing endogenous development. As elaborated in this chapter, with definite variations per partner, the impact at village-level has generally been positive in terms of ecological situation, capacity to experiment and improve traditional knowledge, social cohesion, cultural identity and to a certain extent income. The methodologies used by the partners has been appreciated pos-itively by rural people, field staff and development professionals, especially because of the attention given to the cultural background of those involved in the process. The capacity of partners in building a good relationship with rural people, and in learning with and from them, was generally very good. It was concluded that this approach leads to a better relationship between field staff and rural people, and to more effective field work.

At the same time, the constraints encountered at the various levels needs to be addressed in future activities. Rather than increasing the number of partners and regions where Compas would carry out fieldwork, it is considered more important to deepen and further improve the quality of the work with the existing group of partners. This includes training of field staff, developing and consolidating robust methods for endogenous development with a focus on poverty alleviation and gender, dealing with the controver-sies within the communities, deepening the understanding of the knowledge concepts used in the different knowledge systems, and strengthening the network with organisa-tions that play a role in rural development worldwide.

The Compas programme wishes to continue its activities at four levels (see box 8c):
- Field activities of rural communities and member organisations to enhance endogenous

development at local level and to develop and test operational approaches for poverty alleviation.

- Regional support activities for backstopping and training carried out by regional co-ordination units.
- Activities at international level for co-ordination, publication, international networking and intercultural exchange.
- Scientific support through a consortium of universities.

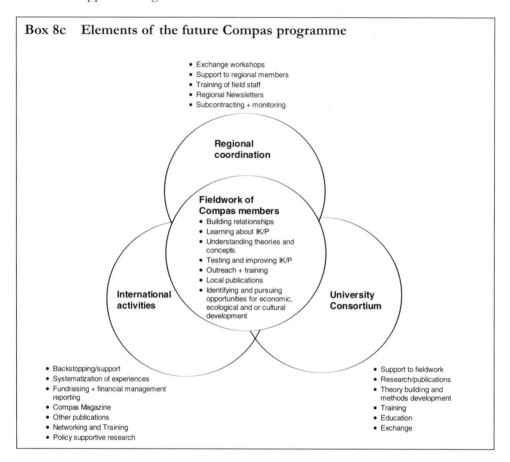

Box 8c   Elements of the future Compas programme

- Exchange workshops
- Support to regional members
- Training of field staff
- Regional Newsletters
- Subcontracting + monitoring

Regional coordination

Fieldwork of Compas members
- Building relationships
- Learning about IK/P
- Understanding theories and concepts
- Testing and improving IK/P
- Outreach + training
- Local publications
- Identifying and pursuing opportunities for economic, ecological and or cultural development

International activities

University Consortium

- Backstopping/support
- Systematization of experiences
- Fundraising + financial management reporting
- Compas Magazine
- Other publications
- Networking and Training
- Policy supportive research

- Support to fieldwork
- Research/publications
- Theory building and methods development
- Training
- Education
- Exchange

The examples described in this book show that new methodologies can work to improve local livelihoods in a sustainable way. Endogenous development is not a theory or a dream: it is tangible in the practical outcomes of activities pursued in the communities. But, due to the constraints mentioned above, the direct environment in which development organisations support local initiatives is often not conducive for endogenous development. This means, that in order to give endogenous development a chance, an enabling environment has to be created. The issues to be addressed in this respect are elaborated in the next and final chapter of this book.

9. CREATING AN ENABLING ENVIRONMENT FOR ENDOGENOUS DEVELOPMENT
Towards a co-evolution of cultures

Initiatives towards endogenous development taken by local farmers and communities are often not support-ed by national policies and hampered by international regulations. Organisations working with endoge-nous development could join forces in order to create a more enabling environment for these local initiatives. Negative effects of globalisation can thus be counteracted by enhancing the sustainable use of local resources, by supporting local alternatives that reduce poverty and migration, and by stimulating the diver-sity of cultures. Options for enhancing endogenous development at a level beyond the rural communities, and the development organisations involved with them, are presented in this final chapter.

The realities of rural people in different cultures vary due to a whole range of reasons, which may include ecological problems, political instability and demographic variables. Increased urbanisation, de-population of rural areas, as well as brain-drain are phenome-na that touch almost all societies, the extent to which may vary in each country and region. The policy contexts can also differ, with different impacts on development initiatives: pol-icy determines the level of import levies and export subsidies, subsidies for inputs, the research and extension agenda, as well as the level of rural infrastructure. Moreover, the local culture and belief systems influence the practices, knowledge, concepts as well as sci-entific methods used. This has considerable implications for the development options within each of the contemporary cultures.

Diversity of worldviews and belief systems. The worldviews and belief systems of the cultures presented in this book have several commonalties, in spite of marked differences in locality and circumstances. The notion of 'cosmos' or universe is perceived in several cultures as an interwoven whole with a sacred nature. In other cultures the universe is con-sidered a combination of units that can be understood separately, all considered to be mat-ter that obey the laws of physics and biology. There are cultures that are based on the belief of a pantheon of Gods, spirits, ancestors and other spiritual beings, while in oth-ers the belief is centred on one God; others doubt or deny the existence of supreme beings altogether. According to the worldview of the different cultures, life after death may be considered not to exist, to exist in a heaven outside this world, to be an ancestral world, or as reincarnation in different life forms.

Similarly, human beings are seen in a variety of ways: as a being totally dependent on the spiritual and natural forces, as a steward or master of creation, or as a miniscule being in an enigmatic cosmos. Animals and plants are seen as pure biological organisms, as liv-ing beings with a soul and feelings, or as beings with a sacred dimension. The way people organise themselves also varies: individually, in families, in ethnic and social structures, or as political entities. Local leadership structures and decision making processes are based on individual choices, family or ethnic ties, as well as religion and culture. It is obvious that, depending on the characteristics of each worldview and belief system, the practices, social structures, values and options for development vary considerably.

The practices carried out by people are based on their values, knowledge, and belief system. People choose between a variety of options, and develop technologies most appropriate for their situation and culture, which meet their requirements and aspirations. Cultural diversity reflects the diversity of agricultural practices, as well as language, religion, foods and consumption patterns, social activities, mechanisms to achieve status and prestige, forms of incentives, sport, art, music, dance, architecture, and the design of tools and commodities.

Diversity of knowledge concepts and scientific methods. Similarly, knowledge concepts show a great diversity amongst cultures. Many traditional knowledge systems have a linear or spiral notion of time, a bi-polar notion of matter (hot-cold, yin-yang), and take into account a variety of powers related to timing of events, locations, specific personal powers, symbols, and sounds. In the scientific worldview developed in Europe in the 18th century, matter is studied within a more mechanistic and linear time concept, while in post-modern approaches more room is given to chance, chaos and diversity. Depending on the scientific concepts, the object and the subject studying it can be seen as separate entities or as an inseparable whole. Depending on this, the role of quantification, measurement, the role of the six senses, conscience, intuition and religious experiences may differ. The attention for that which is manifest and that which is not can differ, as well as the role of mathematics, linguistics, and intuition. The researcher may be appreciated for the capacity to measure and interpret data in scientific terms, or be judged for his or her freedom from prejudice and high morale.

All the factors mentioned above, and many more, determine the extent to which endogenous development can take place. The margins to manoeuvre thus varies, and the strategies to be followed too.

Creating an enabling environment

In this book we have described endogenous development from two different perspectives: the local activities of rural people in using their resources to reduce poverty, and the process of supporting these activities by NGOs and farmers organisations. In the previous chapter we concluded that a number of issues cannot be solved at the level of an individual farmer, community, or development organisation. Local initiatives may not result in effective changes if not enhanced by a supportive legal, economic and policy environment. Analysis and intervention at higher levels are required, new policies need to be developed. The deepening crisis with poverty, environmental degradation, and cultural alienation throughout the poor countries of the world requires a look beyond the modernisation paradigm of agriculture and food production. Some lessons may be learned from the European experiences (see box 9a).

Re-thinking the way forward in agriculture and food production is taking place throughout the world. The multifunctionality of the farm, including off-farm income, innovative forms of cost reduction and on-farm activities, diversity of agricultural production, organic farming, local marketing systems and nature management are common place in the strategies of most poor farming families. Yet, as mentioned several times in

---

Box 9a   Some lessons learned in Europe

European agriculture has been struggling for more than a decade with an ever-deepening crisis. The many expressions of the crisis are perceived more and more as outcomes of the dominant model of agricultural modernisation. This is characterised by government policies directed at intensification, larger scale, monocropping, specialisation, increased inputs, external technology development, and dependency on market chains. Over the past years, the negative effects of these policies have become increasingly clear. Industrialised livestock farming, for example, puts enormous pressure on natural resources, food safety, animal genetic diversity and welfare. Farmers' incomes have declined and now largely depend on subsidies of the European Community Support programmes, while the costs of external inputs increase steadily due to expensive new technologies and numerous regulations.

A recent overview and analysis of the rural development processes throughout Europe [van der Ploeg et al., 2002] clearly indicates, however, that many new responses are being developed to overcome this situation. Europe is moving from agricultural modernisation towards rural development as the guiding principle for policy formulation, enterprise development, and the design of new institutional arrangements. Initiatives have been taken and are sustained by farming families to combat increasing costs and find new sources of income. For them, rural development represents a 'way out' of the limitations and lack of prospects intrinsic to the modernisation paradigm. The initiatives mentioned in the study include agri-tourism, environmental management on agricultural farms, diversification into energy crops that can provide 'bio-diesel', care giving to the handicapped people on farms, regional production and marketing of high quality foods, direct marketing mechanisms, ecological and organic farming, establishment of new types of co-operatives, and new forms of low-external-input farming. Support to these initiatives varies among the different European governments. Romano Prodi, current president of the European Commission, indicates the importance of supporting these efforts: *"The overall findings of the research stress that the maintenance of the heterogeneity and flexibility in Europe's agriculture requires a strengthening of rural development policies. The improvements of such policies should, on the one hand, build upon the impressive variety and heterogeneity that already exists and, on the other, reflect the richness of rural values and knowledge systems which together constitute the common roots of our European heritage. The result of such policies are well worth the effort."*

---

this book, the knowledge bases of these systems are depleting rapidly. International market mechanisms and policies of national governments often hamper the initiatives towards endogenous development.

Supporting local initiatives towards endogenous development can be stimulated by networks of development organisations, farmers' groups, consumer groups, groups of concerned citizens, and religious organisations, to name but a few. In the case of the Compas programme, the local communities, Compas partners, universities and regional networks, as well as other national and international agencies for sustainable development can join hands in developing operational approaches and effective programmes to support local initiatives.

Compas fieldwork with endogenous development has shown, however, that a number of elements have to be taken into account in this process. These elements, presented in the wider circle of box 9b are: stimulating local and regional economies, dealing with controversies, securing intellectual property rights, joint learning and capacity building, enhancing inter-cultural dialogue, stimulating policy supportive research, and enhancing the co-evolution of sciences. These activities have to take place both at field level and at a wider level of negotiation, lobby, and dialogue.

Box 9b   Supporting and enabling endogenous development

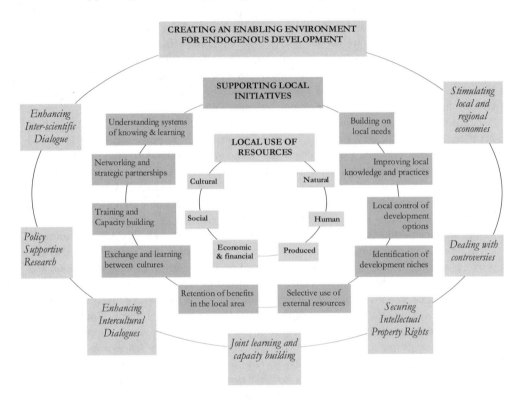

Stimulating local and regional economies. The individual farmer has limited possibilities to influence the conditions of local and national economies. Marketing, transport and storage facilities can be organised between several producers. NGOs can support groups of farmers and marketing organisations by making feasibility studies, elaborating business plans, or mobilising capital, as well as by training, lobbying and public relations. The opportunities for producing region-specific quality products, processing of food and fibres or village-based tourism can be explored. National networks of NGOs or farmer organisations can play a role in the identification of possible products, finding ways to produce them and by providing support in training, product development, infrastructure and marketing. Governmental bodies can support these efforts by creating a favourable environment through legislation, price mechanisms and research.

Access to international markets and securing better prices for agricultural produce and inputs is more difficult, given the restrictions placed by international trade relations. At this level, national networks of NGOs for endogenous development can look into the possibilities for linking with international trading opportunities, and addressing the structural inequity of access to the international market. They can be the voice of farmers in the marginal areas and lobby for changes in the trade regulations.

Dealing with controversies. All cultures have aspects that can be looked upon as positive or negative. Some traditional cultures expect subservience of youth to elders, or of lower castes to higher castes. Culture can often be a culprit that keeps creative energies trapped by conformity and compliance. Children sometimes are told: "*don't ask questions, you will find out later*", and later on they may not find out. Modern practices often emphasise consumerism, leading to increased neglect of social cohesion and respect for nature.

Several philosophers from different continents have called for an assessment of the strong and weak points of each tradition through a process of internal reflection and debate. Hountondji [2000] for example, a philosopher from Benin, refers to specific African traditions and practices he considers unjust, and not sufficiently challenged from within. In order to get this process started, he argues, it is necessary to be mentally liberated from the view other cultures hold of one's culture. This can allow the reflection on why certain practices have emerged and why they may or may no longer work today. Also a respectful and straight forward interaction with other cultures is helpful in this process. In other cultural traditions, such as in the western countries, a critical reflection on issues like the destruction of nature and biodiversity, increased social alienation, the negative effects of industrial agriculture, as well as the effects of international trade relations on the economies of the poorest countries can be stimulated.

Several controversies related to traditional cultures stem from the role and functioning of local leaders. Traditional functionaries often act as judges in legal problems, or guide spiritual and religious activities. In many countries the national governments have experienced difficulty in recognising and accepting these traditional leaders after colonial independence. These leaders may control traditional land use systems in a way incompatible with the government's rules and regulations, while others have become instruments of central government. The traditional spiritual leaders may represent a belief system unacceptable to representatives of formal religions. Moreover, spiritual as well as other traditional leaders may display serious undemocratic (and gender-biased) attitudes. In such instances, a respectful dialogue with a diversity of social categories in the community is an important option.

In endogenous development, the gender issues need to be brought more to light by including a gender dimension in each of the components. Strategies are required for gender specific endogenous devel-

Three generations discuss the potentials and pitfalls of eco-tourism in southern China. A process of internal reflection and debate is needed within cultures to deal with possible controversies and to allow creative ideas to emerge.

opment, including an analysis of the difficulties in finding appropriate female field staff and methodologies to address the specific needs of rural women. Dealing with these issues poses an ongoing challenge within the process of endogenous development.

Another important controversy related to strengthening the cultural identity of traditional societies is the possibility of enhancing ethnocentrism and fundamentalism. This risk is higher when the movement for reviving traditional values and cultures are a response to collective frustration. Organisations involved in enhancing endogenous development should be aware of this risk in their work. Intercultural dialogues could be used to identify and discuss fundamentalist tendencies.

Securing intellectual property rights. Over the last two centuries, traditional knowledge and practices have been used without any acknowledgement or benefit sharing with the traditional communities from where they originated. Examples abound of pieces of traditional knowledge being 'modified' and afterwards a patent claimed on the modification as if it were novel and new. Though the Convention on Biodiversity has made recommendations to stop these unfair practices, the economic liberalisation and globalisation perspective of the General Agreement on Trade and Tariffs (GATT) and its Trade Related Intellectual Property Rights (TRIPS) practically forces poor countries to accept these practices. This has given rise to important debates. For example, the declaration of action of the UNESCO-ISCU World Conference on Science contains the following recommendation: *Intellectual property rights need to be appropriately protected on a global basis, and access to data and information is essential for undertaking scientific work and for translating the results of scientific research into tangible benefits for society. Measures should be taken to enhance those relationships between the protection of intellectual property rights and the dissemination of scientific knowledge that are mutually supportive. There is a need to consider the scope, extent and application of intellectual property rights in relation to the equitable production, distribution and use of knowledge. There is also a need to further develop appropriate national legal frameworks to accommodate the specific requirements of developing countries and traditional knowledge and its sources and products, to ensure their recognition and adequate protection on the basis of the informed consent of the customary or traditional owners of this knowledge.* The regional and national networks on endogenous development need to link up with existing national and international organisations that strive for protection of intellectual property rights. In the Compas network several local initiatives have been taken to protect intellectual property rights: the Village Biodiversity Registers (Green Foundation, India), and Peoples' Biodiversity Register (FRLHT, India). The fight against certain patents has achieved success in some cases in the past. For example, in July 2000, the European Patent Office in Munich rejected a patent claim by a US company for Neem oil, which has been known in India for its anti-fungal properties for centuries both in Ayurvedic medicine and agriculture.

Joint learning and capacity building. The way pupils and students throughout the world are taught in schools is quite diverse. Yet, many curricula are based on western worldviews. This is especially the case in universities and colleges, though often the education in secondary schools includes mathematics, physics, economy and religion based on a western worldview and value system. This was the reason for various Compas partner organisations to focus part of their activities on young people from primary and secondary schools, as well as university students. AGRUCO in Bolivia is an interesting example of how university education can be enhanced by including the worldview and experiences of local communities.

Establishing a more inter-scientific education system implies systematic re-training and re-schooling of professionals in agriculture, health, education and research, who have been trained in a one-sided system. Examples of the re-training process of field staff engaged in endogenous development, as mentioned in this book, could stimulate this process. In the long-term, curricula for colleges, secondary and primary schools could be redesigned. The regional networks could take up the tasks of building curricula, writing handbooks and training trainers.

Enhancing intercultural dialogues. The intercultural dialogue that is part of the Compas programme suggests an engagement of the partners in the processes of joint learning with an open attitude towards a co-evolution of the diversity of cultures. The partners within Latin America, Asia, Africa and Europe learn from each other, as well as from organisations outside the network. Differences can be seen as a way to explore possibilities for learning. In this process the relationships that have grown historically - and that implies professionals from the North having the most influence in international dialogues - need to be changed into a situation where all partners involved have the same rights and possibilities. The Compas Magazine and other publications can be used as a platform for this dialogue. Workshops could be organised around specific themes; policy dialogues could be organised between politicians, religious leaders and scientists.

Policy supportive research. The aspects mentioned above such as stimulating economic development at regional levels, dealing with controversies, securing intellectual property rights, and joint learning and capacity building require policy support. This includes policies of national and local governments and legislative bodies, of major economic stakeholders and social organisations, and of scientific and educational organisations. Motivating these organisations to change their policies in favour of endogenous development calls for data, based on practical research, that substantiates the potentials of this approach. In this process, each of the agencies involved can identify the key questions and formulate these into research questions.

The notion of co-evolution of cultures and sciences implies that specific solutions need to be developed for each specific situation. This requires systematic reflection, problem identification, fact-finding, and reflection on options as well as attitudes of all involved.

Good research can help in clarifying the reasoning behind endogenous development, which is essential in he dialogue between the actors involved and in getting the support of stakeholders in creating the room for change. This type of policy supportive research could be planned and implemented by networks of organisations. International and national organisations can play important roles, and the Compas network needs to build up strategic partnerships with many organisations, both nationally and internationally.

Enhancing inter-scientific dialogue. Science is considered to be knowledge that has been compiled in a systematic way. This implies the way it systematically observes, describes, explains, establishes claims on truth, expands and represents knowledge, and builds up theories to explain the relationship between cause and effect. According to the Study group on Science and Traditional Knowledge of the International Council for Science (2002), *"science has an in-built dynamic towards improvement of knowledge"*. The study group concludes that there is growing awareness about the extraordinary diversity of sciences. Different sciences are far more dissimilar to each other than previously thought, and there is no 'unity of science' nor a 'unique scientific method'. What counts as good scientific practice in one science, may be outdated or even inappropriate in another.

Box 9c   Declaration of the World Conference of Science

This conference, organised in Budapest in 1999 by UNESCO, in cooperation with the International Council for Science (ICSU), accepted a declaration in which western scientific knowledge, with its remarkable innovations that have been of great benefit, are recognised. But the declaration also stresses the challenge to use this knowledge in a responsible manner in addressing human needs and aspirations. The declaration observes that traditional and local knowledge systems, can make, and historically have made, a valuable contribution to science and technology. Its Science Agenda Framework for Action is based on the notion that there is a need to preserve, protect, research and promote this cultural heritage, and presents a number of guidelines for the relations between modern science and other systems of knowledge. Governments, for example, are called upon to formulate national policies that allow wider application of traditional forms of learning and knowledge, while ensuring that its commercialisation is properly rewarded. Governments should support the co-operation between holders of traditional knowledge and scientists in exploring the relationships between different knowledge systems, and in fostering linkages of mutual benefit.

We believe that an important way to address the differences between scientific traditions is to undertake joint research, and to discuss the outcome of such research in a critical but constructive way. If the idea of a diversity of sciences is accepted, this can be an asset rather than a setback. Through inter-scientific research and dialogue the problem definitions and perspectives on solutions can be exchanged. In this way synergy can be built whilst the contradictions based on different conceptual frameworks can be made clear, thus offering opportunities for mutual learning and innovative approaches. Assessment of modern and of traditional practices could then be done by each of the participating sciences. The dialogue would allow sciences to make constructive comments on the basic points of the different research methods, in an attempt to improve methods and theories. As a result of this process certain elements from one scientific tradition can be incorporated into another's paradigm.

If the notion of a diversity of sciences is taken seriously, any knowledge that is considered a science from anywhere in the world can enter into the dialogue. The University Consortium for endogenous development, started by the Compas network in 2002, can play an important role in carrying out policy supporting research, making publications, and organising scientific conferences.

Towards co-evolution of cultures

Co-evolution is the process wherein a number of different systems exist and evolve simultaneously, based on their own dynamics. Each system evolves partly due to its own learning experiences and partly as a response to the interaction with other systems. The concept of co-evolution lies at the heart of endogenous development. The impressive diversity in cultures throughout the world, including values, technologies and development approaches, is now considered by many to hold important keys for counteracting the complex problems the world is facing today. A world in which a wide diversity of sciences and practices can co-exist and co-evolve has more potential for survival, than a world where one approach of development is expected to solve all problems. In endogenous development, therefore, the options and solutions are experimented with according to the existing diversity of ecological situations and cultures. Mutual support and intercultural dialogues are required to enhance the complementarity and synergy between these systems.

We have seen that intercultural contacts can lead to dominance, control and disappearance of cultures. But, we have also experienced that contacts established in a respectful way can lead to productive and positive learning about, from and with each other. They can result in increased local productivity, welfare and reduction of poverty. In this process, respect for differences in cultural values and concepts is a precondition for all involved. Respect does not imply the unconditional

Respectful dialogues imply the willingness to listen, openness to learning, responsiveness to information, questions and suggestions as well as the courage to criticise when necessary.

acceptance of all differences. Respect means the willingness to listen, openness to the possibility of learning, responsiveness to information, questions and suggestions, as well as the courage to criticise when necessary.

We hope that through the historic analysis, the presentation of the approach as well as the practical experiences with endogenous development, we have been able to put forward a perspective for rural communities and development agencies in the forefront of reducing poverty and environmental degradation and in enhancing bio-cultural diversity.

DEFINITIONS

Basic religions: Religions of contemporary people whose religious ideas are not presented in written form, and the religions of prehistoric peoples, about whom we know little. Embraces a great variety of beliefs and practices, including animism, totemism, and poly-theism.

Biodiversity: The variety, distribution, and abundance of different plants, animals, and micro-organisms, the ecological functions and processes they perform, and the genetic resources they contain in a certain locality, region or landscape.

Cartesian worldview: notion that nature functions according to mechanical laws, developed by Descartes during the period of Enlightenment in Europe in the 18th century.

Classical knowledge: Knowledge of ancient cultures derived from classical texts or other cultural expressions such as designs or architecture.

Co-evolution: Process in which a number of different systems evolve simultaneously, partly on the basis of their own dynamics, and partly as a response to their interaction with other systems.

Cosmovision (or worldview): The way a certain population perceives the cosmos (or world). It includes assumed relationships between the human world, the natural world and the spiritual world. It describes the perceived role of supernatural powers, the relationship between humans and nature, and the way natural processes take place. It embodies the premises on which people organise themselves, and determines the moral and scientific basis for intervention in nature.

Culture: The human made environment including all material and non-material aspects, such as food, tools, religion, customs, laws, art, myths, that are transmitted from one generation to the next.

Endogenous development: Development based mainly, though not exclusively, on locally available resources, local knowledge, culture and leadership, with the openness to integrate traditional as well as outside knowledges and practices. It has mechanisms for local learning and experimenting, building local economies and retention of benefits in the local area.

Epistemology: The study of the theoretical background and dynamics of a knowledge system, including its nature, origin and scope.

Global knowledge: Knowledge which has resulted from global processes of knowledge generation and technology, processes of regional specialisation and global integration of communication, production and trade. This knowledge cannot claim exclusive regional origins. An example of global knowledge is the information and communication technology.

Indigenous or local knowledge: Knowledge generated, used and developed by people in a certain area. It is not limited to indigenous peoples and can include knowledge originating from elsewhere that has been internalised by local people through local processes of learning, testing and adaptation. It forms the basis of the art of identifying, combining, unfolding and protecting local resources. It is rooted in and stems from local practices, hence it is specific to the local context and often gender specific.

Intercultural dialogue: Exchange of experiences, ideas and values by representatives of different cultures, with the aim of mutual learning and enhancing the co-evolution of a diversity of cultures.

Interscientific dialogue: Exchange of ideas, experiences and concepts related to scientific paradigms and knowledge generation, with the aim of joint learning and the co-evolution of the diversity of sciences.

Modern knowledge: Knowledge that results from a systematic process of fact finding and understanding, based on methods that uses sensory experience and quantification. Predictability and control are important goals. It uses mechanistic models and follows the principles of Descartes, and is therefore often labelled as Cartesian. This knowledge is developed further in formal research centres and taught at formal educational institutes.

Paradigm: A compact outline of the major concepts, assumptions, theories, methods, procedures and propositions used in a certain scientific school.

Post-modern knowledge: Knowledge resulting from a diversity of concepts that aim for organic, holistic and ecological understanding of reality. As a reaction to modern knowledge, it integrates insights from various scientific sources. It accepts uncertainty, lack of control, and limitations, as well as the complementarity of different knowledge systems.

Traditional knowledge: A cumulative body of knowledge, know-how, practices and representations, maintained and developed by peoples with extended histories, and (originally) transmitted orally. It encompasses understandings, interpretation, classification systems and language, is based on a worldview with its logic and values, and has mechanisms for learning, experimenting and adaptation.

Scientific knowledge: Knowledge that results from systematic processes which include observation, understanding, description, explaining, fact-finding and experimentation. Abstract concepts and symbols are linked with reality through experimentation. Traditional, indigenous, modern and post-modern knowledge can all be considered scientific

REFERENCES

Adas, 1997. *Colonialism and Science* In:. Selin, H. op.cit.

AICRPE, 1996. *Technical Report on All India Co-ordinated Research Project on Ethno-biology* (Unpublished).

D'Ambrosio, U. 1997. *Colonialism and Science in the Americas.* In: Selin, H. op. cit.

Apfel-Marglin, F. with PRATEC, 1998. *The spirit of Regeneration - Andean Culture Confronting Western Notions of Development.* ZED books, London & New York.

Balasubramanian, A.V. (ed.) 2000. *Indian Health Traditions.* A Special issue of Folio, Supplement to The Hindu, 8th October 2000.

Balasubramanian, A.V. 1997. *Knowledge Systems in India.* In: Selin, H. op.cit.

Balasubramanian, A.V. and Radhika, M. 1989. *Local Health Traditions: An Introduction.* Lok Swasthya Parampara Samvardhan Samithi, Madras.

Bartle, P.F.W. 1983. *The Universe has three souls; Notes on translating the Akan Culture.* In: Journal of religion in African.

Bebbington, A., 1999. *Capitals and capabilities: A framework for analysing peasant viability, rural livelihoods and poverty.* World Development vol.27 no.12

Beek, P. van and Blakeley 1994. *Religion in Africa.* Heinemann, New Hampshire.

Beemans, P. 2000. *Foreword in The Lab, the Temple and the market – Reflections at the Intersection of Science, Religion and Development* S.M.P. Harper (ed) IDRC – CRDI, Kumarian Press

Berg, H. van den 1989. *La Tierra no da así no más - los ritos agrícolas en la religión de los Aymara-Christianos.* Hisbol-UCB/ISET, Cochabamba, Bolivia.

Berger, K. and Yang di Sheng, J.E. 1997. *Environment and nature: China.* In: Selin, H. op cit.

Bernal, M. 1987. *Black Athena: The Afro-Asiatic roots of classical civilisation.* Free association books, London.

Biakolo, E. 1998. *Categories of cross cultural cognition and the African Condition.* In: Coetzee, P.H. and Roux, A.P.J. op.cit.

Biko, S. 1998. *Some African cultural concepts.* In: The African Philosophy Reader. Coetzee and Roux, A.P.J. op.cit.

Bilbao Paz, J. D. 1994. *Caracterización y análisis del sistema ganadero en la comunidad de Japo. Tesis de grado para ingeniero agrónomo.* (CIDASC-AGRUCO), Cochabamba, Bolivia.

Breemer, van den J.P.M. 1984. *The diffusion of dry rice cultivation among the Aouan of Ivory Coast.* In: Sociologia Ruralis 29, 3-4, University of Glouchestershire, England.

Bruun, O. and Kalland, A. 1995. *Asian perceptions of nature; a critical approach.* Curzon press Richmond.

Capra, F. 1983. *The turning point. Science, society and the rising culture.* Flamingo, London.

Coetzee, P.H. and Roux A.P.J. (eds) 1998. *The African Philosophy Reader.* Routledge, London.

Delgado, F. and Ponce, D. 2001. *Local markets and indigenous logic.* In: Compas Magazine no 5, December 2001.

Earls, J., Grillo, E., Araujo, H. and Kessel, J. van 1990. *Tecnología Andina - una introducción.* Breve biblioteca de bolsillo, HISBOL, la Paz, Bolivia.

Emeagwali, G. 1997. *Colonialism and science in Africa* In: Selin, H. op. cit.

Evanson, R.E. 1986. *The economics of extension.* In: Investing in rural extension: strategies and goals. G.E. Jones (ed.). Elsevier publishers, London.

Fairhead, J. 1993. *Representing knowledge; the 'new farmer' in research fashion.* In: Practicing development; social science perspectives. Pottier (ed.). Routledge, London.

Fay, B. 1996. *Contemporary philosophy of social science; a multicultural approach*. Blackwell publishers. Malden, Massachusetts.

Freidel, D., Schele L. and Parker J., 1993 *Maya Cosmos: Three Thousand Years on the Shaman's Path*. William R. Morrow, New York

Fukuka-Parr, S., Lopez, C. and Malik, K. 2002. *Capacity for development; new solutions to old problems*. UNDP/Earthscan, New York.

Garcia, M.A, Huet, A., Solís, B., Saquic, J., Tiney, J. 2000. *Tierra y Espiritualidad Maya*. II Encuentro taller sober "Cultura y espiritualidad Maya", Guatemala

Garcia, H. 2000. *Mayan and Chinese health systems compared*. In: Compas Newsletter no 3, July 2000.

Garcia, H. 2001. *Word of Wind - building bridges between health education and culture*. In: Compas Magazine no 4, March 2001.

Gonese, C. 1999. *The three worlds*. In: Compas Newsletter no 1, February 1999.

Guha, R. (Ed.) 1994. *Social Ecology*. Oxford University Press. New Delhi, India

Gyekye, K. 1996. *African Cultural Values: An Introduction*. Sankofa Publishing Company. Accra, Ghana.

Hatse, I. et al. 2000. *The Q'eqchi' Cross - cosmovision as a basis for development*. In: Compas Magazine no 4, March 2001.

Haverkort, B. and Hiemstra, W. (eds) 1999. *Food for thought; ancient visions and new experiments of rural people*. Zed Books, London/Books for Change, Bangalore, India.

Hopfe, M and Woodward, R 1998 *Religions of the World*. Department of Religious Studies Arizona State University. Prentice Hall, Upper Saddle River, New Jersey

Hountondji, P.J. 2001. *Tempting traditions*. Compas Magazine no 4, March 2001.

Hultkrantz, A. 1997. *Religion and science in the native Americas*. In: Selin, H. op. cit.

Kaphagawani, D.N. 1998. *What is African Philosophy?* In: Coetzee and Roux. Op.cit.

Kinsella, J., Wilson, S., Jong, F. de and Renting, H. 2000. *Pluriactivity as livelihood strategy of Irish farm households and its role in rural development*. Sociologia Ruralis 40: 481-498.

Leach, M. and Mearns, R. 1996. *The lie of the land; Challenging received wisdom on the African environment*. IDS, Sussex.

Levy Bruhl, L. 1923. *Primitive mentality*. Allen and Unwin, London.

Levy Bruhl, L. 1985. (1910). *How natives think*. Princeton University press, Princeton.

Levy Strauss, C. 1966. *The savage mind*. Weidenfeld and Nicolson, London.

Lorand, A. 2001. *The biodynamic movement: the complexity of being both esoteric and exoteric*. In: Biodynamics 234, March/April 2001. USA.

Lovelock, J.E. 1979. *Gaia*. Oxford University Press, Oxford.

Mbiti, J. 1969. *African Religions and Philosophy*. Heinemann, London, Ibadan, Nairobi.

Melita, F. 2000. *Organic farming in the Netherlands*. Stiftung Okologische Landbau, Germany.

Millar, D. 1993. *Farmer experimentation and the Cosmovision paradigm*. In: Cultivating Knowledge: Genetic Diversity. Farmer Experimentation, and Crop Research. A. W. de Boef et al. Intermediate Technology Publications, pp. 44-50.

Millar, D. 1994. *Experimenting farmers in northern Ghana*. In: Beyond Farmer First. I. Scoones, and J. Thompson (eds). Intermediate Technology Publications.

Millar, D. 1996. *Footprints in the Mud: Re-constructing the Diversities in Rural People's Learning Processes*. Ph.D. thesis - Wageningen Agricultural University – Holland. Published by Grafisch Service Centrum Van Gils BV, The Netherlands.

Mouton, J., 2001. *How to succeed in your masters and doctoral studies. A South African guide and research book.* Van Schaik Publisher, Pretoria.

Opata, D.U. 1998. *Essays on Igbo worldview.* Nsukka. AP express Publishers, Nigeria.

Orchardson-Mazrui E. 1993. *Janngamizi: spirit and sculpture.* In: African Languages and Cultures 6, 2.

Oruka, H.O. (ed.) 1990. *Sage philosophy: Indigenous thinkers and modern debate on African thinkers.* Brill, Leiden.

Parrinder, E.G. 1969. *African Traditional Religion.* Sheldon Press, London.

Ploeg, J.D. van der 1990. *Tussen bulk en kwaliteit.* Van Gorkum, Assen.

Ploeg, J.D. van der 1999. *De virtuele boer.* Van Gorkum, Assen.

Ploeg, J.D. van der 2000. *Revitalizing agriculture: farming economically as starting ground for rural development.* Sociologia Ruralis 40: 497-511.

Ploeg, J.D. van der and Renting, H. 2000. *Impact and potential: a comparative review of rural development practices.* Sociologia Ruralis 40: 529-543.

Ploeg, J.D. van der, Long, A., Banks, J. 2002. *Living countrysides – Rural development processes in Europe: the state of the art.* Elsevier, Doetinchem

Polman, N.B.P. and Slangen, L.H.G. 1999. *Environmental cooperatives in agriculture: institutional concepts and empirical evidence.* Paper presented at the 64th EAAE seminar, Berlin.

Posey, D.A. 1999. *Cultural and Spiritual Values of Biodiversity.* UNEP, Nairobi.

Prigogini, I, and Stengers, I. 1984. *Order out of chaos.* Bantam, New York.

Radhika, M. and Balasubramanian, A.V. 1990. *Mother and Child Care in Traditional Medicine.* Lok Swasthya Parampara Samwardhan Samithi, Madras.

Ravikumar, K. and Ved, D.K. 2000. *Illustrated field guide to 100 red listed medicinal plants of conservation concern in southern India.* FRLHT,

Reijntjes,.C., Haverkort, B. and Waters-Bayer, A. 1994. *Farming for the Future, Introduction to Low External Input and Sustainable Agriculture.* MacMillan, London.

Rey, C. 2001. *Farmer Innovation in Africa: Source of Inspiration for Agricultural Development.* Earthscan, London, England.

Richards, P. 1985. *Indigenous agricultural revolution. Ecology and food production in West Africa.* Hutchington. London.

Rist, S., San Martin, J. and Tapia, N. 1999. *Andean cosmovision and self-sustained development.* In: Haverkort B., and Hiemstra W. op.cit.

Roep, D. 2000. *Vernieuwend werken. Sporen van vermogen en onvermogen.* PhD thesis, Wageningen University.

Röling, N. 1992. *The emergence of Knowledge System Thinking: changing perception of relationships among innovation, knowledge processes and configuration.* In Knowledge and Policy, vol. 5/2

Saccomanchi, V. 1998. *Agriculture Market Economics: a neo-institutional analysis of exchange, circulation and distribution of agricultural products.* Van Gorkum, Assen.

Salas, M.A. 1996. *Acerca de la interacción de sistemas de conocimiento en los Andes del Perú.* Doctoral thesis of the Catholic University of Nijmegen, the Netherlands.

Scarre, C. 1991. *Past Worlds. Atlas of Archeology* Times books, London

Schulte Nordholt, H.G. 1971. *The political system of the Atoni of Timor.* Martinus Nijhof, Den Haag.

Schultz, M., Soederbaum, F. and Oejendal, 2001. *Regionalisation in a globalizing world. A comparative perspective on forms, actors and processes.* Zed Books, London.

Segal, A. 1997. *Technology in the New World.* In: Selin H. op.cit.

Selin, H. 1997. *Encyclopaedia of the history of science, technology and medicine in non western cultures.*

Kluwer publishers, Dordrecht.

Shankar, D. 1992 *Indigenous Health Services: the State of the Art* In: State of India's Health, A. Mukhopadhyay (ed), New Dehli, Voluntary health Association of India.

Sheldrake, R. 1994 *The Rebirth of Nature – the Greening of Science and God.* Inner Tradition International Ltd.

Sinha, R and Sinha, S. 1998. *Renaissance of Traditional Herbal Medicine in India – Fulfilling the Promise of Health for All in the 21 Century.* In: Curare

Srinivas, M.D. 1987. *The Methodology of Indian Mathematics and Its Contemporary Relevance.* PPST Bulletin 12: 1-35.

Stavenhagen, R. 2002. *La Diversidad Cultural en el desarrollo de las Américas - Los pueblos indígenas y los estados nacionales en Hispanoamérica.* Organización de Estados Americanos, 2002

Steiner, R. 1924. *Agriculture,* Rudolf Steiner College Press, Fair Oaks, California

Steiner, R. 1993 *Agriculture Spiritual foundations for the renewal of Agriculture.* Tonckwood books.

Swanson, R.A. 1980. *Development interventions and self-realisation among the Gourma.* In: Indigenous knowledge systems and development. Brokensha, Warren and Werner. University press of America, Latham.

Tengan, E. 1991. *The land as being and cosmos.* Peter Lang, Frankfurt am Main.

TIRD, 2000. *Report on the exchange visit to India.* Kefamenanu, Indonesia.

Turnbull, D. 1997. *Reframing Science and Other Local Knowledge Traditions.* Futures Pergamon Press, Cambridge, U.K., 29, no. 6.

Walsche, P. de, 1992. *Interview with José Serech.* In Bijeen, November 1992, Wereldwijd.

Warrier, P.K., Nambiar, V.P.K. and Ramankutty, C. (ed.) 1997. *Indian Medicinal Plants: A Compendium of 500 species Volume IV.* Orient Longman, Madras. Reprint pp. 409-411.

Wijsen, F. and Nissen, P., 2002. *Mission is a Must. Intercultural theology and the mission of the church.* Editions Rodopi, 2002

Wilber, K. 1998. *The marriage of sense and soul: integrating science and religion.* New York, Random House

Wiredu, K. 1998. *The concept of truth in the Akan language.* In: The African philosophy Reader. Coetzee and Roux. Op.cit.

Wilgenburg, H.V. 1998. *Pharmaceutical treasures in the South.* In: Problems and Potential in International Health – Trans-disciplinary Perspectives. Pieter Streefland (ed) Amsterdam, Het Spinhuis.

Wilkinson, J.R. 1998. *What's African about African art and African thought?* Fourth International Congress of Aesthetics. Ljubljana. Slovenia.

Yang Di-Sgeng 1997. *Knowledge systems in China.* In: Selin, H. op.cit.

YTM, 1999. *Official record of Management of the Natural caves of Popnam.* YTM, Kefamenanu.

Zahan, D. 1970. *The religion, spirituality and thought of traditional Africa.* The University of Chicago press, Chicago and London.

Zoysa, A. de 2002. *Understanding what we know.* Paper for the planning workshop for the University consortium, Compas.

COMPAS PARTNER ORGANISATIONS

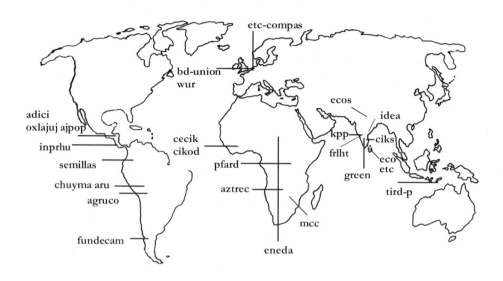

Core Members

ADICI-WAKLIIQO
Mr Oscar Pacay Caal
2a Calle 6-23, Zona 2
16001 Cobán
Alta Verapaz,
GUATEMALA C.A.
adici@c.net.gt

AGRUCO
(Latin American
Coordination)
Mr Freddy Delgado
Agroecologia Universidad
Cochabamba
Av. Petrolera km 4½
Casillla 3392, Cochabamba
BOLIVIA
agruco@pino.cbb.entelnet.bo

AZTREC
(Southern African
Coordination)
Mr Cosmas Gonese
Private Bag 9286
Masvingo, ZIMBABWE
e-mail: aztrec@mweb.co.zw

BD Union
Mr Jos Pelgröm
Postbus 236
3970 AE Driebergen
THE NETHERLANDS
bd.vereniging@ecomarkt.nl

CECIK
Mr David Millar
(Western African
Coordination)
P.O. Box 607
Bolgatanga U.E.R.
GHANA
cecik@africaonline.com.gh

CIKS
(Asian coordination)
Mr A.V. Balasubramanian
30, Gandhi Mandapam Road
Kotturpuram
Chennai 600 085, INDIA
ciks@vsnl.com

ECO
Mr G.K. Upawansa
Hyneford
Dekinda, Nawalapitiya
SRI LANKA
pasasa@sltnet.lk

ECOS
Mr Maheswar Ghimire
P.O. Box 4
Narayangarh Chitwan,
NEPAL
e-mail: ecoce@mos.com.np

ETC-Compas
(International Coordination)
Mr Bertus Haverkort
Mr Wim Hiemstra
Mrs Katrien van 't Hooft
Mrs Marijke Kreikamp
P.O. Box 64
3830 AB Leusden
THE NETHERLANDS
compas@etcnl.nl

ETC LANKA
Mr James Handawela
12, Tickell Road
Colombo-8, SRI LANKA
etc@sri.lanka.net

FRLHT
Mr Darshan Shankar
50, MSH Layout, 2nd Stage,
3rd Main, Anandanagar
Bangalore 560 024, INDIA
darshan@frlht.ernet.in

GREEN Foundation
Mrs Vanaja Ramprasad
Mr G. Krishna Prasad
#G503, Infosys Pride
Bilakahalli
Bannerghatta Road
Bangalore 560 076, INDIA
van@vsnl.com

IDEA
Mr Gowtham Shankar
Flat no. 6A, Maharaja Towers
R.K. Mission Road
Visakhapatnam 530 003
INDIA
gowtham@satyasaionline.net.in

KPP
Mr A.S. Anand
Mr Aruna Kumara
Krishinivasa, Kuruvalli
Thirthahalli 577 432
Karnataka, INDIA
aruna_kpp@yahoo.com/

TIRD-P
Ms Veronika Ata
Yayasan Konsultasi dan
Bantuan Hukum Justitia
Jl. Samratulangi II, No. 28
Kota Baru, Kupang NTT,
INDONESIA
ykbh_justitia@yahoo.com

Associate Members

CHUYMA ARU
Mr Nestor Chambi Pacoricona
Jr. Oroya 114, Casilla Postal
762 Puno, PERU
chuyma@terra.com.pe

FUNDECAM
Mr Jaime Renato Soto Navarro
General Mackenna 080
Temuco, CHILE
jasoto@ufro.cl/
fundecam@telsur.cl

OXLAJUJ AJPOP
Mr Felipe Gomez
9 calle "A" 0-62 zona 3
Ciudad de Guatemala,
GUATEMALA
oxajpop@terra.com.gt

INPRHU
Ms Gladis Caceres Leyva
Parque Central 1c. Al Oeste
Sotomo, NICARAGUA
inprhuso@ibw.com.ni

SEMILLAS
Mr Germán Alonso Vélez O.
Calle 25C no. 3—81A (oficina
301) Edificio la Raqueta
Bogota, COLOMBIA
semil@attglobal.net

MOSHI COOPERATIVE COLLEGE
Mr O.T. Kibwana
Sokoine Road
P.O.Box 474, Moshi,
TANZANIA
iswcp@africaonline.co.tz

PFARD
Peasant Farmers' Association
for Rural Development
Mr David Nkanda
P.O. Box 508 Iganga
UGANDA
idaac@utlonline.co.ug

CIKOD
Mr Ben Guri
P.O. BOX MD 68
Madina
Accra
GHANA
byguri@yahoo.com

Wageningen U.R.
Research School for
farmstyles and endogenous
development
Mr. J.D. van der Ploeg
P.O. BOX 8130
6700 EW Wageningen
The Netherlands
Jan.DouwevanderPloeg@
ALG.SWG.WAU.NL

COLOPHON

Concept, realisation and editing:
Compas - Bertus Haverkort, Katrien van 't Hooft and Wim Hiemstra
P.O. Box 64
3830 AB Leusden, The Netherlands

Language editing
Chesha Wettashina

Lay-out
Marijke Kreikamp

Photography
The photos in this book were made by Compas and:
Bulu Imam (page 42); Jaap Postuma (page 134, bottom); Yingyong Un-Anongrak (page 136, bottom); Robert Estall (page 150/151); Hans Dijkstra (p. 217); Wim van der Ende (page 219); Chris Pennaerts (page 215, page 238); Chris Wollaert (page 224); Ilse Köhler-Rollefson (back cover, bottom left).

Printing
BDU, Barneveld, The Netherlands

Distribution
Zed Books, United Kingdom